Artificial Intelligence and Human Institutions

The Springer Series on

ARTIFICIAL INTELLIGENCE AND SOCIETY

Series Editor: KARAMJIT S. GILL

Richard Ennals

Artificial Intelligence and Human Institutions

Springer-Verlag
London Berlin Heidelberg New York
Paris Tokyo Hong Kong

Richard Ennals
School of Operations Management and Quantitative Methods
Kingston Business School, Kingston Polytechnic, Kingston Hill,
Kingston upon Thames, Surrey KT2 7LB, UK

British Library Cataloguing in Publication Data
Ennals, J. R. (John Richard) 1951–
Artificial intelligence and human institutions.–
(Artificial intelligence and society).
1. Artificial intelligence. Social aspects
I. Title II. Series
306.46

Library of Congress Cataloging-in-Publication Data
Artificial intelligence and human institutions/Richard Ennals.
p. cm.
Includes Index
ISBN-13: 978-3-540-19579-5   e-ISBN-13: 978-1-4471-1735-3
DOI: 10.1007/978-1-4471-1735-3
1. Artificial intelligence. 2. Artificial intelligence–Social aspects. I. Title.
Q335.E56 1991
006.3--dc20   90-10011
                                                                   CIP

2128/3916-54310 Printed on acid-free paper

Contents

Introduction

The title of this book may suggest a detached academic treatise, while the intention is to show the practical applicability of ideas and tools of artificial intelligence in the working of human institutions. The early years of research in artificial intelligence involved pulling together ideas and experience from diverse fields of academic endeavour. The work reported in this book is based on action research case studies in many varied institutional settings, and the work continues as the ideas and tools of artificial intelligence are taken up within institutional cultures.

The book has been written from a perspective of active involvement in collaborative projects with non-technical partners using affordable technology. There is a consistent methodology underlying each of the specialist areas of work reported in the chapters which follow, which focus on the development of working models of social interaction, intended to be taken and repeated by others in different settings. As far as possible the experimental situations should not depend on the skills and talents of a particular individual, but should be available for replication. This leads to a concern for structures of institutions and modes of interaction, and for means of describing such structures and modes to others who may share a common commitment to shared goals.

The presentation here will be inherently fallible. The test of the utility of the work reported will be whether ideas are taken up and used better by others in new situations. In certain specialist areas such as education we can point to a network of international projects spawned in this way. In the case of applications of artificial intelligence in the voluntary sector it is at present a question of empowering motivated individuals to seek their objectives more effectively, taking advantage of available technology. It has been harder to communicate the more general thesis concerning artificial intelligence and human institutions because in conversations and projects over the years the natural concerns of interlocutors have been focused on particular domains or theoretical perspectives. The challenge in this book is to communicate the general thesis while retaining the linguistic and cultural connections with the specialist communities with whom the different parts have been developed.

Some particular debts should be acknowledged. Michael Sorenson and Richard Grover of the Peter Bedford Project taught me some of the disciplines of experimental social work, and introduced me to the ideas of John Bellers. Don Thompson was a supportive tutor in classroom history teaching at the London University Institute of Education. David Giles and John Waddleton provided a stimulating experimental environment for social studies teaching at Tamworth Manor High School, Mitcham. Robert Kowalski and the logic programming group at Imperial College gave me a formal and computational framework within which to develop my ideas deriving from simulations in the classroom, ideas previously formed as a student in the United States and as a teacher in Nigeria and Essex. Anthony Tomei and the Nuffield Foundation provided support for experimental classroom work in Wimbledon, Exeter, and Kingston. Brian Oakley and David Thomas in the Alvey Directorate gave me experience of research management at a national level. Arthur Cotterell and Kingston College of Further Education have provided a haven in recent years, a rich environment for collaborative work with industry, education and community groups using a range of technologies including expert systems tools. Jonathan Briggs and David Hopson have been superb research partners, always happy to try new practical challenges and provide technical support.

John Watson of Springer UK has demonstrated commitment to the social applications and context of artificial intelligence by supporting this book and the work of Karamjit Gill both as editor of the journal *AI and Society* and as editor of the series in which this book appears. The journal and the associated Artificial Intelligence for Society Club have provided a stimulating intellectual and practical environment in which to work.

Hampton   Richard Ennals
Spring 1990

Chapter 1

Approaches to Artificial Intelligence

A Reassessment of Artificial Intelligence

The novelty value of Artificial Intelligence (AI) has worn off. It has not transformed the world as some early evangelical enthusiasts anticipated, and the flow of miracles has apparently dried up, at least temporarily, together with the flow of financial support. With the recent resurgence of interest in neural networks and connectionism, once dismissed as an intellectual cul-de-sac, AI and symbol processing no longer have a monopoly in the field of modelling human mental activity. It is time to reassess what AI is about in human terms. A similar reassessment has had to be done for other "conversion" changes such as Evangelical Christianity, Marxism, Natural Gas, Decimal Coinage or the European Common Market. Each, having attracted public attention and support, has found ways of toning down its claims in order to become an accepted part of modern life.

Writing on AI has usually focused on the technology, and has largely ignored the institutional, social and cultural context, except in the vaguest of terms. This is partly because many AI technical innovators have themselves forsworn normal social interaction in the cause of perceived progress, and have become very specialist and intellectually remote, coping as they do with many levels of abstraction at once, stretching their own intelligence ahead of the computer. Marriages and families have been sacrificed in the cause of research.

AI has been regarded in the West as a tool for profit in the Capitalist system. Expert systems in particular have been seen as prime candidates to strengthen the hand of strong management, maximising short-term profit and easing the planned process of trimming the work-force of excess capacity, while not requiring expensive long-term investment in plant or personnel. Some UK expert systems companies undertook to fund socially useful projects once their profit figures exceeded a million pounds per annum, only to go into receivership first: this book argues that an early emphasis on socially useful projects would provide the foundation for later profit. To ignore the social dimension is not only intellectually bankrupt: it also prevents systems from being practically useful, and condemns them to remain as either research playthings or expensive irrelevancies.

As governments and companies reconsider their positions and cut their research and investment plans, ignoring institutional aspects of the use of AI, they risk throwing the baby out with the bath water, ending basic research in AI because massive short-term profits have not been made, and causing irreparable damage to the long-term development of human institutions. In this AI acts as a microcosm of the economy and society, combining as it does elements of education, training, research, development, sales, marketing and publishing.

Similar arguments can be found in the Software Engineering (SE) community, which is embarking on the construction of information systems factories, which involve the combination of men and machines, technology and institutions, with AI at the core. Integration takes time, and there is still a need for bridge-building between the AI and SE communities, after decades of abuse and distrust. Intercultural bridge-building is no easy matter. Gandhi had similar problems in the early days of Indian Independence, with the Hindus and Muslims! The Irish Question defies easy answers after centuries.

Radical critics of the new technology have not necessarily helped the cause of basic research, lending apparent weight to the arguments of Treasury economists by emphasising the inherent limitations of the technology when set against the complexities of problems of human knowledge. They have neglected the examination of human interaction in an institutional context enhanced by AI. The mistake has partly been to accept the financial definitions of the Treasury accountants, and to restrict evaluation to mere financial monitoring and quantification: there are many respectable alternative characterisations of the performance of technologies and institutions, which we will examine in this book.

At present there is a skilled community of practitioners, equipped with modern computer hardware and software. There is also a wealth of human problems in need of solution. Many of the practitioners would like to use their skills in a beneficial manner, but do not have practical experience of real-world problems, and those with the problems would like assistance in their solution, but are unfamiliar with the ways of academia and advanced technology. The challenge is to bring the two together.

The way one makes practical progress in this area is by doing the experimental work first, next writing up the case studies, then revealing the underlying theoretical framework for those who want and need to know. In this respect human institutions and computer technology are handled in the same way by those who wish to effect change. The danger in each case is also the same: a knowledge based system working uncontrolled in real time is simply an ideology, irrespective of the technology used in implementation. Systems must remain under human control.

Leaving matters to market forces has not proved successful: those with the real human problems tend not to have the financial resources to enter the market, and those with the technology have proved reluctant to share or transfer it at less than a competitive price. Concepts of property and ownership do not always fit easily with changing technology, particularly information technology. The underlying questions are not new. We need to find, develop and test new ways of working together so that problems can be addressed and, if not solved, at least better understood.

These issues concern AI, but go far beyond the theoretical domains which are normally covered by that phrase. AI is simply the technology of thought which enables us to make sense of the complexity of human thought, action and interaction. It is a dynamic intellectual medium which enables us to share and explain abstract concepts, some of which may come from fields such as social science, history, archaeology, linguistics, philosophy, politics, economics, law and theology. Thinkers and activists in these fields need to meet and exchange ideas: AI provides a meeting ground. It can teach us to learn from our failures, to share our insights and to clarify our representations.

Artificial Intelligence and Human Institutions

Human institutions provide the "missing link" which makes AI systems "work". AI systems can be represented ultimately, if not entirely completely, in the form of facts and rules, symbolic representations of reality. These representations have to be accepted as such, and accorded a common interpretation by the community of users, with an implicit recognition of their limitations. It would not be sufficient to add further facts or rules in the hopes of attaining completeness: the AI system can only ever be a model.

An understanding of human institutions enables us to overcome conventional philosophical obstacles confronting the individual thinker. Within the closed worlds of human institutions an "is" becomes an "ought", as the accepted rules of the institution dictate what can and what cannot be done. Frequently these institutional rules are tacit, and beyond observation by the participant. In this way a "total institution", such as a prison, a boarding school, or a dictatorship, is enabled to work, together with "partial institutions" such as clubs, companies and educational establishments where participation is nominally by consent. Western science itself can be seen as falling under such a description, once it is viewed as a human social activity. AI will be no exception, but may be more reflective and self-critical, as has been the case with history and philosophy in the past.

The techniques of the social anthropologist have proved valuable in eliciting such "social knowledge". How many of them have seen themselves as "knowledge engineers", even in the last decade, when AI has been gaining currency? Instead, they tend to resist the very notion of an association with computers or AI. This is surely mistaken, as their trade is similarly abstract, dealing with metaphors, symbols, and decoding of human behaviour. The European structuralist tradition links the two domains: in France advantage can be taken of this, unifying the Chomskian computational linguistics of Colmerauer [1,2] and the social anthropology of Levi-Strauss [3], the cognitive psychology of Piaget [4] with the mathematics teaching of Papert [5], while in Britain the structuralist link is rejected at both ends. The British tradition is predominantly empirical rather than theoretical.

Creative expression, in whatever medium, enables the artist to make his knowledge and feelings explicit, but often in a way which falls outside, or goes beyond, the normal bounds of scientific discourse. Here we call upon the skills of the literary, dramatic, musical or theatrical critic, who can bring to bear a frame of reference and a set of critical criteria. Such influences are rarely felt in information technology education. The current work of Hilton [6] and Goranzon [7–9] is exploring ways of remedying this deficiency, examining current myths and metaphors, and in particular Pygmalion. AI provides a medium in which ideas can be discussed, modified and developed. Freed from the sequential constraints of speech and writing, and with the opportunity of combining representations as appropriate, a greater range of possibilities are opened up. Among these are the applications of hypermedia.

These possibilities, and the continuation of the activity of AI itself, depend on the existence of a community which participates in the discourse. Powerful ideas in isolation are of no effect: knowledge must be shared in order to grow. As computer technology falls in price, community access and use become practically feasible, if individualistic habits can be overcome. AI as a means of communication helps to determine the nature of the resulting community. Where communication is by electronic network and not accompanied by human contact, the resulting communication may appear correspondingly partial and unbalanced. Electronic networks are no substitute for human networks, but may support them. It may be that electronic publishing [10], and the sending of discs between friends, could offer the desired support for interactivity and personal contact in an environment where access to electronic networks is not seen as a priority. A number of these questions are raised by bringing together "Artificial Intelligence" and "Society" for consideration in discussions, in a journal, or by seeking to apply new intelligent technology to real social problems in the Artificial Intelligence for Society Club. Just as modelling knowledge domains requires experimental work, trial and error, the same applies to social applications projects. For the intellectual concept to achieve practical real world fruition, real world experience will be required: a novelty for thinking academic researchers. "Artificial Intelligence" needs "Society" just as much as "Society" needs "Artificial Intelligence", though this has not been appreciated.

AI has seemed to adhere to the myth of individual knowledge and independence, and commercial companies set up in the rush of the 1980s have made it hard for individuals to talk and exchange ideas without prejudicing "intellectual property rights". Indeed, the whole concept and legal framework of intellectual property is in need of recasting. We have much to learn from the precedent of humour: who can claim copyright on a joke, and how could you define what constitutes a variation on an original theme? Jokes require someone to laugh: they are not funny in themselves. Given that knowledge only exists once shared socially, its "ownership" cannot be said to reside with an individual. The traditional model of property, derived from physical possessions and then applied to the abstract forms of money and finance, does not fit well with knowledge and "intellectual property" .

Applying market forces and disciplines means little when those who have the greatest need for knowledge lack the financial means to enter the market-place. Thus, if AI is to be made available to all irrespective of financial resources, the market must be transcended. Powerful tools need users. Some may be financially well-equipped (like banks or major companies). However, they may be reluctant to talk openly, to share their knowledge, or even to give the necessary time to developing intelligent systems to address their problems. Community groups do not usually share such reluctance, and may in fact have needs for applications systems which closely resemble the needs of banks and major companies in terms of providing access to information with usable interfaces. Many AI applications projects would benefit from the addition of community groups to the collaborative teams. Unrestricted by the constraints of finance within the collaborative project, community groups and their interactions with other team members can accelerate the progress of applications development, and the beta-test systems can perform socially useful functions. This insight has been tested by teams of AI systems developers at Barclays Bank, British Telecom and TSB, under the umbrella of the Artificial Intelligence for Society Club.

In order to establish a new paradigm, in the terms described by Kuhn [11], one first has to achieve success according to the rules of the old. For AI to be taken seriously in the different contexts where it has potential it has to be seen to deliver according to conventional criteria. Some anomalies are inevitable during the transition phase. Similar problems have been noted with other paradigm shifts [12]. For AI to be taken seriously by software engineers it has to achieve standards of reliability and performance which, on some definitions, would disqualify it from consideration as AI, if our view of AI encompasses the activity of exploration of a poorly understood domain with incomplete knowledge. For AI to be taken seriously by humanities researchers it may be expected to capture the modes of representation and inference which are particular to the domain in question [13]. If it does so, however, it may be accused of "dehumanising" the discipline and reducing it to stereotypical forms [14].

There is a real sense in which AI cannot win, but may seek to achieve toleration and continued existence for itself and for those whose medium of communication it has become.

An Alternative Model of Artificial Intelligence

This book seeks to present a unified alternative approach to AI, challenging conventional technocratic assumptions, and casting light on new directions for development.

AI concerns human collaborative activity, and must be pursued collaboratively. It is not properly a "solitary vice": though it can be practised in private it takes at least two to tango. AI is about the exchange of ideas and making sense of utterances and actions, about communication and debate, about the modes of interaction that are essentially human and define our institutions. Human knowledge and the representation of knowledge is at the centre: this distinguishes AI from natural science. Without representation there is nothing available to discuss, but human activity and interaction continue at the level of actions and tacit understandings.

Our concerns are qualitative. Quantification is at the heart of predicate logic: we can use rules to describe patterns and regularities, but the entities about which we reason must be distinguished qualitatively. Any recourse to numbers or statistics should be resisted unless qualitatively justified and explained. Measures of probability or certainty may be better replaced by knowledge based approaches, including the identification of different conditions or criteria according to which conclusions will be different.

We are concerned with dialogue, not monologue. This may include by extension the dialogue of the scholar with his subject [15,16].

We are working with models, and could never capture the full complexity and detail of the real world in real time mechanical systems. There are fundamental logical limitations on our models, as identified by Godel [17].

AI provides tools for understanding complex human behaviour, but not for its complete replication. Human thought and action have to be located in a cultural context which no computer systems could fully share.

Natural language is our most powerful tool for describing our world, but there will always be limits as to the extent to which our computer systems can be said to "understand" natural language [18,19]. By the same token, the quest for a universal underlying "natural logic" is doomed to failure, or rather, to only partial success [7,20,21].

We are here concerned with what Searle called "weak AI" [22], tools to aid the understanding of human problems, rather than "strong AI", the enterprise of building "computer brains". The tools for "weak AI" are available today, but are not being used to their proper potential. The reasons for this are more to do with human institutions than with AI. We can explore these problems through action research case studies.

In order for AI tools to work properly in a collaborative context, we suggest that some necessary conditions must be satisfied:

1. Knowledge must be freely transferred at the point of need. The exchange of money and the exchange of knowledge must be separated. This may be done through common membership of a community or club: at the most general level, the human race.
2. There must be parity of esteem between supplier and recipient, working towards common objectives but also with independent motivations.
3. A supporting network of collaborators must be available on call.
4. All systems must be deemed to be provisional. There could be no such thing as a final version of a knowledge based system addressing real world problems. Once development of a system ends, and it is frozen and commercialised as a product, the system dies like a cut flower.
5. The process of collaboration must be seen as being of comparable importance to the product at any given stage.

Artificial Intelligence as Tool and Institution

Using AI as a tool enables one to stand back from institutions, considering their structure and their operation with a degree of abstraction, and developing models with which one may be better equipped to understand, work within, change, innovate and explain.

There are dangers. A banal view is none the less banal for being expressed in an expert system or an "Intelligent Front End". The impact of ideas and their expression may be amplified by the technology, and a degree of arrogance is required in order to assert that one's own naivety and ignorance may not be amplified by technology. At least it is made explicit.

Using AI depends on a social context: each of the activities above requires an audience, with a degree of response or feedback. An AI model, of itself, is entirely empty unless authenticated by a third party as bearing some correspondence to the real world. AI is not unlike pornography, whose value lies in the mind of the beholder. In newsagents we find computing magazines competing for space with soft pornography and amateur photography, perhaps providing titillation for the intellectual voyeur. The corruption of pornography for personal financial profit betrays but does not remove the beauty of the human body. The corruption of AI for personal financial profit betrays but does not remove the beauty of the human mind. Ideas once sold cheap can no longer grow freely, but wither.

By virtue of their social nature, each of the activities above is ongoing and could never be logically complete. This realisation sits uneasily with the conventional scientific language in which AI is considered, with the implicit Western scientific model of the individual rational observer, seeking objectivity. Any conclusion in AI must be seen as provisional: we may decide that this should also be true for science in general.

AI has itself become something of an institution, a form of life. It has its own characteristic languages, metaphors, power structures and expectations. Once fully immured in the AI culture it can be hard, or impossible, for an individual to see it in context. Each new observer in turn becomes involved and sullied: AI spreads with a form of intellectual cultural syncretism, within which for many the medium has become the message. Gurus and high priests abound, though they are usually far more in the eye of the beholder than of the individual to whom oracular powers are ascribed. One irony of the AI phenomenon is that the original researchers were largely nonconformist radical dissenters, at least in academic and often also in political terms, yet the perceived success of the technology has forced them into the roles of authority figures. They have then, unsurprisingly, been unable to live up to the expectations of sycophantic followers, instead appearing to justify the criticisms of sceptical, frequently jealous, onlookers.

If you stop in a busy street and look up towards the top of a building opposite, it is likely that others may stop to see what you are looking at. After a while a crowd will have gathered, comparing notes on what is going on. At this stage the original person may slip away unnoticed, leaving an ongoing activity though there may in fact have been nothing to look at at all. There might once have been a loose brick or tile, now falling onto the crowd below. It could even have been a dream of a perfect programming language, bringing together logic and natural language.

If students or young researchers run short of money, they may be tempted to take up a musical instrument and go "busking" in the underground or on a busy shopping street in a tourist area. Any passer-by will only hear a brief snatch of music, which may be performed to a tape-recorded background or even just mimed. If it is sufficiently impressive a donation may be made. A limited repertoire may last a busker all day, offering misleading evidence of a potential which may be wholly synthetic. A portable instrument and a begging bowl, with a plausible demonstration: this characterises the beginning of so many AI projects. Andy Warhol described the phenomenon of being "famous for fifteen minutes". Many in the world of AI know what he was talking about. The announcement of a new machine or programming idea can catch the headlines – that may indeed be its purpose, as the headline can be used to land the contract.

It can be hard to separate AI from its customary economic, military, media and even political environment in California. Insufficient attention has been paid to the European AI culture, and to the alternative culture epitomised by AI and society. In the reaction against consumerist high technology, the tools of powerful thinking and questioning may be in jeopardy. There have been attempts to effect a separation and revision, as in La Reunion and Scandinavia, but it is too soon to assess the long-term results.

We must analyse the changes in the culture of AI brought about by the expansion of collaborative activity since 1981 [23]. What are the implications of industry and academia working together, of different government departments, of different academic institutions, different companies submerging their traditional competitive instincts in joint activity? What would count as success? What would be indices of cultural change? Does it have something to do with management, or more generally with personal relations?

It may the case that the alternative culture of AI and Society and the modern academic perspective of the role of higher education have a great deal in common, yet this commonality is under-appreciated. While we continue with the cultural divide between the Arts and the Sciences, both sides will decline. Only when the forces of thought are brought together will the present monolithic philistine political order be questioned.

It is thus particularly important to be able to point to successful institutional working models of AI in practice. For a model, as opposed to an instance, to be judged successful, there must be a framework of action research case studies and illuminative evaluation.

The Artificial Intelligence Debate

AI emerged from the research laboratories in the United States to become very big business, with commercial and military applications often obscuring the intellectual issues and debates on which the technology is founded. Now is the time to return to those issues.

John Haugeland's *Artificial Intelligence: The Very Idea* [24] introduces and explores the central ideas and claims of AI in non-technical terms for the general reader, with the central theme the idea that human thinking and machine computing are "radically the same" and that thinking can be simulated on a computer. His examples are original, down to earth and often amusingly expressed: when illustrating problems of representation he develops a formal stereotype for "Cocker Spaniel" and introduces the classical "frame problem" of coping with change over time through the story of "The Three Boxes and Goldiwires". Haugeland gives ample references to more technical introductions to the field, for which his work is both a preparation and a corrective. Is Good Old Fashioned Artificial Intelligence really possible? "After thirty years", he concludes, "the hard questions remain open".

The Artificial Intelligence Debate: False Starts, Real Foundations, edited by Stephen Graubard [25], has distinguished contributors, including Seymour Papert, Hubert Dreyfus, Daniel Dennett, John McCarthy and Sherry Turkle. The debate is brought to life by the challenge presented to AI by connectionism and neural networks, involving not just ideas but careers and high finance. No longer is AI, symbol processing, presented as the only current model for human thinking, as a successor to the telephone exchange. Logic and problem solving are contrasted with simulations of the working of human neurons, formerly derided by Minsky and Papert [26] as impractical and misconceived, but now sufficiently impressive to form the basis of companies and military projects. This involves a welcome reassessment of the claims and achievements of AI theory, very much in the tradition of what Searle has called "strong AI", modelling the working of the human mind. The debate is not concerned with spin-off products such as expert systems which, while technically simple and theoretically unambitious, can be of use in helping to solve practical problems ("weak AI"). That process of enhanced problem solving holds considerable interest, but is neglected in the literature.

More practically oriented discussions of "weak AI" come from Europe, where there has been less access to the most advanced computer systems but more concentration on the human user.

Logic and Problem Solving

A recurrent bone of contention in the AI debate has been the status of logic. In the early years the debate was somewhat abstract, concerning whether human beings really do think in a logical way. The implementation of logic programming, building on the tradition of Frege [27] in predicate logic and of Robinson [28] in the development of the resolution principle in automated theorem proving, complicated matters by providing the means of producing working systems based on logic. Early work on PROLOG [29] was further derived from Chomskian linguistics and formal grammars [2].

The debate on the role and status of logic raged in the academic journals in the 1970s [e.g. 30–32], but with little impact on the world of commerce or social institutions. Demonstration systems were few in number and highly specialised, the domain of post-doctoral research. Where logic was applied to problem solving this was in the classical tradition of Polya [33], where problems were well-fomed, providing a series of bench-mark microworlds against which new mathematical formalisms could be tested. This approach is exemplified in Kowalski's *Logic for Problem Solving* [34], where the formalism under consideration was the Horn clause subset of predicate logic. Many of his examples would not in fact run as printed on commercially available implementations of PROLOG.

There was a major change of tone in the 1980s. Partly this was due to the adaption by the Japanese of logic programming as the basis of their Fifth Generation computer systems, with PROLOG as the starting point [35]. Partly it was due to the microprocessor revolution which brought powerful computing systems to those for whom computing had been an object of distant study. In 1980 PROLOG was implemented for microcomputers [36], symptomatic of the fact that AI, expert systems, logic programming and rule-based systems were leaving the research laboratory and entering everyday life. LISP did not prove so amenable to transportation to microcomputers, because of the scale of the programming environments which began to require special purpose hardware, so the systems which became commercially available, particularly in Europe, reflected the emphasis on logic programming and rule-based systems.

In the 1980s, therefore, a new generation of powerful software products and tools was in the hands of a new kind of user, who was not necessarily familiar with the research background from which they had come. This research background included long consideration of logic and problem solving, before the two were brought together in theorem proving and logic programming.

A further complicating factor was undoubtedly money. Among the academic community ideas can be exchanged relatively freely through lectures and publications, and controversy can be both vigorous and friendly. Once companies are established to exploit those same ideas commercially, as happened from the late 1970s and increasingly in the early 1980s, the profit motive distorts discussion. Someone wishing to sell a new system tends to emphasise its strong features, glossing over its weaknesses. Purchasers will use a tool with different expectations and motivations from researchers and developers. Where a researcher has stated, correctly, that a tool could be used to build a successful and profit-making system for financial transactions, a customer may assume that use of the tool itself will guarantee the production of profitable results. As with all tools, it is a question of how they are used. Paraphrasing Wittgenstein, tools have no meaning in themselves, the meaning is seen in the use. Use will be in an institutional and economic context, beyond the jurisdiction of the tool builder.

The problem of tools and their use is further complicated where the tools in question are rule-based systems, and the use purports to be problem solving. Apart from the surface issues of user interfaces and acceptable knowledge representations, there are deeper questions concerning rules and problems.

Philosophers have argued over the status of rules for centuries. It is now not in question, whether by philosophers or modern AI scientists, that different forms of logical notation, such as first order predicate calculus, are extremely effective for the representation of knowledge [37]. It is further acknowledged that many other modes of representation, such as semantic networks and frames, can themselves be expressed in predicate logic form and are thus potentially equivalent [38]. This should not surprise us, for it corresponds to the way in which accepted forms of natural language can be used to describe knowledge in everyday life, and can themselves be re-expressed in a logical notation.

A major step forward was taken by Kowalski in proposing a procedural interpretation of declarative sentences of logic. This gives new power to expressions of the form

conclusion if condition and condition...

Where these expressions concern logical truths or relations, the new power of logic programming simply displays dynamically what was already inherent in the paper formulation. However, where we depart from the realms of strictly logical systems, expressions in the form of rules may not support the interpretation suggested by their being run as programs. Our rules may be generalisations based on experience, or they may have implicit qualifications in terms of probability, uncertainty or narrow context of application which do not appeal in the Horn clause formulation.

In order to advance the field of logic programming and its applications Kowalski and his colleagues employed a research strategy which has often been poorly understood, and which in some application domains was inherently hazard-prone. Kowalski's first assumption would be that the rules in a given domain could be made explicit. Secondly, these rules could be represented adequately and appropriately in the Horn clause subset of predicate logic. Thirdly, this set of rules could make a useful contribution to work in the application domain. His strategy, which could be modelled at the meta- level, is to seek to carry out the task using Horn clauses, in order to attract objections concerning areas where this approach is allegedly inappropriate. Having flushed out particular objections, he seeks to meet them by rationally reconstructing problematic areas in logic, and representing them in Horn clauses, if necessary combining object level and meta level in the same logic program. This strategy has been used to address issues of temporal and modal logic, which he has sought to deal with within Horn clauses.

Kowalski and his fellow researchers, such as Sergot, have neatly circumvented the first assumption by focusing attention on knowledge which has already been made explicit in the form of laws, rules and regulations [39]. In their view, much of the hard work has already been done by those who codify the laws, and regarding laws as programs is relatively straightforward thanks to the technology of logic, thus bearing out the second assumption. It is not surprising that Kowalski is vulnerable on his third assumption, for logic programmers and AI scientists focus their attention on the theory of problem solving, rather than on addressing problems in the real world as they arise in specialist application domains. His chosen area of the law is instructive. Kowalski is a meta-mathematician and computer scientist. His colleague Sergot has focused his attention on the law [40], but with a background in mathematics and computer science rather than law. His approach in rationally reconstructing the work of Stamper and his colleagues in LEGOL in terms of logic programming [41] attracted initial hostile reactions from lawyers using computers who were not familiar with logic programming. Work at Imperial College on representing part of the British Nationality Act as a logic program [42] attracted vigorous objections from Leith [43], who carried his concerns to the pages of academic journals. It is interesting that Susskind [44,45], who undertook doctoral research at Oxford in AI and the law following legal training, sees practical utility in Kowalski's approach, while acknowledging that there are many aspects of the law which are not addressed by representing the law as programs, seen within the context of jurisprudence.

At the root of the controversies over logic and the law are conflicting perspectives on problem solving, inherent in the coming together of theory and practice that is entailed by the procedural interpretation of descriptions. Logicians start with a model of problem solving that is abstract and formal, dealing with discrete domains that are derived from understood models of reality, and seek representations and formalisms from which solutions can be derived. Specialists in a knowledge domain see problems differently. Problems arise where a unified description cannot be given, and there is some unresolved complexity or inconsistency. Systems and legal frameworks have to adjust to changing realities, without the possibility of achieving perfection. It is therefore empty to expect the application of logic and AI to provide complete solutions to problems in the real world, though light may be cast on new aspects and details. Logic may been seen as a tool for problem finding as much as for problem solving.

The case of the British Nationality Act is particulary instructive in this regard. The objective of the Conservative government in drafting the 1981 Bill, which became law as the Act in 1983, was to allow particular categories of people to be accorded full British nationality with right of abode, to regulate others to the status of British subjects with no right of abode, and to exclude others. The law needed to be drafted in such a way that it could be explicable, defensible, and amendable in light of changing circumstances. With all the implicit references to previous legislation over the century, the new Act not only had to be consistent with past legislation but it also had to provide a new unified environment for the consideration of individual cases in the highly charged area of immigration. Government was turning to the law to provide systematic solutions to human problems, in the same kind of way that companies turn to computer systems. Just as company financial systems are used to help to maximise profits and reduce costs, the British Nationality Act was intended to reduce immigration and maximise political benefits. The problems for the legal draftsmen was thus to find rules which would admit preferred groups while barring those groups, many of them large in number, whose entry was not politically expedient or desirable.

The Act was chosen as an interesting example by the Imperial College group in 1981, following small scale experimental work on supplementary benefits legislation. This work had shown that sets of regulations could be regarded as programs to solve queries about benefit entitlements, used flexibly to provide advice to claimants and their advisers. In early 1982 Sergot developed the Query the User facility for logic programming [46], which enabled the system and user to engage in dialogue to solve a problem, with the user supplying factual information when needed in order to test the conditions in particular rules. Many of the research group were not British Nationals, and they had more than an academic interest in immigration law given that it determined their future careers as researchers in the UK. Of the team of authors of the paper presented at the Royal Society and published in the communications of the ACM, Therese Cory and Peter Hammond are British, while Robert Kowalski is American, Marek Sergot of Polish extraction, and Kave Eshgi and Fariba Sadri Iranian. Early modelling exercises indicated that while the conclusions of the Act were closely correlated with racial background of the applicants, the conditions were expressed in much more complex terms, and very often depended in case of difficulty on decisions of the Home Secretary. Hammond's and Sergot's APES system (Augmented PROLOG for Expert Systems) [47] provided a useful vehicle for the knowledge representation exercise on personal computers, and a large part of the Act was encoded in this way as an unfunded academic exercise.

I was involved in demonstrating the prototype system to officials from the

Home Office, who were excited by the potential of the system as a tool for the legal draftsman and the senior immigration officer. Off the record, senior civil servants were aware of the delicacy of problems concerning the nationality and citizenship status of the residents of the Falkland Islands, Gibraltar and Hong Kong. Following the 1982 Falklands War it was agreed to amend the Act to allow Falklands residents right of abode in the UK, though they had been specifically excluded under the 1981 Act. The amendment had to be phrased in such a way that could not be taken as a precedent by Gibraltarians or, more significantly in political and numerical terms, the people of Hong Kong whose territory would return to Chinese control in 1997. The law was being drafted, implemented and amended to deal with a major human problem. Logic could clarify the nature of the law, and could help experts and critics to focus attention on remaining areas of difficulty, raising the potential quality of discussion, debate and decision-making.

The Imperial College British Nationality Act system never went beyond the stage of a provocative unfunded demonstration. The work on logic and the law, with an emphasis on issues in knowledge representation such as time and open texture, continued in association with the Alvey Programme Large Demonstrator System on Intelligent Decision Support with the Department of Health and Social Security. Susskind, first at Oxford, then at Ernst and Young, pursued the issues of expert systems and the law in the context of jurisprudence [44]. Controversy continued, fanned by papers and correspondence from Kowalski and Leith, on logic and problem solving in the law. The controversy retained more heat than is usual in academic debate through Kowalski's adherence to his research strategy of bold assertions modified in the light of debate. A strategy derived from the seminar room proved uncomfortable for some when logic programming was considered as a tool for solving real world problems, for which it had never been designed.

Logic programming derives from automatic theorem proving, and a concern for reasoning about sets of axioms and theorems, models of reality. Changing axioms raises complex logical problems of non-monotonic reasoning. Answering questions about systems involves the closed world assumption, that only knowledge derived from the model can be considered, and the model could never include complete real world information on a subject. Logic programming to date is based on the Horn clause subset of predicate logic, and thus will not encompass temporal or modal logic, nor will it handle truth values other than true and false. Full negation as in classical logic is not available, merely negation as failure, whereby an assertion is held to be false if it cannot be shown to be true.

There are, therefore, inherent differences between what can be accomplished by logic programming in problem solving in the traditional sense, and what non-specialist users may expect of intelligent computer systems operating in the real world. There is no logical reason why systems based on technologies other than logic programming should be exempt from these logical weaknesses, which we can turn into practical strengths once they have been understood. This conclusion will be frustrating for the devotee of "strong AI" but liberating to the practical worker in "weak AI".

Developments in Applied Artificial Intelligence

Applications of AI are not possible without prior consideration of research issues in AI, unless there are to be serious consequences. This suggests the prerequisite for a developed scientific research and development culture [48,49]. Applications will only be as strong as the theory which underlies them, unless they deliver immediate, unquestioned success, which is then sustained over time. Once a given research product performs reliably, however, it loses the classification of AI, and is subsumed into computer science or information technology. A theory which has been developed with the support of AI may then achieve an apparent stability which enables the intellectual scaffolding to be withdrawn. The concepts may pass into the language, with the origins obscured.

There is a tendency among industry and government to want to proceed to commercial applications without passing through the research stage. Research is somehow seen as academic, distant, uncommercial and unnecessary. Government, for example in the United Kingdom, sees near-market research as to be paid for by industry, and plays down the role of basic or fundamental research. In turn industry seeks to focus attention on product development, assuming that public sector funds will cater for research. The dangers of this approach are numerous.

Nobody wishes to pay for research. It is hard, if not impossible, to guarantee a healthy short-term return on research investment. In a world of short-term accountancy, research is sacrificed. In consequence, the culture of research is weakened, and in turn the likelihood of later research funding is reduced. It is straightforward for accountancy-driven evaluations of research programmes to recommend their termination, and the examples are multiplying.

The user or sponsor loses the distinction between the model and reality. The marketing conventions of modern commercial practice are in direct contradiction to scientific principles. Claims will be made to gain effect, but may be subsequently denied or modified. Language will be used metaphorically rather than literally, which impedes verification by normal means. There is a tendency to describe a system in terms of the problem it is intended to solve, rather than its own characteristics as demonstrated in practice. At the global level this applies to "defence" systems, for which contracts are issued defined by identified needs, but whose details remain classified: it is understood that these systems will rarely work, but are intended to deter through their very names. More mundanely, descriptions such as "user friendly", "expert system", "integrated", "natural language front end" and "intelligent tutoring system" are the names of aspirations, not achievements. We learn to discount the claims in practice. We have seen a similar problem in politics, where political movements or parties take their names from their chosen objectives, but find the name applied to their current practice. Thus "Communist", "Democratic", "Socialist", "Liberal", "Radical" all carry ambiguous connotations: they describe an aspiration rather than present reality.

The user and commissioning patron lose touch with what is possible, and imagine results can just be bought. Financial currency is readily understood: it can be cashed in for real goods. Price provides an index by which different items can be compared, with the underlying assumption that greater price denotes greater value in qualitative terms. (This is often the $64,000 question.) It is an easy step to assign a price to a problem, and thus to assume that a solution can be bought given the appropriate efforts, technology and management skills. A large sum of money can be broken down neatly into smaller sums: the same may not apply to problems of knowledge, where shifting representations are common, and it may not be possible to predict how the different pieces will come together.

All too often human consequences of the introduction of particular systems are not considered. Systems should be seen as merely implementations of ideologies or belief systems, and analysis in ideological terms will not usually give priority to human consequences. To take a "systems view" is to risk human damage: even the purported attention to human factors may conflict with the system requirements. The language of system description does not accommodate accounts of external consequences of use.

Increasingly, the unified nature of the core of work in AI is neglected, and obvious lessons are ignored. There will be sound pragmatic reasons for glossing over the areas of uncertainty and theoretical weakness in AI, and focusing on commercially exploitable results in a given area, but the risks are great. AI researchers, using a unified set of tools and concepts, will be quick to apply advances in one area to problems in another. Narrow specialisation in content terms is obsolete and insufficient. Fleck's account of the early development of the AI community [50] bears out this view.

Policy statement can be confused with outcome. AI researchers have helped confound this confusion by overplaying the power of the declarative description or specification. Fifth Generation computing and logic programming are open to this criticism. Classical planning problems emphasise the difficulty of moving from a given described current state to a desired goal state, even within toy domains with agreed objects and language. The real world is enormously more complex, and cannot be relied upon to comply. Criteria for evaluation become confused: for example, Treasury financial criteria and scientific judgements become blurred under a short-termist regime. Quantitative criteria are far easier to check, and to automate with computers. We must reflect on the criteria by which we evaluate our own activities and those of others: by what criteria will we judge our quantitative criteria? At some level the account must be qualitative: why not at the level of human interaction and discourse?

The general low level of scientific knowledge means that research advances are not put in a proper perspective, and undue ill-informed optimism is engendered. British companies lack the culture of AI research, and do not know how to interpret and deal with claims from this area. There is a shortage of university post-doctoral scientists. Salary structures do not reward post-doctoral entrants to industry, and financial skills are regarded more highly than science and technology. Indeed, a large proportion of graduate engineers are recruited into accountancy and financial services.

There is a lack of AI workstations in industry. Technology and information technology directors rarely have board status and control over significant budgets. The pressure from finance directors is to economise, and personal computers are significantly cheaper. There is a lack of electronic networks, compared with the availability of systems such as ARPANET in the USA. Research workers and groups in the United Kingdom continue to work in isolation, and have not acquired the habits of electronic communication and collaboration which are well established in the United States. The foundations were laid by the Department of Defense in funding DARPA and ARPANET, used for wider purposes.

There is no established research and development culture. Successful research depends on a process of what Popper called "Conjecture and Refutation". This in turn presupposes an ongoing environment of informed scientific and technical discourse, with a mixture of free exchange of ideas and progressive advances in expertise and maturity with experience. This cannot come about with short-term projects and temporary contracts, or repeated changes in research policy and funding patterns.

Crucially, there is a lack of technical expertise among management. There is an arrogant and mistaken assumption that specialist training is not required for the development of management skills, and that management skills, once acquired, can be applied across any domain. Thus, many board members and senior managers in British industry may have a background in accountancy, but not in either management or the technologies of production which they manage. There is an unmistakable class aspect to this: managers in major firms may have a public school and university background, but are unlikely to have studied science or technology, while managers of smaller firms may have risen from the shop floor, with minimal formal education prior to work. Either way, the critical mix of technical and management skills is lacking. Compounding the problem is a lack of research management. It has only recently been perceived that scientific and technical research itself requires management, and that research management skills take years to acquire.

The situation has been complicated for many British companies by their reliance on defence contracts. Not only have defence contracts provided an assured income, but the profit element has largely financed the research and development base for civil products. This has meant a feather-bedding from civilian market conditions. The civil market involves competition on price, quality and delivery times, none of which have been stringently applied in defence contracts. Where defence firms have launched civil products, they have probably subsidised the process from military products with common technology components. Indeed, for governments publicly opposed to state subsidy for industry, this has been an obvious route to industrial supremacy, particularly in the United States. US firms have the added benefits of protection by the Pentagon and Department of Commerce under COCOM terms, interpreted to benefit American companies by comparison with their Western competitors. Normal production methods have not been followed in the high performance, high unit cost tradition of defence. Military technology is unlikely to work in practice, but in principle it must meet the highest standards, almost regardless of price, as the dangers of defeat in war far outweigh financial considerations. The culture of defence work virtually precludes technology transfer on security grounds. If we believe in the efficacy of military technology, it is hardly sensible to let it fall into the hands of potential enemies, or those who might pass the technology to them. Unfortunately, computer technology combines military potential with civil applications, and dramatic research advances make socially useful applications less likely. Such a situation has been compounded by the fall in price of computer hardware, and the vast scale of production and take-up internationally. Complete control of technology transfer is out of the question, but the Pentagon continues to apply restrictions to the movement of any components of American origin. Normal commercial discussion and academic teaching is impaired, for militarily funded work cannot be freely drawn on in discussion with students and colleagues.

Where AI is applied, and systems are implemented to run automatically in real time in the real world, there are considerable dangers. Users need to be aware of the constraints on the application of the system. It could help if users had a model of the belief system of the designers, given that their use is within that system. In the case of military systems, security probably precludes disclosure of the underlying belief system, which is beyond interrogation or revision. Such rigidity is incompatible with the underlying exploratory foundations of AI. To follow an underlying belief system without question is to be bound by an ideology, and must be acknowledged as such. To use such a system to test a hypothesis is a different matter: hypotheses can be refuted and replaced.

Applied AI can negate the exploratory foundations of AI, as it implies the possibility of complete and certain solutions to problems in a complex and changing world. AI is only ultimately as strong as its critical reception. AI is process, not product: if all AI products are accepted without dispute, AI is dead.

Chapter 2

Perspectives from the Humanities

Knowledge, Information and Data

Do we want to explore the theoretical foundations of the humanities with the aid of intelligent information technology, or just play around with data? How do we distinguish the levels of data, information and knowledge, or is this an idle distinction? Some clarification is in order, if we are to locate the different levels in the context of human use.

"Knowledge" is a term much abused in information technology, particularly where claims are made regarding knowledge based systems. Often emphasis is placed on the manner in which knowledge is made explicit in a representation for use by both the user and the system. Knowledge will necessarily have a qualitative character, though this may be implicit, hidden behind a quantitative exterior appearance. Knowledge makes no sense when divorced from the consideration of someone who knows. We expect the holder of knowledge to feel some personal association with it, as part of himself. What is the status of tacit knowledge? Can I be said to know something if I am unable to demonstrate that knowledge to others? This demonstration could include performing tasks for which particular knowledge would be required, enabling the observer to infer the presence of that knowledge.

Can we escape from social and cultural criteria for the possession of knowledge? If not, then the ascription "knowledge based system" must properly be applied to the human social context in which the computer system is developed and used, and not more narrowly to the software component. The software system can then be said to be based on the socially constituted knowledge which it seeks to represent. When used it will be located in a different social context of knowledge. Thus, though the code will be unchanged, it will be given a different interpretation by "users". Knowledge based systems would thus appear to fall into the same category as books, plays and films, with the additional features of interaction, including responses to questions and the provision of partial explanations, in terms of the structure within which particular propositions are located.

"Information" presupposes some semantic component, some explicit or implicit question to which the information could be seen as the answer. Management information systems tend to have a quantitative emphasis, used for statistical purposes, and presuppose the existence of institutional structures and qualitative categories. Again, for a management information system to work it must bring together people and technology: the computer system itself is not enough.

"Data" are given, but were not necessarily asked for. Like unwanted Christmas presents, the origin may be clear but the reception may be passive rather than interactive. Data may be in the form of low level signals, which require interpretation before contributing to our knowledge. Data may be regarded as evidence if considered as possibly forming part of an answer to a question, but data does not acquire the status of evidence, or of information, without human intervention.

Our levels of information handling and system use will be associated with our level of expertise in the given domain. "Expertise" is a term we often use, but rarely define, except by pointing to examples. How could we define expertise? How can we distinguish the humanities scholar from the intelligent layman? Could the scholar make the basis of his expertise explicit? Does the historian do more than merely process data? If we cannot characterise expertise in the humanities, what is the foundation of our elaborate structure of course and qualifications? How can we justify the salaries paid to humanities teachers and lecturers? It may be worth assembling our ideas and trying to build models of the reasoning performed in the humanities.

Models, ideas and programs are related to the real world of applications through individual and social interpretations. Work has begun, through logicist analysis [13,51–54], in reconstructing and simulating such interpretations. Archaeology has been the primary focus of attention, and the early successes may be due to the fact that archaeological evidence cannot answer back.

Can AI be applied without in some sense prostituting the domain of application? Must it be diminished by successive approximations? Does it threaten or subvert the professional standing of the established exponent? Is that subversion entirely a bad idea? Have academics maybe found it too easy to slip into a routine of publishing unread papers in obscure journals for the sake of academic prestige? Academic communication should again be interactive, through AI, and with rules and patterns of discourse made newly explicit. We could hope for a resurgence of research activity and critical debate.

Interpretation and Codebreaking

Collingwood [15] argued that:

History is a science whose business is to study events not accessible to our observation, and to study these events inferentially, arguing to them from something else which is accessible to our observation, and which the historian calls "evidence" for the event in which he is interested.

Historical knowledge must be shared and explained; it cannot be individual property:

The historian is not allowed to claim any single piece of knowledge, except where he can justify his claim by exhibiting to himself in the first place, and secondly to anyone else who is both able and willing to follow his demonstration, the grounds upon which it is based.

The activity of the historian is seen as scientific, and based on the asking and answering of questions:

Scientific historians study problems: they ask questions, and if they are good historians they ask questions which they see their way to answering.

In particular, history is seen as the key to the investigation of "mind":

The right way of investigating mind is by the methods of history.

Carr [55] attacked the objective, espoused by Acton, of "ultimate history". He ridiculed the approach typified by Mr Gradgrind in Dickens' *Hard Times*: "What I want is Facts.... Facts alone are wanted in life", an approach which enjoyed a revival in Downing Street in the 1980s. Carr drew attention to the fact that even our records of ancient and medieval history are, quoting Bury "starred with lacunae". We are the recipients of the interpretations of others:

Our picture has been preselected and predetermined for us, not so much by accident as by people who were consciously or unconsciously imbued with a particular view, and thought the facts which supported that view worth preserving.

There is no respectable escape from the "fetishism of facts" into the "fetishism of documents":

No document can tell us more than what the author of the document thought – what he thought had happened, what he thought ought to happen or would happen, or perhaps only what he wanted others to think he thought, or even only what he himself thought he thought. None of this means anything until the historian has got to work on it and deciphered it. The facts, whether found in documents or not, still have to be processed by the historian before he can make any use of them: the use he makes of them is, if I may put it that way, the processing process.

In short, Carr concludes that "History means interpretation".

Laslett was influenced by the work of French social historians of the Annales School in his work in Cambridge on population and social structure. He made enthusiastic use of quantitative methods, but with explicit concern for the genuine significance of quantification for historians [56]:

Whenever a statement is made about a plurality of persons and it is claimed that they are more this than that or mostly the one and not the other, on average like this rather than like anything else; whenever a proposition is made in social terms, whether it is about votes, or prices, or length of life, or the number of heirs likely to live long enough to succeed, or even about the distribution of opinions, or preferences, or beliefs, then quantities are in question.

He showed an acute awareness of the limitations of the quantitative approach [57], when considering the position of the educated priest or literate parish clerk whose entries form the raw material for so much local history:

Whether or not a sense of duty in the mind of a priest, duty to his order or duty to his flock, was sufficient to keep him at his task of registration consistently enough to earn our praise so long after he is dead, it is impossible to imagine that he could ever have anticipated being judged on our criteria.

Macfarlane, both historian [58,59] and social anthropologist [60], has attempted the reconstruction of many past communities over time. His work follows the insight of Collingwood [15] that:

The historian is not interested in the fact that men eat and sleep and make love and thus satisfy their natural appetites; but he is interested in the social customs which they created by their thought as a framework within which these appetites find satisfaction in ways sanctioned by convention and morality.

He led an exhaustive study of the village of Earls Colne 1400–1750 [58], reconstructing the lives of individuals from the records of the Church, the State and the Estate on which they lived:

In order to understand what these fragments mean it is essential to understand how the information came to be collected; for what purpose and with what assumptions it was written down .... Furthermore, we need to know not only what remains but what else was written at the time and has since been lost; not only what was recorded but what was omitted because it was common knowledge or unknown .... The significance of every word is decreased if we do not understand the process of the institutions which created the documents .... What we have is the dismembered reflection of many individual lives in records created for a multitude of purposes.

Collingwood argued in his *Autobiography* [61], that the historian needed to maintain hypotheses, to expect particular answers to his questions:

If you want to know why a certain kind of thing happened in a certain kind of case, you must begin by asking, "what did you expect?" You must consider what the normal development is in cases of that kind. Only then, if the thing that happened in this case was exceptional, should you try to explain it by appeal to exceptional circumstances.

Macfarlane, in *The Origins of English Individualism* [59], explains how he felt obliged to discard conventional models of social change in England. He came to the work on Earls Colne after historical studies of witchcraft and sexual behaviour in Essex, and anthropological study of a Himalayan village, giving him a broader basis for comparison. His analysis of the Earls Colne documents required a general theoretical framework, but:

There was a very considerable gap between what I was discovering and what I should have been finding. Instead of relatively "closed" and integrated "communities" at the start, which gradually broke apart with the gradual penetration of the market, increasing geographical mobility, the break-down of kinship groups and other changes, it began to appear that there was no long secular trend .... It was just not possible to use the models of community-based societies which historians and anthropologists had devised in relation to many parts of the world...

He was thus obliged to seek a new interpretive framework:

This work is thus a search not only for a revised framework which would make some of my own previously unsolved theoretical problems soluble, but one which would help to explain whether and when England became different from other parts of Europe and the nature of the social structure which we have inherited.

In past decades this approach to history, increasingly seen, in Collingwood's terms, as "the science of mind" rather than a mechanical process of scissors and paste assembly, was contrasted with the methodology and aspirations of the natural sciences. The confidence of scientists was such, in the early years of the century, that they aspired to full understanding of all natural phenomena, and promised the replication of many through the use of advancing technology. Reflective modern scientists recall that science is a matter of organising knowledge, and that the laboratory must always be distinguished from the real world. Chemical experiments, as with Collingwood's thought experiments, can only be described in terms of what we know, and we cannot control real life.

Ziman [62], professor of physics and of science policy, has attacked the complacency of those who hide behind the facade of neutral science, a flawed ideology, adherence to which can mask less worthy objectives.

Science is held to be perfectly rational – i.e. logically irrefutable, from its observational premises to its theoretical conclusions, and perfectly objective – i.e. representing the point of view of an abstract intellect free from the defects and vices of any single human mind .... In reality, science grows by processes that are far more fallible, far more subjective, far less disinterested, far less logically watertight than this ideology would allow. Reliable as it may be in most of its main lines of argument, and in numerous details, science nevertheless maintains many errors of fact and interpretation. Much of its rationality is superficial – little better than special pleading for an interpretation that is far from proven by the evidence. Much of its objectivity is spurious – little better than a depersonalised abstract formulation of the prejudices and interests unconsciously shared by a particular group of scientists working in a particular field.... The scientist who depends solely on "scientific method" for his or her opinions tends to adopt an inhumane attitude which is not sufficiently responsive to historical circumstances, moral values, the diversity of human aspirations and other untidy realities that cannot be "rationalised" and "objectified" out of the way.

We must puncture the myth of scientific objectivity: science is as much a product of its cultural context as any other human social and economic institution. Science and technology do not necessarily operate in the same way in different cultures, though practitioners will normally act as if there were no language and cultural barriers, and we operated in a single intellectual market.

We are accustomed in the Anglo-Saxon world to the divide between the arts and the sciences, described by C.P.Snow [63] as the "Two Cultures". Such a division is less extreme in the rest of Europe, where philosophy and theory are held in greater respect, and history is numbered among the "human sciences". It may be that the prominence given to AI in the Anglo-Saxon world may lead to some healing of the rift between arts and sciences, as well as an intellectual bridging of the Channel.

A useful framework is offered by Simon [64] in *The Sciences of the Artificial*, where he sees AI as giving visible coherence and structure to human activities in the social and economic sphere and the social sciences. He outlines his thesis in the Preface:

Certain phenomena are "Artificial" in a very specific sense: they are as they are only because of a system's being moulded, by goals or purposes, to the environment in which it lives.

As a Nobel prize winning economist Simon had seen the power of abstraction and simulation, and he could immediately see the potential for the computer:

The computer becomes an obvious device for exploring the consequences of alternative organisational assumptions for human behaviour.

He found that the computer enabled him to deal with ideas as he was accustomed to dealing with administrative structures:

Computers have transported symbol systems from the platonic heaven of ideas to the empirical world of actual processes carried out by machines or brains, or by the two of them working together.

His focus on human problem solving involves the breaking down of conventional barriers between subject areas:

The real subject of the intellectual free trade among the many cultures are our own thought processes, our processes of judging, deciding, choosing and creating. We are importing and exporting from one intellectual discipline to another ideas about how a socially organised information- processing system like a human being – or a computer, or a complex of men and women and computers in organised cooperation – solves problems and achieves goals in outer environments of great complexity.

Boden [65] has argued in similar terms for philosophy and literature. AI enables us to give form to abstract ideas, making them explicit and opening them up for scrutiny:

This field of research has a potential for counteracting the dehumanising influence of natural science for suggesting solutions to many traditional problems in the philosophy of mind, and for illuminating the hidden complexities of human thinking and personal psychology.

Explanations and interpretations can be modelled and scrutinised:

The computational metaphor helps one to ask whether an interpretation of a psychological phenomenon is a possible explanation of it, without implying that validation must involve detailed predictive tests.

Logicist Analysis and Artificial Intelligence

Wittgenstein was concerned with the foundations of knowledge, and never wanted detail to obscure his view. He wrote [66]:

What interests me is not constructing a building, but having in front of me in a transparent way the foundations of possible buildings ... for me such clarity or transparency is a goal in itself.

Gardin et al. [13] have challenged the assumption that computer formalisation might be applicable to the natural sciences but was precluded from the humanities by their very nature:

The unbridled character of the literature of the humanities, compared with that of the more precise sciences, has been put forward as an obstacle to all hope of a formalisation of reasoning in the sense, and to the extent, required by AI.

In a perceptive insight, they noted that many scholars might find exemption from computer technology curiously convenient:

In addition, some see in this contrast a fortunate protection from the encroachments of technology; for them, the study of human conduct and creative behaviour should be a kind of intellectual conservation area, protected from science, where ways of thinking and forms of language hold sway which are irreducible to those computational mechanisms which are, in their view, incarnate in expert systems.

Gardin, a computer user whose humanistic credentials are beyond impeachment, turns the argument round against the sceptics:

The very peculiarities of ways of thinking which are specific to the humanities means that a computer simulation can bring to the surface stimulating intellectual problems which have been more or less evaded in the conventional restriction of the applications of computers to highly specialised technical areas.

He argues the case for more rigorous thinking in the humanities, with the computer as an invaluable aid:

The reproduction of certain types of reasoning on the computer imposes a preliminary analysis of mental processes in terms and at a level of precision which is rarely encountered in the humanities.

This opens up areas of research and discussion not normally available to humanities scholars, concerning the nature of their own reasoning. Such questions are not merely raised by the use of expert systems, but must be addressed prior to the responsible use of such systems:

There is little chance of understanding much of the role of expert systems in the humanities if one does not pose preliminary questions on the nature of the reasoning process which these systems are expected to reproduce or replace through computational means.

Argument in the Humanities

Arthur Stutt [67] carries the debate further, building on Gardin's insights to explore the nature and processes of argument in the humanities. Skills in argument are somehow taken for granted in the humanities:

We all know how to argue. We don't have to be taught how to argue any more than we have to be taught how to talk. It is a natural consequence of our competitive natures and the rich semantic complexity of our language that argument is both necessary and possible. Of course we provide training for specialised forms of argument. For philosophers, say, and lawyers. But the arguments they provide, while perhaps more formal in their expression and more profound in their importance nevertheless depend on the tracing or creation of a web of semantic as well as logical interconnections between the concepts which make up a particular context of discourse.

Close analysis of arguments suggests that knowledge is used in many different ways:

There are differences ... in the sort of knowledge made use of by different arguers in different domains, the common sense or background understanding which is tacitly appealed to, the different value systems and the particular context of an argument.

There are immediate practical implications for the designers of systems which are intended for use in a humanistic knowledge domain:

What does matter is that the designer of a knowledge based system has experience of the domain or close and prolonged contact with someone who has such experience.

Knowledge base design takes on a new level of demands once the perceptions and argumentation patterns of intended users are considered:

It is necessary for the designer of knowledge based systems to have a clear understanding both of the domain and of the problems in using advanced computer systems as perceived by users in the domain.

By such criteria current programs offered for use in the humanities tend to seem inadequate, or even inappropriate:

It is not simply that the programs are felt to be inadequate (though they are) nor that they are felt to be authoritarian (though they can be) but that their existence changes not only accepted procedures but accepted ways of thinking.

Once it is accepted that it would be valuable to clarify areas of difficulty in developing a model of a problem, the case for interactive use of a program is strengthened:

Interpretation will always be an uncertain, plausible and provisional process. At the same time certain elements become clearer when exposed .... This clarity can be enhanced by a computer program which automates the analysis by prompting the user for all the necessary elements in building up an argument.

Stutt emphasises the inherent limits in the extent to which computers could ever represent human arguments:

Insofar as argumentation is the meat and bones of many of our discourses both in our everyday life and in our specialised pursuits (academic and non-academic) this attempt is important. However, for the same reason, the attempt must ultimately fail. In order to be able to "argue" as a human can a machine would need to be the isomorph of a human being. Arguing is not something we do independently of our other capacities and attributes. Thus the model I produce must of necessity only approximate to a human being.

What the computer program offers is the possibility of externalising key issues, and presenting intellectual structures for scrutiny:

The computer imposes a degree of objectivity on the attempt which is of importance and, when coupled with AI techniques of representation and manipulation, a model and a simulation of arguing can be produced which, while formal in that a computer language is used, is also human-like in taking account of more than the merely mathematical aspects of logic. I am aware that computer technology is in itself determined by particular social and political constraints. But then this is true of any form of expression which I might attempt to use. The computer, like natural language, can be used as a means of exposing its own determining factors. The automation of arguing processes also allows the possibility of exposing and manipulating the processes which shape our arguments.

Representation

Representation is central to AI and its applications, but has far broader ramifications. The outcomes of AI research have successively been incorporated into computer science, which has served to obscure the theoretical foundations on which the research was built. Whereas natural science has been concerned with the formulation and testing of hypotheses and models, technology has been used to effect change in the real world.

For scientific models to relate to practical human activity in the real world, they must be represented in terms which mediate between the user and the postulated model or machine. AI can be seen as the "technology of thought", giving form to the otherwise abstract or haphazard function of mediation, resulting in alternative representations. How else would we have scholarly discourse as distinct from ordinary language? We have learnt to accept competing representations, but with emerging criteria of adequacy.

An important research area concerns the use of computational tools for the elucidation of problems in the humanities. Where a representation can be agreed upon, the problem may become computationally tractable. This involves a critical shift in the definitions of problems and problem solving. In the humanities we solve a problem by achieving a satisfactory representation. AI techniques enable us to process the knowledge as represented, giving answers to specific questions. Humanities researchers have sometimes feared that their purity is somehow sullied by the use of computational models and representations. They have remained content to consider periods of history in terms of the reconstructed lives of families in institutional contexts, or to adopt structuralist approaches to literary criticism.

Representation concerns the making explicit of underlying presuppositions, the exposure of hidden structure. To address issues of representation is not to abandon one's judgement or interpretation in favour of a machine, but to be prepared to reflect on one's practice, and to allow others to join in that reflection. As such it may come to be seen as an indispensable stage in the social reconstitution of knowledge.

Quantification

Quantification is not a matter of numbers, but of generalities. Rather than taking each case individually, as a matter of convenience we identify common characteristics, or predicates, which can be ascribed to sets of individuals. Such predicates can only provide partial descriptions, and are themselves artificial, though some practical utility maybe derived.

The choice of predicates will be culturally and socially influenced. Within a given human institution it will be customary for particular predicates to be used, and in conventionally accepted structures and ways. A new arrival to the institution will be deemed eligible for membership if he uses the predicates "correctly", if he "speaks the same language" or participates in the same "form of life".

Where numbers are used within quantification they cannot denote an additional level of objectivity or scientific reality, for the numbers are merely used within culturally derived predicates. This will not usually be perceived by the audience for the display of numbers, for whom the numbers, or statistics, constitute a confirmation of the orthodoxy to which they are subject. A request to explain a set of statistics is normally answered, if at all, in terms of further statistics within the same cultural model. As such, it is rarely an explanation proper, and more usually a redescription within the hermetic seal of quantification. Where objective reality is ascribed to a set of statistics, it will be because the statistics have been assembled to present a point of view. Government figures on unemployment are regularly cited by the press, who fail to point out that the basis on which they are calculated has been changed some thirty times in ten years, meaning that none of the figures are strictly comparable. Even Laslett's parish clerk [56] was writing for the record.

The obsession with numbers is clearest when it comes to money. Britain produces more accountants per head than any other advanced country, and fewer engineers and scientists than major competitors. Our company directors often know how to make nothing but money. They no longer read literature, but restrict themselves to balance sheets. To look at a company or process simply in terms of the balance sheet is to take a partial and distorted view. Certain unhelpful assumptions are embedded within the belief system of the accountant, which must be made explicit, and in some cases challenged. Analysis tends to be solely in terms of those aspects of a company or process which can be quantified in financial terms. All other aspects drop out of consideration. It is notoriously difficult, for example, to mix business and ethics, or to ascribe value to personal characteristics. It is much easier to "stick to the facts", by which is meant selected numbers. When different choices are considered, the likely outcomes are usually compared quantitatively rather than qualitatively.

The balance sheet mentality tends to corrupt the language with which the functioning of institutions is described. We talk of profit and loss, of costs and benefits, as if quantities could change while qualities somehow continued unaltered. An understanding of the financial language of the auditor or accountant enables the "creative accountant" to assemble a statistical picture that conforms with external requirements, but which says little about the reality of the institution. Creative accountancy can be a substitute for activity.

Any statistical comparison will only be valid if all other variables are assumed to remain unchanged. This could only ever be true of a model, and not of the real world, which we have only ever partially described in arbitrary categories and quantities. The financial interpretation of numerical information tends to impose a two-dimensional or even linear view of reality. When situations are modelled in terms of two-person games, they tend to be seen in confrontational terms, with a zero-sum view of outcomes. This ignores both the benefits of co-operation and the dynamics of change.

There is an implicit assumption of individualism rather than collectivism. Items are bought and sold, but never shared. This model does not fully capture the power of knowledge or "intellectual property", as it has to be called when financial considerations are applied to ideas.

Conventional hierarchical management, with vertical lines of control, may be endangered by the spread of AI tools and techniques. If the lower ranks can model the policies and practices of their superiors, what is to prevent them from replacing them? What are the implications for policy on technology and training? If an administrative system is inherently able to explain itself in terms of its rules and regulations, then what happens to those bureaucrats whose role has been to act as a buffer between government and people? Can they be replaced, or is their role merely changed? What happens to management consultants as their expensive advice is made available through expert systems on personal computers? Should consultants seek to make themselves obsolete?

Would finance directors be threatened if management took an intelligent interest in decision support systems? Would there be pressure to look beyond the simple certainties of the balance sheet? Is there at present a cosy conspiracy between finance and computer staff, playing on the ignorance and idleness of management?

Is there a parallel with defence policy, where experts present figures on the threat facing the nation, in justification of ever increasing expenditure on arms? How would industrial relations be affected if both employers and unions could work through simulations of the problems they both face, exploring the different outcomes and appreciating the mutual gains to be made from collaboration rather than conflict? Would strategies of bluff and counter-bluff be modified if each side knew more about the other? How much is management a question of the efficient use of information, and how much does it involve people and expert knowledge?

Where management has the use of intelligent decision support tools, are they made available to their employees as well, or is a competitive advantage preserved? Should any more credence be given to management decisions made with the aid of expert systems technology: or should we in fact dismiss them if we have doubts as to the validity of the tools used? Who is to blame for decisions made using expert systems? Auditing is not merely a financial operation, though that is how it has been traditionally regarded. We now hear talk of skills audits, curriculum audit, medical audit. Often this is accompanied by talk of cost centres and devolved financial decision-making, and it may turn out that the terms in which the audit is designed are predominantly financial. This should not be so, for to accept a financial model as the basis for considering the working of an institution is to accept the full set of underlying financial assumptions.

What, then, is the acceptable alternative? We may object to discussions of institutions in terms of money, but it at least provides an apparently universal "currency" for debate. If we discard such an established approach what can we put in its place? Qualitative descriptions can be criticised as collapsing into value-judgements. People who object to the standard approaches may be thought to have something to hide.

If we are to audit or evaluate an institution we must have, albeit implicitly, a model of the cultural context. Institutions, even total institutions, do not operate in a vacuum. From within they may appear consistent and complete, but from outside they have limits, points of contact, input and output, exchange and communication.

Modelling with Artificial Intelligence Tools

We may wish to represent such a model using AI tools and techniques. A number of approaches are available:

1. Declarative logic [68]: we describe a set of facts and rules, showing the state of the world and conclusions that can be drawn.
2. Procedural [69]: we identify particular processes, and show what actions or events are triggered by particular combinations of causes or preconditions.
3. Frame-based [70,71]: we identify stereotypical models and situations, in terms of which we can make sense of a particular set of circumstances.
4. Semantic network [72]: we identify nodes and links, to give structure to a mass of detailed information, highlighting relationships between different elements.
5. Distributed AI [73,74]: we identify several actors working at once, drawing attention to their different backgrounds, beliefs and actions, and to their interactions.

No model is going to achieve complete correspondence with observed reality, but attention may usefully be drawn to the differences, to the anomalies which are not fully understood. We may wish to use several different models, or representations, in turn in order to gain new insights. It may be hard to give statistical measures of the "degree of fit": that, too, is a knowledge based concept in this account. We should be able to describe the senses in which a model is inadequate, and in a way which motivates further effort and enquiry.

The process of reflection and self-scrutiny implicit in the conduct of such a knowledge based institutional audit is likely to be healthy and beneficial for the institution, though disconcerting in the short term for those unaccustomed to the process. All participants, including external agents, have to be prepared to answer direct questions.

Computational Politics: Modelling Bureaucrats

Policies can be modelled and tested, building working models of manifestos. Manifestos can be seen as declarative statements, given procedural interpretations by politicians in the environment of political institutions. Policy proposals can be run past a series of model institutions or officials, like metal components in a finishing shop or automobiles undergoing quality control testing.

Qualitative modelling of policies goes much deeper than Treasury statistical quantitative models. Underlying belief systems must be made explicit if the figures are to have meaning. Revealing such belief systems is likely to contradict Official Secrets legislation.

Colby [75] and Abelson [76] modelled the Cold War Warrior with their "Ideology Machine", which was subjected to the test of responding to questions put to a White House spokesman on foreign affairs. We could now model the Downing Street spokesman, the senior civil servant as satirised by Sir Humphrey Appleby in *Yes, Minister* [76,77]. Such an official will always be "economical with the truth". This can be described in more formal terms to cast light on the "closed world" of the civil service.

A civil servant is trained to reveal the minimum of information, carrying out a minimal search and seeking to avoid possible further questions. When in doubt, a civil servant will prefer to address the syntactic structure of a question rather than the semantic content or the pragmatic context, as this strategy will often obviate the need for providing a substantive answer. The closed world assumption is used in association with negation as failure: it is assumed that open civil service files contain the sum total of relevant information, and thus a failure to find evidence is equated with there being no evidence, inhibiting the asking of questions lest evidence be found. Given the role of preparing ministerial briefs, which constitute models of the problems to be addressed, greater emphasis is placed on consistency than on overall coherence. A brief needs to withstand attack through supplementary questions, a large proportion of which can be anticipated and catered for. Given that the purpose of a brief is to provide a sustainable and watertight model, questions of truth or falsity have little relevance. The civil servant encourages his minister to remain within the civil service model rather than venturing into the real world with which it only partly corresponds. The intervention of political advisers can thus be extremely disruptive, eroding the neat boundaries and categories devised by the civil service for administrative convenience. The civil servant learns to give answers which discourage further questions, or which set the challenge of a new knowledge hurdle to be overcome before another question can be put. He learns the use of the public record, and the means of keeping official papers from public scrutiny. Secrecy is a major tool for preservation of the status quo. When challenged beyond approved limits, the civil servant learns to speak in a code which is only understood by the few, yet has an apparently acceptable interpretation to the many.

This could be effectively modelled at the meta-level, giving a "Civil Servant Expert System Shell", or a series of such shells for more specialist areas. Experienced civil servants have served in many ministries dealing with many knowledge domains, but with common meta-level strategies and approaches to the user interface. However, this account could be misleading. Senior civil servants are far from automata, rather they have acquired considerable tacit knowledge from their participation in the governmental form of life, so that they know how to act in a given situation. It could not sensibly be left to a machine to determine how a situation should be characterised, though this might appear straightforward in retrospect. The "Civil Servant Shells", however, could perform a valuable function in assisting the preparation and submission of funding proposals, planning applications, etc. They would offer a means of making explicit what the "official beliefs" are, together with the disclosure of the consequences of their acceptance. The same shells, having performed a job support role with policy makers and administrators, could support advice giving and training. Perhaps this concept of the "Civil Servant Shell" corresponds to the generalist civil servant, but with the difference of a bias towards generosity, rather than economy, with the truth.

Chapter 3

Education

Education Before Computers

Long before the first working computers the concepts of reasoning and computation offered powerful metaphors to assist in learning. Children have been obliged to learn their tables in order to compute the answers to arithmetic problems, and to learn the linguistic and grammatical forms of dead languages in order to process and understand texts in modern languages. Powerful formal structures were identified which underlay the academic content to be mastered, and traditional education could be conceived as a form of programming, where the outcome of the process was intended to be matriculating students who were younger conforming versions of their master. In software and social engineering terms it was important to inculcate structures and bodies of knowledge which were both powerful and amenable to change in the light of changing circumstances. Particular knowledge was required to be held by all, while certain advanced subject matter was to be restricted to the elite few. In a world where change was gradual, control and standards could be maintained over the process, and the repeated stages of selection through examination and financial means ensured a high degree of quality control on the product. Within the education system there was a correct answer to every question, and thus increased efficiency could be sought by instituting payment by results and automating assessment through standardised questions. Education could thus be administered along business lines, providing those within the system with the certainties and constraints of a total institution. Automation offered the prospect of considerable benefits: the power of the few over the many could be enhanced with the support of the technically skilled.

When practical computer systems were first implemented, it was not to advance the cause of learning. Wartime codebreaking and defence requirements accelerated the process of development, and over the past forty years the role of computers in business and industry has grown ever greater. In the early days communication with computers was through low level machine "languages", but as time has gone on it has been possible to use more "natural" modes of communication, including higher level computer languages, graphics and voice input. The performance and capacity of computers have increased dramatically, while their size and cost have fallen beyond the wildest imaginings of the early pioneers. Whereas the few early systems were based in air- conditioned isolation and operated by scientists in white coats, we now see lap-top machines sold by the millions from corner shops, and few areas of modern life have not now been affected.

Generations of Computer-Assisted Learning

I would like to identify four "generations" of Computer-Assisted Learning (CAL), with which I have been associated since the 1960s.

Mainframes: Machines

Computers were at first a scarce resource, with "mainframe" systems being installed at privileged locations. Access to hardware was opened up through the development of time-sharing which allowed a number of users to use the same central processing unit from terminals in different locations. Advances in software technology also increased access. From the early machine languages specialist languages were developed for particular purposes: FORTRAN for scientific and numerical work, and COBOL for business data processing. Dartmouth College in New Hampshire developed the language BASIC as an introduction to programming for users of their time-sharing system. Accordingly, as one such user at Phillips Academy, Andover, in Massachusetts, I could write programs to help me in my work on statistics and probability, and my classmates experimented with the generation of computer poetry.

To program such a machine one had to learn to think like a machine. A program was a sequence of numbered instructions, and no scope could be left for doubt or ambiguity if the system was to "run". A program could be made interactive by requiring the user to type in particular prescribed responses, each of which had been anticipated by the program. The interactive systems were thus closed, and limited in flexibility although numerous permutations of iterations and branching could be used. It took little imagination to model stereotypical classroom treatment of particular educational issues into such program moulds, as long as one was prepared to insist on the absolute correctness of answers, and prepared to abandon the consideration of alternatives. My own work concerned the tree representation of decision and game theory, modelling both problems of history and philosophy and their heavily simplified program equivalents.

In educational systems where simple certainties still reigned and mainframe computers with terminals were accessible, notably in North America, the new field of CAL bloomed. An early objective was to make systems "teacher proof", as there was great concern over the low calibre of schoolteachers, whose failings might be circumvented through the centralised provision of automated systems. The theoretical basis for CAL work was often derived from the behaviourist work of Skinner [79], and his techniques developed with rats were readily applied to teachers and students. However, rats do not answer back, ask for explanations or grow up to program other rats.

Europe was in general more sceptical, but saw that the potential technology needed to be explored. Accordingly, in the United Kingdom the National Development Programme for Computer Assisted Learning (NDPCAL) was established, combining a research base and classroom practice in a number of projects across the country and across the disciplines. Few schools had regular access to mainframe systems, so these were very much pilot projects.

Microcomputers: Programs

Technological advances are rarely predicted, and their consequences may take decades to become clear. The development of microcomputers in the late 1970s suddenly brought computer power within the reach of schools and colleges, without there being a clear perception of what was to be done with it.

In the UK the NDPCAL results were cautious and not widely disseminated [80]. As is so often the case, the pilot projects were not followed up by sustained support. Instead, as part of Whitehall interdepartmental warfare, the Department of Trade and Industry announced a scheme to support the acquisition of microcomputers by schools and colleges, later followed by the damage limitation exercise from the Department of Education and Science in what became the Microelectronics Education Programme (MEP) [81], giving support for teachers and students. Few teachers had prior experience of computers, and little help was available from higher education. There was no strong base in educational research on which to build, so teachers were left to improvise.

As head of a history department at an Essex comprehensive school, I entered a competition in a computing magazine, offering a Research Machines computer (RML 380Z) for the best ideas for computers in education. My proposals for work in historical simulation [82] won us the computer, followed by a second from the Department of Trade and Industry scheme which was launched using photographs of our Wedgwood simulation. The RML 380Z allowed us to program in BASIC, which I quickly saw was not adequate for my needs: for example I needed rich data description and explanation of events and decisions, with easy access to information for my students for use in classroom debates and decisions.

There were expert groups in the UK, producing valuable CAL software for the Research Machines computer and the BBC Micro. In particular the Schools Council Computers in the Curriculum Project, based at Chelsea College, had long experience carried over from NDPCAL, and the necessary critical mass of programmers and teachers with current classroom expertise. Their work, together with that of the Advisory Unit for Microtechnology in Hatfield, the Computer-Based Learning Unit at Leeds University, and the Institute of Educational Technology at the Open University, predated MEP, and had the central administrative backing from the Council for Educational Technology (CET). When MEP suffered the customary fate of UK national programmes, abolition without either replacement or securely funded follow-up, many of the MEP 14 regional centres collapsed or reverted to their previous functions. Much of the work in the MEP period was at the cottage-industry level, without the level of funding necessary for sound development methods and quality control [83], and designing software for UK microcomputers whose export potential proved to be limited, never reaching an international mass education market. The Microelectronics Education Support Unit (MESU) lacked a defined role or significant budget, and in 1988 was subsumed into the National Council for Educational Technology (NCET), providing an administrative structure similar to that before MEP.

One spin-off of the proliferation of microcomputers was the vast expansion in school teaching of "Computer Studies", which often meant simply programming in BASIC on BBC Micro or Sinclair Spectrum. Given that the teachers were themselves untrained in Computer Studies, and the versions of BASIC offered on microcomputers were many and various, the result was akin to the computational equivalent of salmonella in eggs: most production of computer scientists was infected, and government support was mainly directed at the producers of microcomputers.

Artificial Intelligence and Education: Tools

Researchers at Edinburgh University Department of Artificial Intelligence were among the first to warn of the dangers of "putting the clock back" [84] through the ill-considered proliferation of microcomputers. Just at the time when educational theory was moving on from Skinnerian behaviourism to Piagetian cognitive development, the use of microcomputers risked reversing the process, restoring a linear and closed approach to instruction, and the use of multiple-choice questions, rather than an emphasis on learning and the learner, opening up possibilities for further exploration.

In the 1970s and early 1980s researchers in AI and education were hampered by the fact that their programs were extremely large and relied on expensive equipment for their use, whereas BASIC and conventional CAL were being offered on current microcomputers. Thus, although they could criticise the poor quality of what was on offer, they could not deliver fully working alternatives. Indeed, what made things worse was that AI researchers were only too aware of the limitations of what could be done. Given that we understand little about what constitutes good teaching, building a good teaching system presents certain difficulties. AI was concerned "to increase our understanding of complex cognitive activities such as seeing, learning, thinking and using language by constructing and testing explanations in computer program form" [85].

In a commercial environment of competition between rival microcomputers, the UK education system could derive limited benefits from AI research. In the United States, there was well-established research on Intelligent Teaching Systems [86], often underwritten by military funding, but even with greater access by American educational establishments to expensive technology it was hard to find systems in practical use, though interesting issues were being raised regarding, for example, student modelling [83,87], error identification [88] and knowledge representation [89].

Regarding the Learner as Programmer

In the United States the predominant model for CAL had in fact been Computer Assisted Instruction, whereby an increasing part of the "curriculum" was "delivered" by computers, diminishing the role of human teachers. Seymour Papert of Massachusetts Institute of Technology [5] objected that this constituted the programming of the student, whereas the student should program the computer:

When a child learns to program, the process of learning is transformed, it becomes more active and self-directed. In particular, the knowledge is acquired for a recognizable personal purpose. The child does something with it. The new knowledge is a source of power and is experienced as such from the moment it begins to form in the child's mind.

LOGO

Papert's ideas led in particular to the development of the computer language and environment LOGO, which has been widely used around the world as it has become available on microcomputers. The first and most popular version is based on "Turtle graphics". Crucial tensions have arisen over just how much control the learner should have. Papert wrote [5]:

Of course the Turtle can help in the teaching of traditional curriculum, but I have thought of it as a vehicle for Piagetian learning, which to me is learning without curriculum.

This sits uneasily with a National Curriculum conforming to central directions!

SMALLTALK

Similar research themes were pursued by Adele Goldberg [90] at Xerox PARC in developing the SMALLTALK environment with children. There was a considerable time delay before the results were available in UK classrooms, again due to software size and hardware expense, but the speed with which

Apple Macintoshes are now being used in educational establishments bears eloquent witness to the twenty years of AI research which had gone before. From the early work on the "Dynabook", their concept of a handheld computer which dates from before the days of the microprocessor, the group wanted to develop [90]:

a system that people themselves, both children and adults, can mould into the kinds of tools that they required … especially in educational settings, we want to be able to handle open-ended situations.

With LOGO, students learn to think procedurally, seeing the importance of taking steps in a particular sequence. With SMALLTALK and on the Apple Macintosh we deal with objects and classes, with an environment which allows us to create complex systems that are inherently nonlinear. In both cases powerful ideas are made available to young minds, and at diminishing cost.

PROLOG

The third AI approach and programming language that has had a major impact on CAL has been logic programming and PROLOG in a project based at Imperial College London from 1980 [91]. The subject of the original research project was "Logic as a Computer Language for Children", based on the ideas of Robert Kowalski regarding the fundamental importance of formal predicate logic, with the present author as teacher. From teaching logic with the aid of the computer the project progressed to supporting logical thinking across the curriculum, driven by the enthusiasms of specialist subject teachers and their students.

I had started with my previous concern to describe and explain historical knowledge, and many of my published examples derive from the humanities [91,92], as does the work of Jon Nichol at Exeter University School of Education [93,94]. However, as the PROLOG Education Group (PEG) has expanded worldwide since 1982, we can find applications in almost all curriculum areas, from ecology [95] to electronics [96], chemistry [97] to geography teaching [98].

Work has been aided by the availability of recent compatible PROLOG implementations on most microcomputers, and the improving sophistication of the interface and environment. This has meant that students and teachers have not needed to be aware that they were using logic or PROLOG as such, but enables them to work with a range of powerful software tools on the computer in the classroom.

Presuppositions: Logic Programming and the Culture of the Classroom

We have been accustomed to reading of Intelligent Tutoring Systems, or Intelligent Teaching Systems, and may have felt incomplete in the PEG community because the products of our labours do not have that status. What has been lacking is an analysis of the alternative pedagogy in which we have been engaged, which can itself be seen as a system in which teachers, students and computers play complementary roles in the exploration of domains of knowledge and experience. In effect the different PEG projects have made explicit particular stages and areas of the educational process within a broader system, and successful use of PEG products has depended on teachers and students sharing certain tacit presuppositions.

It is no coincidence that the concept of "tacit presuppositions" draws on a philosophical foundation in the work of Collingwood [15,61] and Wittgenstein [66,99–102] and concepts of exploration relate to the work of Piaget [4] and Foucault [103–105]. Such a philosophical framework has provided a tacit meta-level context for our object level products for classroom use. It has also been explored in work coordinated by the Swedish Centre for Working Life under the theme of "Culture, Language and Artificial Intelligence" [7–9]. Here we sketch the form of the alternative pedagogy in which we have been engaged in separate but associated projects.

Work Should be Seen as an Environment for Learning

This observation links our work with the developing "Human Centred" perspective on manufacturing and computer systems. As working teachers and educationalists we have turned to computers to assist our own process of learning as well as that of our students. We are increasingly aware of our continual need for development, and for support of a system of continuing education across society. As we consider the needs of the workplace and of vocational education and training, we must address the arbitrary distinction between the working environment and the learning environment. Our classrooms should be working models of the fusion of work and learning.

Fusion in the classroom, as in the test-tube, has potentially revolutionary and explosive implications. Giving the learner the experience of autonomous working in the classroom may not be reversible in the workplace. Encouraging the learner to ask questions may not instil habits of unquestioning obedience in the worker.

The first stage of industrial working concerned the processing of physical materials. Recent years, particularly in the United Kingdom, have seen the decline of manufacturing industry and the rise of service industries, processing money. Internationally, the trend is towards the processing of knowledge. Our classroom work with knowledge based systems has developed in parallel with national and international programmes in new generation computer systems: our pupils are the true Fifth Generation.

The Teacher Often Learns More Than the Student

The traditional model of classroom interaction was of the decanting of knowledge from the expert teacher to the ignorant pupil, often accomplished through the dictation and transcription of notes, a process which required the intellectual involvement of neither donor nor recipient. From this arose the view that "learning" could be "delivered", much as an organ could be transplanted.

The work of PEG is located firmly in the tradition that a child is "a torch to be lit, not a pot to be filled". We have been concerned with the level of classroom interaction and pupil involvement, and with the process of learning in the classroom rather than just the final external product.

Working at the individual project level, another general principle may have escaped notice. PEG projects are initiated by teachers with an abiding sense of curiosity, wanting to learn more about education and learning with the help of the computer, and themselves learning in the classroom. Lessons become joint activities of exploration with the pupils. Roles can be reversed. The first pilot class at Park House Middle School [91] wrote their own programs from November 1980, enabling them to play the role of teacher, while their subject teachers became their pupils in the art of writing declarative programs in PROLOG. The true teacher is simply an experienced learner who will share his knowledge and enthusiasm.

Learning is a Collaborative Process

PEG projects have been collaborative at a number of levels. We have normally worked with class groups, and though the increased availability of computer hardware has facilitated access by individuals, we have retained an emphasis on class discussion and group work away from the computer.

Within educational institutions the use of the computer has necessitated collaboration across normal subject and departmental barriers. Once breached, these barriers cannot be rebuilt. Use of the computer in teaching and learning history, for example, has required a degree of team teaching that has been destructive of the conventional pattern of the single teacher as sole master in his classroom. Once seen to be successful, the model has been available as an option in other subject areas.

Information Technology can Provide Mediating Representations

Information technology (IT) can be the means of bringing together teacher and student, teacher and teacher, student and student. It can also ease the interaction between subject matter and student, cultural context of subject and of student, and language of subject materials and of student.

These Representations can be Shared by a Group to Facilitate Collaborative Activity and Learning

IT allows different participants to deal with different but consistent representations of the same underlying subject matter, and can help them to recognise inconsistencies and contradictions. IT allows the modelling of abstract concepts, rendering them open to critical study. AI techniques allow us to model belief systems of individuals and groups, making explicit issues such as racism and discrimination.

Simulation and adventure game systems, where the student is the creative author modelling and describing his/her own world, offer us insights into tacit knowledge and cultural experience that otherwise pass unnoticed.

Intelligent IT can authenticate nonconformity, dignifying it with a comprehensible form. Intelligent IT offers new insights into language, its power, richness and diversity. IT offers assistance in understanding and acquiring competence in foreign languages in a practical or vocational context.

IT can in principle support individual, distant or open learning. The provision of the right conditions for learning remains as a practical challenge.

PEG has highlighted the possibilities for collaboration between institutions and across national boundaries. Software and documentation developed in one educational setting can be developed further in another, and that further development can be regarded as a form of active participative evaluation. We can see this by following the history of particular classic program ideas in the PEG literature, notably the murder mystery "Who killed Susie?" [91], the historical problem of the Body in the Bog [93], and the family of food programs derived from the Marseilles restaurant menu [106,107]. Whereas the collaborations started, through PEG, on an informal basis, it is gratifying to note the spread of major funded collaborative projects, often forging new links across educational sectors.

The Exchange of Knowledge Should be Separated from the Exchange of Money

PEG may have benefited from its unfunded foundation. Rather than being driven by the demands of external funding agencies, PEG has developed organically, based on the commitment and enthusiasms of its members. From the time of the first courses for teachers in 1982, financial barriers have not been allowed to stand in the way of the exchange of knowledge and the establishment of new pilot projects.

There have been sound reasons for this approach. There is no point in relying on "market forces" when the lack of funding for education, particularly in the United Kingdom, prevents teachers and their students from entering the market-place to buy, and prevents commercial software producers from regarding the nation's education system as a viable market.

More generally, the financial model does not fit comfortably with the exchange of knowledge. Whereas if I give somebody £100 I am thereby £100 poorer and he is £100 richer, the same does not apply with knowledge. If I share my knowledge with someone else, not only is he richer, but I am likely to gain by his reactions and responses, meaning that the total knowledge increases. To apply the financial model is to assume a fixed or shrinking cake to be divided. To share and exchange knowledge is to facilitate productive growth.

Technology Transfer is Often Accomplished Through People Transfer

The New Testament gives a graphic account of how new ideas were developed and spread across the known world by a small group of disciples, who worked together then founded a network of communicating churches. Powerful ideas were encapsulated in memorable examples, saved in the collective memory and passed on through oral tradition. Disciples usually worked in twos, and travelled light, relying on finding hospitality in the towns they visited. They were empowered to show small working examples, but relied on the faith of the audience that these small examples could be scaled up to accomplish personal salvation. As they established new churches they were sensitive to local conditions, and incorporated aspects of the indigenous culture in the institutions they established. Their gospels and letters long outlived them as testimony to their efforts in a cruel and hostile world, but served to authenticate the work of their later successors when the prevailing intellectual climate had changed.

PEG has indeed spread and grown through people transfer, through individual visits, courses and conferences. The pattern of dissemination resembles that charted by Fleck for the first years of AI [50].

Our Systems will Always be Provisional

In a market- and product-oriented world, it is unconventional to describe systems as provisional and incomplete. The strongest part of PEG has been the "Provisional Wing", achieving guerilla-style victories with lightweight computational tools, but resisting premature institutionalisation.

It is not that PEG tools and systems are weaker than their commercial rivals: quite the reverse. Computer systems can only ever embody partial models of the reality with which they seek to deal, and by being issued as commercial products their development is ended and their flexibility sacrificed. This will not be stated in the marketing literature.

It is the essence of the PEG philosophy of systems and of the classroom that what we do is provisional. We have more to learn, in company with our students, and in a changing world our learning could never be finished. Our view must be more clearly articulated: where we depend on a closed world assumption or a particular belief system we should attempt to make that dependence explicit. Only if we adopt such standards can we expect the practice to become established.

Knowledge Should be Open and Explicable

In the past it has been easy to demand greater openness in education and from authorities in society, and to receive partial concessions. Now we have technology which is based on the representation of knowledge in a form in which it is automatically "explicable" to some extent, the debate has ceased to be abstract and academic. In meddling with the technology of knowledge and power we are playing with fire.

PEG applications tend to be developed in areas where the teacher has established expertise which is to be shared with students. Human intelligence has paved the way for artificial intelligence. The teacher has an instinctive feel for what is "safe", and where the boundaries of the subject lie. Students can explore within these boundaries with impunity, but they venture beyond at their peril. The explanations which they receive will be couched in the language and descriptive framework provided by the teacher, and they should be aware of this.

Unstructured forays into the unknown, which may result from student-initiated exploration, place great demands on the teacher as "native guide" or "Sherpa". The current cult of "playing" with knowledge based systems, as opposed to using them to address real problems, carries attendant hazards, akin to the recreational use of drugs. Neural networks on personal computers, inherently inexplicable and based on machine rather than machine intelligence, are likely to compound the problem.

Knowledge based systems place new demands on education. As Piaget outlined [4], we have to equip students with the cognitive tools for structuring complex knowledge and experience, assimilating and accommodating over time. However, as Godel showed [17], there are limits to logical explanation within the confines of a particular system. We have to locate our systems and explanations within what Wittgenstein [66] called our "form of life".

There will Always be a Crucial Residue of Tacit Knowledge

The theory was that knowledge engineers would one day succeed in eliciting all the knowledge of human experts so that it could be represented in expert systems which could take on their functions. In order to be an expert one must have "known" the facts and rules which comprise the area of expertise. On this basis, highly complex projects were launched, including a number in the field of Intelligent Tutoring Systems. A financial justification for research and development was that teachers could be replaced by computer systems: indeed this outcome has been built into the forward expenditure plans of the British Government.

The realisation is growing that this theory is fatally flawed. We can produce rules using particular knowledge structures and descriptions, but these could never be more than models of reality, and incomplete models at that. Some knowledge will be missing because it is not known, or not available, but some knowledge cannot be expressed. We "know how" to do particular tasks, such as riding a bicycle, but could never fully express that in words. Often we share certain knowledge and experiences with our interlocutors: there is an unspoken frame of reference or shared set of presuppositions, which may be seen as a common culture. Finally, given that knowledge is socially constituted, and expressed in a common language of discourse, we can say nothing of the private experience which lies behind the use by different individuals of a common language.

Such realisations are not new, but have to be encountered anew following the over inflated expectations of knowledge based systems in the world outside the classroom. New dogs must learn old tricks.

Education and Training Should Adopt a "Human Centred" Perspective

There are great pressures at present for Education and Training to conform to the model specified by "market forces" and to seek to meet the needs of industry and commerce. These should be resisted. Industry in the age of mass production has sought to maximise efficiency and output by breaking down problems and people into narrowly specialised components. Such components, on the model of machine tools, have been designed to perform a specific function, and not to be transferred to other tasks. In the United Kingdom we see the development of a system of National Vocational Qualifications based on this model, by which a trainee or student will be described in terms of the atomised functions which he is deemed to be competent to perform, rather than in terms of his potential, interests and abilities.

International studies suggest that the world of machine tools has changed, and that greater output is achieved where multipurpose tools are wielded by flexibly trained expert craftsmen than when single purpose tools are watched by unskilled machine minders. Developing the understanding and skills of the human operator is crucial, and this involves providing a congenial work environment, a degree of autonomy in how the work is undertaken, and enhanced participation in decision making.

Logic programming has proved a powerful tool in education, by providing a common interactive medium and the building blocks for a growing set of tools which we share. It has obliged us to make declarative knowledge explicit in order to play with classroom examples. Declarative logic programming is not enough. Nor is it enough to add the appropriate procedural facilities and advanced software engineering to produce efficient working systems. We have to go beyond software engineering to social engineering. This has long been the business of teachers, socialising students into the society of the present and future. We have the technology, but with it comes responsibility.

New Partnerships for CAL Researchers

In 1981 the Japanese announced their plans for a new Fifth Generation of computers, prompting the establishment of major research and development programs around the world [108–110]. In many cases this meant that researchers in educational computing, starved of funds for their own work, were led to join collaborative research projects, particularly in the field of Expert Systems or Intelligent Knowledge Based Systems. In the UK in particular, this involved researchers at Edinburgh, Sussex, Lancaster, Leeds, Aberdeen and the Open University. The habit of collaboration has been acquired, together with some hardware and software. Some educational issues have been seen as of wider research significance: for example work on student modelling is significant to the development of intelligent interfaces to commercial systems. Typically, however, research collaborators display little understanding of the practical realities of education, and its crippling resource limitations.

Many of the problems addressed have clear implications for education [111,112]. Work at Sussex University developed an "Intelligent Help System" [113] for users of the POPLOG system. At Sussex, Edinburgh, the Open University and Strathclyde systems were developed to teach programming and debugging skills. At Imperial College an "Intelligent Front End" was developed for the GLIM statistical modelling system [114], and at Edinburgh for an ecological expert system [115]. At the Open University a tutoring system for quadratic equations [116] has been developed and implemented for the Archimedes computer, while work at Imperial College, Exeter University and Kingston College of Further Education, with Logica and the Engineering Industry Training Board, concerned a knowledge based engineering training system [117], using expert systems and interactive video.

More generally, work in expert systems, with its concern for representation, inference, dialogue and explanation [118,119], is clearly of great relevance to education and training, and as expert system shells have become available for microcomputer systems the range of tools potentially available to schools and colleges has increased. It had been supposed that tutorial "front ends" could trivially be added to working expert systems to meet the needs of education, but this has proved not to be the case both through practical research and theoretical analysis of the processes of knowledge representation and explanation [120].

In 1983 a conference on Artificial Intelligence and Education was held at Exeter University [111], with the avowed intention of resolving differences of emphasis and establishing common ground amongst practitioners in the different traditions outlined above. Since that time we can detect a new maturity in the field, and fewer unrealistic claims made for the educational potential of the technology.

It is now generally accepted that we can provide useful models, but could never hope to capture the full details of an area of knowledge and its application in a complete system. Debates as to which is the ideal computer language are idle, as each offers a different perspective and insights, and features of each can be implemented in the others. Educational or tutoring systems are perhaps more complex than other knowledge based systems, as we have to represent both a growing student model and our teaching and learning strategies. Our present job is to provide powerful tools for the learner and teacher, to assist them in developing their own models and representations of knowledge areas. The facilities for the user are more important than the language in which they are implemented.

Some of the academic community engaged in AI together with new commercial and industrial partners, are now working on the Training Agency (formerly Manpower Services Commission and Training Commission) programme for Artificial Intelligence Applications to Learning. Projects include the "Learning with Expert Systems" Starter Pack from Kingston College of Further Education [110, 121], and the evaluation of work using a Training Expert System (TRAINER) [122] by Advanced Training Research at Kingston Polytechnic with Royal Insurance, in association with a Training Expert Systems Club involving 15 major companies and supported by the Department of Trade and Industry.

Integrated Systems: From Theory to Practice

The influence of AI research has now been so all-pervasive over the past twenty years that it cannot sensibly be considered in isolation. Similarly, the spread of computer technology has been such that CAL applications can no longer be isolated from other modes of use. Developments of time-sharing, operating systems, graphics interfaces and natural language front ends all derive from AI research, and AI languages such as LISP, PROLOG and SMALLTALK have become standard system development tools, or have been the implementation languages for standard tools or shells. Word processing, databases, spreadsheets, graphics packages and expert systems tools are now in regular educational use (at Kingston College of Further Education all are included in an open access core course for all full-time students), and may almost be regarded as part of the standard furniture [123]. Furthermore, with millions of home computers and terminals installed, CAL may no longer be the monopoly of educational and training institutions, but is increasingly used at a distance or as part of open learning. As has been investigated on the Open Tech Stewart Wrightson Embedded Computer Based Training Project [124], a tutorial training system may be built into the introduction of new technology in an area such as the insurance industry.

Authoring packages are among the products of the new integration, whereby a software system with an attractive interface and appropriate mode o interaction is offered with the facility for the teacher/author to simply add th information about his chosen subject to be taught or learnt. The packages cai be deceptive, as each will support only particular teaching strategies o knowledge structures, but they enable the teacher/author to concentrate on authentic issues rather than details of programming. Current contender include ECAL (Extended Computer Assisted Learning) [125] from the Opei University, and TRAINER (a Training Expert System Shell) from Advancec Training Research, Kingston Polytechnic. More generally, teacher/authors will find the facilities of Hypercard on the Macintosh exciting on first impression, though the excitement may fade. Software developers tend to use Hypercard to build fast mock-ups of system interfaces, then build the equivalent real system using more powerful programming tools. Rapid prototyping and user testing has now become commonplace.

How, then, do we characterise CAL in the age of integrated systems? We may find unexpected users and initiators: at Kingston College use of the Macintosh system has been pioneered by a graphics technician in the Educational Resources Section, rather than a computer specialist. His ablest assistants are often students, themselves owners of similar systems. Normal power relations are distorted in an atmosphere of creative tension.

The realisation has grown that collaboration is essential if the necessary diversity of skills are to be brought together and managed to produce a successful working system. For Further Education Colleges the collaboration needs to involve subject experts and computer specialists together with graphic designers in the College, and links with Higher Education research. For real success a commercial user/sponsor will be added and a commercial publisher/distributor. It is dangerous to rely exclusively on public sector funding.

Evaluation of CAL

Central government in particular is inclined to support the evaluation of CAL projects, but often without a clear statement of the basis on which the evaluation is to be conducted. It may be useful, in light of the foregoing analysis, to clarify the different considerations which may be involved.

Educational Criteria: Rationale

The evaluation of an educational activity can only sensibly be conducted with respect to stated educational criteria. For example, will the use of a particular technology or approach increase pass rates in particular examinations by comparison with a control group, or increase the period of retention of particular knowledge or skills? Is the evaluation to be with respect to an existing curriculum, or is the technology itself defining a new curriculum whose operation is to be monitored against known standards? Are we concerned with the level of student involvement and response, or merely with some paper record of attainment? Can the evaluation be performed through on- line monitoring, or must there be observation of classroom interaction? Are we evaluating the performance of teachers and/or students, or merely the acceptability of a particular form of educational material? How can we take account of the effect of the novelty impact of CAL (though this is much diminished as students take sophisticated computer graphics for granted)?

Among the classic cases of evaluation in this field must be the work in

Edinburgh and France monitoring the effects of the use of LOGO. In Edinburgh [126] success was to be measured in terms of performance in a particular section of the mathematics syllabus, ignoring wider issues as outlined by Papert [5]. When compared with a control group, the experimental group were found to perform to the same level, though other aspects of their behaviour differed. In France a more holistic and ambitious approach was adopted, wherein it was expected that LOGO would transform the educational performance of its users. The evaluation led to the cessation of the project [127].

In the case of projects of the PROLOG Education Group [94], evaluation has been in terms of the effectiveness of the tools used by teachers in pursuing their existing curriculum objectives. Innovators are disqualified from evaluating their own work, so dissemination to second and third generation projects has been important.

Institutional and Cultural Context: Situation

CAL is not used in isolation, and evaluation has to take full account of the situation. American CAL systems often assume the availability of a terminal for each student, and early LOGO work relied on a high ratio of researchers to students. In contrast, the default assumption in the UK has often been the availability of one computer for a class of thirty students, led by one teacher without technical support. First generation experimental use tends to be in the context of an externally funded project, and after the cessation of external funding CAL has to compete for time and resources with other methods and technologies.

Classically, the evaluation of innovation should take place in a context where other variables are held constant. An environment where curriculum require-ments are changing, where financial resources are being reduced, where there are no strictly monitored control groups, and where staff, not to mention computer technology, is changing, is not appropriate if long-term and apparently scientific judgements are to be reached.

Two related approaches can then be adopted. One, following practice in NDPCAL [80] and the Nuffield Humanities Project [128], is to undertake illuminative evaluation of the institution as a whole in the context of the particular innovation, using ethnographic methods. The other, favoured by the Swedish Centre for Working Life [7–9], is the observation of extended case studies over time, tracing the impact of technological change and innovation beyond the first enthusiastic months or years. This has uncovered major implications for education and training of the changing skill requirements of new technology.

On occasion a project may be established to explore institutional and cultural contexts. In 1983 the Island of La Reunion in the Indian Ocean launched a project to develop a system bilingual in French and Creole [129], among the objectives being the sheltering of users of Western computer technology from the obligation to consume American culture and values. The Information

Technology Development Unit at Kingston College of Further Education was established in January 1985, following a report to the Further Education Unit (FEU) [108], to explore effects of the use of Advanced Information Technology on the culture of the college.

More generally, we have to accept that we cannot separate the use of information technology from its cultural context [130,131]. Many of our CAL systems embody assumptions about student users and the knowledge areas they are exploring which appear anomalous when the systems are run in a different cultural setting. This raises important issues when we consider both multicultural classrooms and the multilingual European Community context. Not merely interfaces and use of natural language, but the structure of knowledge and its mode of communication are open to question. As CAL development projects become increasingly multinational with support from the European commission, UK CAL has to end its cultural and linguistic isolation.

Benefits and Attitudes: Outcomes

Piaget's influence on primary school education can be seen in the encourage-ment of students to ask questions, to explore their world. In contrast, conventional CAL tends to encourage conformity, with the system requiring the correct answer to be given and not deigning to offer explanations. Computer use cannot be evaluated in disregard of the prevailing ethos of the classroom. If the computer reinforces the prevailing ethos it may be deemed effective by the teacher, who is otherwise unlikely to sanction its continued use.

Evaluation must therefore address questions of educational philosophy and staff development, whether or not these have been considered by CAL users. It may be that issues are raised in the classroom which serve to identify new training needs for staff and/or students, and to change the direction of the use of CAL.

If the only criteria for evaluation are based on cost-benefit analysis of a short-term financial nature, summing financial quantities and ignoring quali-tative issues, then conclusions are easy to predict but devoid of utility except to accountants. Innovative activity tends to have a high front-end financial loading, especially where technology is concerned, and tends to produce diverse outcomes in the longer term, including institutional disruption and change. Educational research has often served to shift the paradigms by which judgements are made, yet has been doomed to be evaluated according to the models it has replaced, wielded by authority figures either without specialist knowledge or from a previous generation.

It may be that governments wish to use CAL systems to replace teachers, to reduce their salaries bill and enhance the degree of conformity of students and remaining staff. To replace a skilled professional by a machine is always a risk: Scandinavian research suggests that some three years later the absence of critical skills is noticed, and that the consequences are immense [132]. We understand so little about learning and teaching that to replace teachers with man-made machines could only be an act of gross and wilful folly, cultural vandalism.

Knowledge Engineering and the Knowledge Society: Process and Structure

As information and knowledge processing assume ever greater economic significance, and the weaknesses of current computer systems in commercial use become apparent, the status of professionals has to be reassessed. Accountancy is amenable to automation, and progress is being made with areas of the law. Minor professionals such as insurance and estate agents find their status under threat. Engineers and teachers (redefined as knowledge engineers), using computers as standard tools, need to realise their potential and responsibilities.

How then, do we evaluate teachers and lecturers as knowledge engineers? This question is particularly pressing in British further education, as we seek to respond to the emerging querulous dictates of the National Council for Vocational Qualifications (NCVQ), for whom all professional or vocational knowledge and expertise can be reduced to competence statements, each of which can be assessed in terms of performance criteria. Indeed, NCVQ policies and the structures and contents of National Vocational Qualifications can usefully be modelled and scrutinised using simple expert systems [133]. Such systems could be of great practical use in aiding the assessment of learning and achievement in an understood area of expertise. NCVQ are irreversibly handicapped by the inability of professionals to understand, make explicit and standardise the nature of their own expertise. The continuing residue of tacit knowledge resists formalisation, so we cannot hope to do more than offer partial models, supporting human judgement and assessment.

Experience of writing and using CAL in the traditions outlined above would be invaluable in this new knowledge engineering consultancy role, as CAL practitioners are required to develop knowledge representations and schemas, to write procedures, to program responses to user inputs, and to incorporate the use of CAL into the regular curriculum. CAL has been a training in dealing with education at the meta-level; rather than just being concerned with the content of what is to be learnt, we have been developing and implementing methods and structures with multiple application. One could conclude that the process itself justifies the expenditure of time and resources, though the products to date may seem largely unremarkable.

Educational knowledge engineering is a form of intellectual management consultancy, dealing with qualitative and changing information rather than mere quantities. Why is it then that in the UK the field has been so poorly regarded, and its expert practitioners treated so shabbily? Why is so much valuable time spent writing lengthy proposals to attract minimal funding to carry out vital work as a succession of "pump-priming initiatives" come and go?

Can it be that those in authority do not really like learners to ask too intelligent questions in case they find out that nobody knows the answers? Calls for freedom of information are met by economy with truth. Piaget becomes politically inconvenient after primary school, and even there the clock is being turned back with centrally determined testing. Innovation is encouraged as long as it is not allowed to change anything to the detriment of those in positions of power. The financial enterprise culture is supported at the expense of intellectual enterprise culture. The bill for today's material affluence and intellectual squalor will be paid by those, our students and children, whose learning we now inhibit by tacit complicity in the philistinism of short-term economies. Unlike experimental rats, we have a professional obligation to answer back.

Chapter 4

Work

Work has somehow been taken for granted in modern societies. IT and AI offer new insights and benefits, if we are prepared to move beyond simplistic approaches, and subject our own assumptions to critical scrutiny.

What are Skills?

Some insight into the conceptual complexity of this field is offered by Wittgenstein in his *Philosophical Investigations* [66, paragraph 150]:

The grammar of the word "knows" is evidently closely related to that of "can", "is able to". But also related to that of "understands" ("mastery" of a technique).

Skills are demonstrated in the performance of a task; they are observed and described by a third party who sees the actions of the agent as constituting the performance of the particular task. If we are seeking to develop the skills of a young colleague, at a certain stage we may decide that he knows how to go on; he has learnt the rules of the game; he has become part of this form of life.

The exercise of skills requires the application of knowledge of the subject domain and the development of competencies (defined in terms of the task). Sometimes these can be formalised in terms Von Wright described as a "practical inference": a certain conclusion or action follows for an agent if he believes that certain conditions hold. In computational terms this approach is adopted in production rules and expert systems, whereby the system takes or recommends particular actions when given conditions are satisfied.

Skills are clearly enhanced by experience, whether through habit, increasing skill, or improvements derived from feedback. The process of skill acquisition is cyclical and recursive, with the practical use of the skills playing an essential role.

Assessments of skills depend on the belief that a particular task, under a particular description, is being attempted, and confidence in both the intentions of the agent and the judgement of the observer.

The Strategic Significance of Skills

The report of the IT86 Committee [134] in the UK was concerned with the future development, application and use of information technology in industry and commerce. It recognised the central importance of skills, and put forward a naive but superficially attractive technological solution:

We are faced with the anomalous situation in the UK where there are a large number of unemployed, many of whom are young people with, at the same time, a shortage of skills in many walks of life. One field in which the shortage of skills is evident is IT itself, and the use of technicians to provide a greater pool of IT skills which, in turn, can be used to create wealth in other sectors of the economy seems, to say the least, very worth while. The mechanism is interactive distance learning and the market for such systems is potentially very large in the UK with considerable export opportunities.

On this view skills are seen in technological terms as a marketable commodity: the human element drops out of consideration. In contrast, if one starts by examining the real practical problems to be solved by humans in a particular social and economic context, the computer or other enabling technology in effect drops out of consideration, having no more than an instrumental function.

Transferring Skills

We can see the transfer of skills at three levels. Skills can be transferred by and with an individual between different tasks, applications or domains. A good education will involve learning skills in one subject area which are then applied in another. Piaget [4] was concerned with exploring the nature, learning and transfer of skills, and with the cognitive development of the individual. The objective of education programmes such as the British Technical and Vocational Education Initiative and the Certificate of Pre-Vocational Education is to develop transferable problem solving skills rather than remaining narrowly task-specific or conventionally subject-based.

Skills can be transferred between people, as in the processes of education and training. When a senior specialist in a company nears retirement there is concern lest his expertise be lost, and there is often an attempt to transfer his key skills to a younger colleague. When an apprentice joins a firm (though the system of apprenticeship itself has weakened considerably in the United

Kingdom in recent years) he is likely to be assigned to work under the direction of an experienced worker, whose skills he is encouraged to acquire. This acquisition will be through practical experience as well as theoretical guidance.

At the social or institutional level skills can be transferred between groups, so that skill and influence is concentrated in a particular area. New technology such as computer-controlled machinery can diminish the requirement for specialist skills from the operative. Alternatively, word processing can put more executive power into the hands of intelligent secretaries.

The following suggested models reflect different emphases on the three levels of skill transfer outlined above, and may offer us insights into the nature of the transfer of skills in institutions.

Transmission

The transmission model assumes the existence of an established body of knowledge, held by the expert or teacher, which is transferred to the novice or student. Such knowledge is likely to be propositional, factual and non-negotiable. It may include knowledge of official procedures which must be followed without question, and thus applies particularly in military training, multinational corporations or an uncritical civil service. The transmission model embodies a one-way system of communication, where neither the expert nor the knowledge is open to question: indeed, the "expert" may in turn have received the knowledge in the same way, and may be unable to answer questions or explain the knowledge even if he wished to, for it is not "his own". Transmission implies the existence of a system of education, training or control that has its own "meta-level" rules concerning who, is entitled to know what information, or to ask what questions, and what constitutes an answer or an explanation.

Transfusion

The transfusion model assumes the existence of an organic institution or system, whose working can be affected by the addition of new knowledge to its "bloodstream", so that it can flow to the different parts. The acquisition of a new skill, or the use of a new technology which embodies a skill, can have radical effects if appropriately applied. Keeping the medical metaphor, certain transfusions can provoke the development of antibodies by the receiving system. Caution must be taken as to the purity of materials used, and as to their appropriateness for the type or group of individuals contained in the institution.

Catalysis

The concept of catalysis applied to transfer of skills is that different individuals within a group or institution will each have skills and abilities which others need, but that conventional institutional structures may not enable those skills and abilities to be shared to the maximum overall benefit. The purpose of the catalyst is to bring individuals together in a constructive social interaction, rather than itself being of central lasting significance. AI technology can perform this function by offering a unifying representation of a common problem to which different individuals with varying expertise can relate. AI, on this view, cannot solve human problems, but it can make them amenable to solution, showing the flies, as Wittgenstein put it, "the way out of the fly bottle".

Infection

Ideas can be catching; certain environments make it more likely that new ideas will spread; association with another person who holds strong ideas can lead first to a breakdown of resistance, and then to acceptance of the ideas. The objective of ideologies is to render the holder immune from infection from outside; however, when a tenet of the ideology appears to conflict with observed reality (cognitive dissonance) resistance may be permeable. Institutions may seek the protection of "conceptual condoms" to inhibit the conception of new ideas and practices, but they can never be fully effective, and the ideas themselves have to be addressed.

Acquisition

Piaget studied the processes of knowledge acquisition and conceptual accommodation in children and adolescents, and considerable work continues in the field, in particular, of AI and expert systems. Piaget wrote of "genetic epistemology" [4] and took a structuralist view of knowledge and social science, thus locating processes of individual action and learning in a broader context. Knowledge cannot be simply, almost passively, acquired in the sense of being taken off the shelf in a pre-packaged form: it requires action by the learner – acquisition without accommodation is worth very little. This view has radical implications for the current explosion in the development of "open", "distance" or "flexible" learning packages, many of which appear to have adopted a consumer marketing approach to skills transfer. We have all seen advertising messages such as:

"Choose any five modules from our attractive range"
"Learn in the privacy of your own car"
"Impress your colleagues with your knowledge"
"A Complete Training Course in 13 weekly instalments"
"Learn from the Experts with an Expert System on your PC"

Revelation

All will be made clear by the international expert at an expensive one- or two-day seminar in a prestigious hotel, possibly targeted at senior management who are too busy to think through a complex problem, but may be persuaded to buy a complete solution from a consultant. Where this revelatory approach succeeds, it tends to result in a contract for the consultant to take on the problem, for a continuing fee. The consultant will not reveal his methods in his answers to questions or his explanations: the element of mystery is maintained as his source of income. Revelation is thus normally partial and phased, with control and profit in the hands of the "prophet" (this is what Mikes [135] has called the "prophet motive").

Preconditions for the Transfer of Skills

Whichever model of the transfer of skills we adopt, there are certain common preconditions.

There must be the potential for the application of the skill in question, or it can never be exercised and thus internalised. This precondition may be met by either a real or a simulated situation.

There must be some motivation in the recipient in order for the skill to be taken on and added to his repertoire. The motivation could take various forms, including:

Personal danger (which can help in learning to swim)
Instrumental need (motivating students to learn typing)
Financial gain (where a bonus payment is made for additional skills or qualifications)
Social concern (for those learning first aid skills)
Personal goals (as with athletes or religious believers)
Pressure from employer (employees without certain skills may be made redundant)

There must be some shared practical context, some common language between those imparting and those receiving skills, though this may well be mediated by a number of different educational technologies of individual or mass communication. In order to learn how to play a game there is a need in some sense to know that the objective is to play the game, though the skill may be imparted before it is named, or fully put into practice. Wittgenstein used to teach the principles of basketball without a ball, showing how it was done by running in and out of the trees by the river in Cambridge. His students should know how to go on if they found themselves in a game. Such insights could not be acquired in conventional texts or lectures.

Technology and Skills

If we regard technology as the partial realisation of particular defined human skills, as implementations of "the extension of man", then there is clearly a dynamic and controversial relationship between the two. Given some understanding of what is technologically possible, it is a social and political issue as to how the balance should be struck, and by whom. Technology is of itself politically, socially and economically neutral: it is inevitably political in its use; reflecting and possibly strengthening the value system as well as the economic and political interests of those who control it.

Many of the terms which are causing concern in present-day industrial relations demonstrate the interconnectedness of technology and skills. We talk of "de-skilling", when the introduction of new technology means that a task no longer requires the same degree of human skill: instead of carrying out a complex process the operative may just press a button. Where the work-force had been trained using one generation of technology, and faces a new generation of technology in the workplace, we talk of "re-skilling". Where the work-force has incorporated so much new technology that the nature of the process and the worker's place in it has changed, we may find discussion of "multi-skilling", where the worker is expected to apply himself to a number of different tasks rather than being a specialist in one.

There is a clear danger in this technological "advance" that the nature of skill becomes defined in terms of technological and industrial processes, as constituting a human response to the needs of the technology, rather than the reverse. When the industrial base collapses, as is happening in the UK at present, it may take with it the narrowly defined human skills which it embodied. Such a drastic form of alienation of the worker from the products of his labour cannot but haveexplosive effects.

Technology and skills are also associated in the sense that both require the support of long-term investment. Neither can be treated as a short-term cost to be cut without calamitous consequences, for which the United Kingdom again serves as an example. Research, development, education and training are inseparable essential elements of a society's continuation.

Technology policy has to be determined with regard to the social and economic needs of society. The newest, most advanced and expensive technology may well not be appropriate. A country with a large working population may not give priority to a technology which replaces human labour: that would not be authentic for the interests of the society as a whole, though it might make a few company directors extremely wealthy. There has been concern, based on the work of Schumacher [136], to identify intermediate, appropriate technologies, which extend the effectiveness of people in meeting their own particular goals. Enabling technology can be liberating; inappropriate technology can provide a form of enslavement. The same physical objects, such as printing presses, steam engines or computers, could in themselves be enabling or enslaving: it is the context of use which is crucial and defines the social meaning of the technology.

Artificial Intelligence and Skills

AI is being applied to the complex process of training and skill transfer. Training clearly happens in particular cases, but the critical elements are not proving easily amenable to automation. There are definite limits to what is possible with AI, and these limits are currently being encountered in both research projects and practical applications.

There were those who thought that the process of Training Needs Analysis could be automated, that from a description of a task to be performed and of the employee who should perform it, an account could be generated of the training required, and that much of the necessary training could then be provided through the computer. Such a view derives from a mechanistic approach to human behaviour, closely related to a Taylorist view of the division of labour in manufacturing processes. If instead we start with an understanding and appreciation of the human, and regard the job descriptions as adaptable, our conclusions and work practices will be different.

When we use AI tools or techniques in a practical situation we are constrained by the extent of our knowledge. Our systems can only be as good as the description of the problem to be addressed, and the chosen knowledge representation. Human experts can never make all their expertise explicit, and we have to resort to various knowledge-elicitation methods in order to try to make up the deficit. As our knowledge of a problem can never be complete, our system can never be fully dependable in the real world. We can thus never build a system which cures all illnesses, solves all business problems or destroys all incoming ballistic missiles. There will, furthermore, always be limits to the extent to which the system can offer acceptable explanations of its behaviour and conclusions. In order to give a satisfactory explanation to somebody else we need to know a good deal about that somebody: there will always be severe limitations on what computers can be said to "know" about their users.

Tacit Knowledge

In AI the literature is full of references to the "bottleneck" in knowledge engineering or knowledge elicitation. In particular much knowledge which had previously been implicit would need to be made explicit, and codified in the form of rules either manually or to be represented in a form which was coherent, consistent and accessible to the user or reader.

Work on tacit knowledge suggests that although it may be possible, through particular techniques, to convert some knowledge from implicit to explicit form, there will always be a residue of expertise or "know-how" for which an explicit rule based representation or explanation cannot be given. Hubert Dreyfus [137] attacks the whole foundation of a complacent approach to expert systems when he argues:

No amount of rules and facts can capture the knowledge an expert has when he has stored the experience of the actual outcomes of tens of thousands of situations. The Socratic slogan: "If you can't explain it, you don't understand it," should be reversed: anyone who thinks he can fully explain his skill, does not have expert understanding.

A number of general questions arise from case studies in the context of working life:

How do I know whether I have an adequate representation of the knowledge of another person or group?
How can I hope to explain my knowledge to others?
What tacit and cultural knowledge is lost when we replace a person with a machine?
How can we appropriately value tacit knowledge?
Can we automate rule based professional knowledge?
Can a robot properly replace a skilled craftsman?
What are the implications for education and training?

Alan Janik worked on a series of case studies with the Swedish Centre for Working Life, reporting his findings at a conference in 1988 [138]. He locates issues of tacit knowledge in the context of power and elite groups:

One aspect of tacit knowledge has to do with the ways in which elites, such as guild masters, maintain their power by political manipulation of knowledge.

It is not sufficient to identify activities of following rules, but studies over time indicate the transitional and formative function performed by a set of rules:

Rule following activity may originate in rote behaviour but it terminates in creative activity ... being able to extend the rules.

This insight gives an added dimension to the knowledge elicitation process: making knowledge explicit helps to appreciate the value of the tacit residue:

It is not incompatible with the notion that skill involves an irreducibly tacit element that we urge the skilled to articulate the basis of their activities. The possibility of radical innovation is, however, the logical limit of description. That is what tacit knowledge is all about. To the extent that work is built upon skill, tacit knowledge is an essential part of the analysis of its internal order.

Janik analyses the findings of Ingela Josefson on the work of nurses as knowledge engineers:

Nurses can say a great deal about what they know at a factual level. It is the process of forming judgements which are accurate that resists precise formulation.

Paradoxically it has been the overreaching ambitions of computer scientists, particularly in the United States, which has shed light on the practical problems and implications of tacit knowledge. Early claims that the knowledge engineering bottleneck would soon be overcome, and automation introduced to many new areas of work, have had to be revised in the light of experience, leaving a trail of embarrassment and disruption where companies were overenthusiastic in their replacement of people by machines.

Diane Berry [139] has drawn attention to the different kinds of knowledge that are required by experts:

Even in a single domain expert knowledge is of several different kinds. Moreover, the different kinds of knowledge require different knowledge elicitation techniques to capture them most effectively.

This simply multiplies the areas in which tacit knowledge arises:

Skilled individuals are often able to carry out certain tasks in an optimal way without being aware of how or why they are able to do so; their knowledge (or particular aspects of it) is implicit in that it cannot be easily accessed or communicated.

A useful mediating function may be performed by reconstructed rules which are accepted as plausible by practitioners. The provisional status of such rules must be recognised:

In order for knowledge engineering to advance as a science it is necessary to recognise the existence of implicit knowledge as well as the constraints that it imposes on system development.

She draws more general conclusions concerning the restricted applicability of expert systems, or their use in association with skilled users:

Because of the problem of tacit knowledge we need to review the likely role of expert systems ... with the current state of the art systems should not be built with the aim of replacing skilled persons. Their only role at present is as aids to increase the productivity of skilled persons, or to replace the relatively unskilled. In both cases the relevant tacit knowledge can be supplied by the user.

Hertzberg [140] places these issues in a broader context, emphasising the importance of practice over scientific terms:

Philosophers have tended to overlook the dependence of understanding on practice because they emphasise scientific terms: concepts that are primarily used in classifying and reidentifying things, rather than in expressing an attitude.

The cultural context cannot be neglected, for knowledge and skill will take different forms in different cultures:

Different cultures may develop different language games, because they live in different environments and their history is different. Human nature, we might say, grows differently in the soil of different cultures. There can be translations from one language to another where the language games are the same, or similar enough. People who live in radically different ways could never speak to us, nor we to them.

This highlights a further limitation of computers:

Computers can only be on the mark, or off the mark. They have no lives into which their judgements may fit.

Cooley [141] locates changes in the workplace in the context of historical change, and identifies a key turning point in Europe following the Renaissance:

Around the 16th century, there emerged in most of the European languages the term "design" or its equivalent. The emergence of the word coincided with the need to describe the occupation of designing. That is not to suggest that design was a new activity, rather that it was being separated out from under production activity and recognised as a function in its own right. This recognition can be said to constitute a separation of hand and brain, of manual and intellectual work; and the separation of the work from the labour process. Above all, the term indicated that designing was to be separated from doing.

Apprenticeship takes on a critical new cultural dimension, and thus the virtual abolition of the apprenticeship system in Britain may strike an irreversible blow to the heart of the industrial culture:

Apprenticeships ... were not merely a means by which one acquired forms of manual dexterity. They were far more the transmission of a culture.

Changing the nature of industrial culture, de-skilling the worker, in turn necessitates the de-skilling of the consumer to accept the downgraded products:

If we have deskilled the ability to bake, then we must deskill the consumer so that they are happy with the cotton wool-like substitute for real bread.

We can unify these concerns with our previous discussion of knowledge by considering knowledge in terms of production and reproduction:

One should not just think in terms of production, but the reproduction of knowledge. Where indeed are the next generation of skill, knowledge and competence going to come from if we destroy the very seedbeds from which they spring?

Cooley is uncompromising in his verdict on the relative values of programming, training, and education:

You program a robot, you train a dog, or possibly a soldier, but you provide educational environments for human beings.

Knowledge Based Systems and Work Based Learning

Vocational Education and Training is increasingly dominated by the demands of work. In the United Kingdom a new system of Vocational Qualifications is to be based on employers' descriptions of the competencies required for the satisfactory performance of the job. Learning is no longer assumed necessarily to occur in traditional courses in schools or colleges, and credit is to be given for prior learning and achievement, enabling applicants to be exempted from lower level courses where they can satisfy tutors in an assessment interview. Such credit is to be recorded cumulatively in a National Record of Vocational Achievement. It is the UK government's intention that the National Vocational Qualifications (NVQ) structure should eventually encompass the whole range of academic and professional qualifications, unified by an emphasis on competence.

We examine the appropriate contribution of KBS in this new environment, drawing in particular on experience using the "Learning with Expert Systems" Starter Pack [110,121]. This pack was developed at Kingston College of Further Education, and initial example applications dealt with Hairdressing, Physics, Business Studies, Home Economics, Electronics, Printing, Chemistry, Mathematics, Computing and Biology. Our interest here is focused in the fields of Motor Vehicle Technology and Electrical Installation, with research work supported by the Further Education Unit and the Training Agency. Work at the Further Education Unit by Jack Mansell [133], addressed issues of the Assessment of Prior Learning and Achievement (APLA) in general, and focused on the particular application area of Electrical Installation, his own area of technical expertise. Kingston College of Further Education contributed expertise in expert systems development and use, supported pilot collaborative projects in different vocational areas to test out approaches suggested by Mansell in his central program, and explored implications for staff development.

Understanding the Application Area, the Individual and the Technology

In order to deploy a given technology we have to develop an understanding of the concepts and relationships in the field of application, and of the potential and limitations of the technology in question. This understanding can in turn be enhanced by the development, using knowledge based tools, of partial models of the problem which are rendered open to criticism and further development [8,9]. The Assessment of Prior Learning and Achievement itself can be seen as a technology falling under the same description as a Knowledge Based Assessment Method, whether or not partially implemented in software. To the extent that we fall short, as we must, of a complete and absolute understanding of the concepts and relationships, or to the extent that we fail to elicit the full knowledge and prior learning of our subject, our conclusions will be inherently fallible. The intellectual technology of assessment can only ever offer a partial model. This might seem to contradict the objective and quantitative aspirations of the "assessment industry", or at least to subject them to a cultural limitation. The acceptance of this conclusion enables vocational education and training to continue in a sensible and culturally-sensible way, free from unattainable objectives and criteria. The stages of our decision-making process regarding prior learning are qualitative rather than quantitative, as illustrated in the following drafting tool program, refined from Mansell's pilot program:

overall APLA credit possible in ...... if
   competent in ...... and
   APLA tutor assessed enough competencies in ......
competent in ...... if
   comprehensive know-how of ...... and
   demonstrated competencies in ......
APL A tutor assessed enough competencies in ...... if
   enough discussions of ...... assessed and
   enough complete assignments in ...... assessed and
   enough experiential learning of ...... in portfolio and
   enough competencies in ...... assessed

comprehensive know-how of ...... if
   knows criteria for ...... and
   knows about ...... and
   knows scope of ...... and
   knows how to select ...... and
   knows how to estimate ...... and
   knows how to design ......
knows about ...... if
   understands ...... and
   describes ......

Considerable attention has been given at Kingston College to the assessment and accreditation of work based learning. There has been extensive staff development on development in Vocational Qualifications, and an expansion of training provision in association with industry in the Kingston Area Training Consortium. Assessment of Prior Learning and Achievement using Expert Systems is one of the themes of the College's contribution to the Training Agency project "Assessment and Accreditation of Work Based Learning", where the application areas include Motor Vehicle Technology, Electrical Installation, Graphic Design, and Travel. Informal Assessment of Prior Learning is a prerequisite for any intelligent and practical conversation between individuals. In order to converse we have to establish a common language, a common set of experiences and interpretations [16]. In order to work together we have to identify common practices. For an expert practitioner to assess the prior learning of someone claiming competence in his craft is to establish whether the applicant is "one of us", a participant in the same culture or "form of life" [8]. Computer systems could never perform the entire task, as they themselves are outside any form of life, though they can be valuable tools for use by reflecting practitioners.

Using knowledge based tools obliges us to make explicit our representations of areas of technical expertise. Instead of an informal interview we are seeking to provide an element of structure and formality. It may be that the area to be explored with the applicant is large and complex, or that the tutor's own expertise is in a different area; the appropriate tool may extend the tutor's capacity for assessment. Much then depends on the representation used, which must satisfy the requirements of the specialist domain expert, the tutor and the applicant. It may be that different but equivalent representations are used, taking advantage of the mutual translatability of different formalisms via first order logic [38].

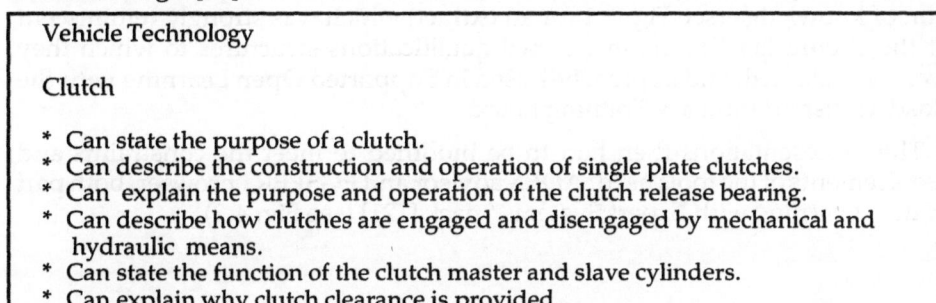

Vehicle Technology

Clutch

* Can state the purpose of a clutch.
* Can describe the construction and operation of single plate clutches.
* Can explain the purpose and operation of the clutch release bearing.
* Can describe how clutches are engaged and disengaged by mechanical and hydraulic means.
* Can state the function of the clutch master and slave cylinders.
* Can explain why clutch clearance is provided.

Fig. 4.1 Extract from representation of knowledge in motor vehicle technology.

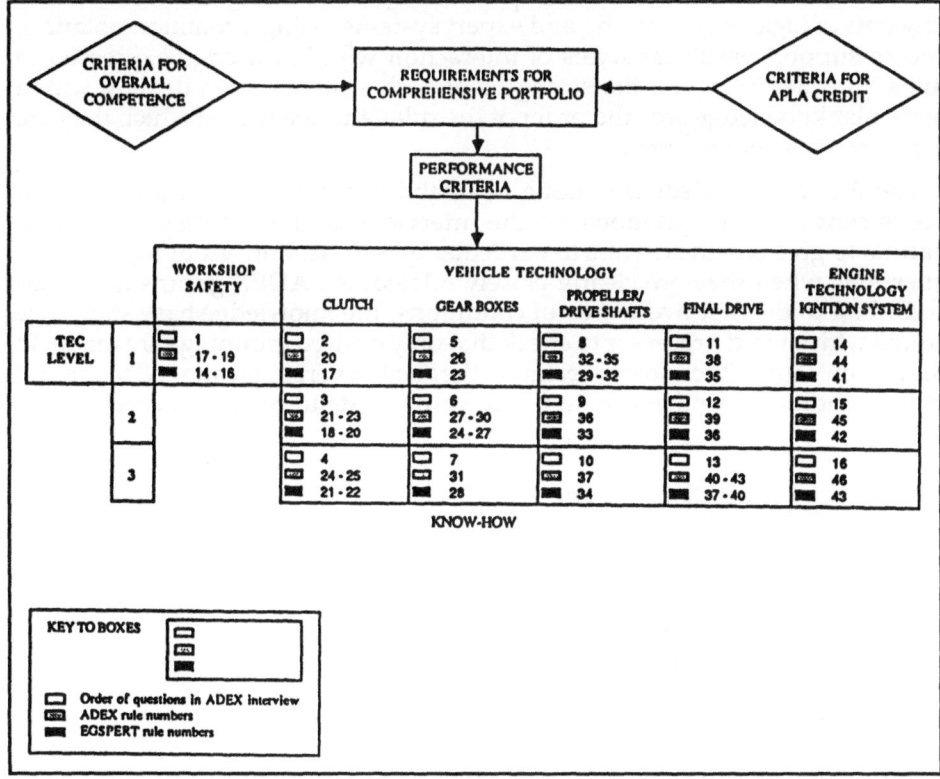

Fig. 4.2 Schematic diagram of motor vehicle technology APLA, ADEX and EGSPERT programs.

In the work on Electrical Installation, Jack Mansell played the three roles of domain expert, tutor and knowledge engineer, without these different roles necessarily being apparent. The successive versions of his system were piloted with lecturers and students in Kingston. In the Kingston work on Motor Vehicle Engineering John Hadjikyriacos (Motor Vehicle Lecturer) was the domain expert, Peter Stevens (Communications Lecturer) the tutor and Richard Ennals the knowledge engineer. Hadjikyriacos and Stevens developed a representation of knowledge (see Fig. 4.1 for an extract) which was strongly reminiscent of the Technician Education Council qualifications structures to which they were accustomed, and approaches used in Supported Open Learning with the Road Transport Industry Training Board.

The representations then had to be modified to meet the constraints and requirements of the tools used: ADEX advisor and EGSPERT browser, both part of the "Learning with Expert Systems" pack [121] (see Fig. 4.2).

Significant Features of ADEX and EGSPERT

Both systems are deliberately simple, having been designed to introduce concepts of logic programming and expert systems, using a common notation, and to support particular styles of interaction with knowledge expressed in rules. In order to exploit the strengths of each system, when dealing with a particular knowledge area the order of the rules and the way in which they are expressed may be changed.

The ADEX supervisor is seeking to establish conclusions, and to do so it poses conditions as questions. In the interview situation it may seem most natural to give yes/no answers to particular questions, only grouping together questions when they are clearly closely related. As ADEX groups questions according to the first two words of conditions, the knowledge base should be edited with a word processor to check that only desired groupings are made. In the Motor Vehicle Technology example the "action verbs" are moved to the end of the conditions, so that the first two words relate to parts of the vehicle, as follows:

Clutch level 1 element achieved if
   1 clutch questions appropriate and
   clutch purpose stated and
   clutch single plate construction described and
   clutch single plate operation described and
   clutch release bearing purpose explained and
   clutch release bearing operation explained and
   mechanical clutch engagement described and
   mechanical clutch disengagement described and
   hydraulic clutch engagement described and
   hydraulic clutch disengagement described and
   clutch master/slave cylinders functions stated and

clutch clearance provision explained and
assignment 2 satisfactory

The EGSPERT supervisor allows the user to browse across the knowledge base, moving from conclusions to conditions, conditions to conclusions or between "similar" conditions. Here we take a view of "similar" that supports the similarity of action verbs relating to processes, but not the structures of qualifications. Again a word processor is used to enhance the appropriateness of the use of this feature.

element clutch level 1 if
    states purpose of clutch and
    describes construction of single plate clutch and
    describes operation of single plate clutch and
    explains purpose of clutch release bearing and
    explains operation of clutch release bearing and
    describes engagement of mechanical clutch and
    describes disengagement of mechanical clutch and
    describes engagement of hydraulic clutch and
    describes disengagement of hydraulic clutch and
    states function of clutch master/slave cylinders and
    explains why clutch clearance is provided and
    completes assignment 2 satisfactorily

---

1. Identify area of vocational competence
2. Identify expert practitioner and tutor in area of vocation competence
3. Elicit competence-based description
4. Represent description in forms of rules
5. Analyse nature and sequence of interactions in APLA interviews
6. Select expert system shell or shell most appropriate for interview style
7. Test rules in current form in selected shell or shells
8. Modify knowledge base to improve interaction, taking advantage of features of selected shell or shells
9. Test pilot system, with expert practitioner and tutor
10. Modify
11. Test pilot system with APLA tutor
12. Modify
13. Test pilot system with APLA tutor and applicant
14. Modify
15. Use system in controlled experimental conditions
16. Modify
17. Release for Beta-site use and evaluation
18. Modify
19. Release for general use
20. Support with staff development

Fig. 4.3 Stages in developing an APLA expert system tool.

The order of advice and rules in ADEX is important, as it affects the nature of the interaction, and the order of questions asked. The knowledge as represented on Motor Vehicle Technology can be approached through interviews using varying sequences of questions. For example, an area such as Clutch or Gear Box could be pursued at all three levels before moving on, or an interview could explore all level 1 competencies (in Technician Education Council terms) before moving on to levels 2 and 3. With a system as simple as ADEX, the order of the rules can be changed using a word processor. A more complex (and expensive) system could allow the user to define his teaching strategy and sequence of concerns in a meta-level program. Here we gain insights into the case for such facilities if we know how to use them.

Different users are likely to have particular requirements, which can be met by the knowledge engineer, modifying the system in the light of experience. The stages in developing an APLA expert system tool are summarised in Fig. 4.3, and have been followed at Kingston College.

Work and Work Based Learning

In introducing a new technology we must be aware of its context of use. This is especially true when the educational use of computers is brought into the workplace, which now has to be considered as a learning environment.

Work is a social and cultural activity; though the observer may prefer to consider it in technical and economic terms it may not be perceived in the same way by the worker [142,143]. We are accustomed to the idea of education as a social and cultural activity [144], of education performing functions of socialisation and social control on the individual. We should not expect a great contrast when we look at work based learning, despite the rhetoric of training and competence. What is at issue is human learning, by individuals but in a social context and assessed in terms of behaviour and performance. For all the talk of competence and competence- based learning, competence is simply defined in terms of what the effective worker does today, so competence-based learning is defining the criteria for tomorrow in terms of what is acceptable today.

A common mistake is to regard the workplace as conceptually straightforward, so that complex tasks can be broken down progressively into ever smaller subtasks, which can be undertaken by individuals in isolation and without a need for overarching understanding [145]. Thus the role and work of the individual is defined in terms of his place in the process. When the industry and processes change, as is constantly the case with modern technology, it becomes critical for the worker's skills to be transferable [146], if he is not to be discarded, like any other industrial component, as obsolete and outdated.

How, then, do we represent areas of technical expertise? Is there some neutral canonical form? It would certainly make life easier, for it would enable us to codify the descriptions of all major forms of employment, and then assign people to likely jobs following a straightforward interview process. Training Needs Analysis would be merely a matter of noting the difference between the requirements of the job and the competencies of the applicant, generating a list of items as an "Action Plan". Indeed, this approach is adopted in the United

Kingdom by the Training Agency. It has provided the underlying assumptions behind the bringing together of "Industry Lead Bodies" to establish definitive descriptions of the competencies in their industrial sectors, to be accredited by the National Council for Vocational Qualifications as NVQs.

The scale of the unsolved problem is suggested by the lack of agreed NVQs, and by the failure to agree on the description of competencies common to many industrial sectors, such as office skills, information technology and interpersonal relations. Part of this problem can be explained in terms of the lack of training and competence at senior management level, but even were this to be resolved there would remain unresolved issues of knowledge and knowledge representation, seen in the cultural context of work. We cannot expect to arrive at a common description language free of connotations from the culture of working life, simply by virtue of using new technology.

In order to represent technical knowledge we must first elicit such knowledge from the acknowledged experts. This is far from straightforward [147]. Technical experts are often reluctant to share their expertise, or to reveal its deficiencies. For a consultant to make his expertise explicit is to threaten his continued livelihood. Lecturers such as those at Kingston cited above are an exception, their professional role is to mediate between the area of technical specialism and the student or trainee, but the complexity of their mediating function should not be underestimated. Although technical domains can be described in terms of rules, expertise can be seen as knowing how to go beyond the rules, using that tacit knowledge which by definition cannot be shared [137,138]. To fall back on reliance on the observation of expert performance, from which rules and criteria are inferred, may be perilous. It is all the more so if we are moving to the goal of assessment on the basis of observed performance: the amateur may look as if he is doing the same as the seasoned professional, but in fact have no understanding of what he is doing, or of its limitations. In such a system the knowledge drops out of consideration.

The knowledge-free approach is entirely consistent with Taylorist approaches to mass production, where workers were seen as inferior to machines, and where the ideal machineminder would be educationally subnormal, content to continue for years on the same repetitive tasks. For the modern world of rapidly changing technology this is not longer adequate: workers have to be prepared to be flexible, to transfer to new tasks as technology and product lines change. This flexibility and transferability necessitates the explicit representation of the technical knowledge required for a task in terms which are comparable with descriptions of other tasks in other industrial sectors. To represent the knowledge in one technical area has possible implications for all other areas. This should come as no surprise, for industrial policies and technological advances have wide-ranging implications: so must the representation of the knowledge on which they depend.

It is tempting to embark on a wholesale structuring of competencies and work based learning. Indeed, this approach has been adopted by the National Council for Vocational Qualifications. The generalist civil service mind would be attracted by the neatness with which levels of vocational qualifications can be identified which correspond intuitively to the official Registrar-General's Classification of Occupations in terms of Social Class. There is a clarity about the decision to regard Vocational Qualifications as covering areas of competence, each of them consisting of elements of competence, each assessable according to performance criteria.

```
award of NVQ in.......if
   achieve unit 1 in ......and
   achieve unit 2 in ......and
   achieve unit 3 in ......and
   achieve unit 4 in ......

achieve unit 1 in ......if
   achieve element 1.1 in ......and
   achieve element 1.2 in ......and
   ......

achieve element 1.1 in ......if
   element description 1.1 and
   satisfy performance criteria 1.1
```

Fig. 4.4 Schematic representation of NVQ structure.

Indeed, the whole model is reassuringly familiar, with its Taylorist fragmentation of industrial tasks and confirmation of the superior status of professional over manual work: it only becomes problematic when you try to apply it to the reality of the workplace.

Modelling Knowledge and Work Based Learning

Modelling knowledge in work based learning is not new, although it may not always have been seen in those terms. Analysis of learning tasks in terms of aims and objectives, action words and competence statements, and the drawing up of profiles all constitute modelling activities. When we animate these models using knowledge based tools [148] we open the models up for scrutiny, laying bare the underlying structure or lack of structure. We are forced to demystify and disambiguate the technical jargon which pervades vocational education and training. This does not always lead to instant popularity, as mystery and ambiguity can be major sources of revenue to examining and accrediting bodies, and they may even want to claim copyright on jargon terms such as "competence", "level" and "transferable", reserving the right to define and redefine them as they wish. Approaching assessment in terms of competencies in vocationally defined tasks, with performance criteria for each of a number of atomic subtasks, has no necessary implications for either knowledge or learning. It may be tempting to change education and provision to a modular basis, offering units of competence for assessment rather than addressing more general knowledge areas, and indeed short-term cost savings may follow, but the risk would be that current occupational patterns would be frozen, and flexibility replaced by narrow specialisation and fossilisation. We still require a strong model of the knowledge itself, and of its institutional applications.

Conclusions

Knowledge based tools have proved to be useful in exploring complex problems of knowledge in work based learning. The explicit representation of knowledge is a necessary but not sufficient condition for the solution of problems concerning that knowledge. Given that expert technical knowledge could never be made fully explicit, some problems will not be amenable to solution by computers, but subject to continuing processes of interpersonal negotiation. In the context of work based learning, both education and the workplace are cultural situations which need to be understood if knowledge based tools, or any other approaches, are to be effective in practice. If we accept the inherent limits of representation and systematisation, we can arrive at ways of enabling students, teachers, employers and unions to make effective use of knowledge based tools in the workplace and work based learning. In particular, the practical work reported here paves the way to new programmes of staff development, where lecturers are increasingly seen as knowledge engineers.

AI tools offer the potential of making social complexity more tractable, if we can arrive at an adequate representation of the institutional structures, problems and interest groups concerned. This involves a shift to seeing AI as a tool for social, or collaborative, problem solving, rather than for individual procedural problem solving of the conventional kind.

The Politics of Skills

Politics is concerned with people and the deployment of human resources. A political philosophy must include some view of the future, in which both the individual and society play parts. Politics includes the pragmatics of the management of change, but in a manner whereby success or failure are not purely calculated in terms of short-term profit and loss, and policies are seen as means to longer- term ends, or goals.

In this context training, and the transfer of skills, must be of central importance in any political programme.

For what future are people to be trained? What skills are to be transferred, and to whom? Are we at present mortgaging our future to finance current profligacy?

Who is being consulted and involved in preparing a solution to perhaps the central problem of our era, and who is left to form part of the problem?

From whom should we elicit the knowledge? How could this be done? To what extent will the shop-floor work-force be involved? Official reports are normally assembled by non-specialist observers, and focus on quantitative data rather than the qualitative descriptions and judgements which we require.

Is there a particularly European cultural approach to manufacturing industry, which will have its reflection both in the skills of the workers and the design of intelligent systems? If so, will this be compromised in contexts which are ever more dominated by American or Japanese technology? Cooley has suggested that there may be a European approach to technology and training, and in the ESPRIT Project on Human-Centred Manufacturing Systems [141] he has sought to develop the foundations for working examples.

Are there key technologies and processes which are core to new generation manufacturing technology, and can be supported with intelligent frameworks? How many people understand the underlying unifying concepts? Can frameworks be fully useful without being understood by some critical mass of participants in the activity encompassed?

Materials Selection, Materials Science and Artificial Intelligence

Materials science raises important practical questions for work which can be better understood by analogy with AI, and vice versa. The following conclusions are influenced by the ideas of Gustaf Ostberg [149] and experience of a research project in materials science with the Further Education Unit and Engineering Industry Training Board, based at Kingston College of Further Education [150], which involved the production of a video and software for teaching.

There are a number of respects in which the two fields reveal similarities. In both there is no absolute perfect answer, merely the best available solution in the circumstances to the problem as described. Selections of materials and knowledge descriptions are not done on a purely scientific basis, but are influenced by external circumstances, beliefs, short-term goals, market conditions, and chance. In both, the medium may become the message: our video featured the use of lightweight portable phones as status symbols. Practical real world products in both fields involve compromise. As we stand back and look at both fields more theoretically, we see more conceptual links. Shells and techniques can be transferred between domains. There is an emerging common terminology: fine grain/coarse grain, shell, modular, frame, structure, construction, top down/bottom up, design and much more. In each case we find that the belief systems of designers and users are different, a point well illustrated by Ostberg, who also shows how systems are always vulnerable to unexpected developments.

The comparison with materials science enables us to see how AI systems can be seen as made up of knowledge materials, and how problem solving involves intellectual materials selection. It would be instructive for each discipline to have access to studies of problem solving methods in the other.

Work, Skill and Management

It would be instructive to undertake a study of the impact of computers and advanced information technology on job design, noting the different motivation behind the introduction of new technology in different contexts and in different countries including, in particular, Scandinavia. This could be a healthy corrective, at least in the United Kingdom, to the assumption that technological change is always imposed on the work-force by the management without consultation and without detailed advanced planning.

Is it significant that many of the directors of engineering companies, especially in the United Kingdom, are not themselves engineers with practical experience of the manufacturing process? Is there a different perception of craft skill and the culture of work which derives from practical personal experience? Does this deficiency carry through to a lack of a common industrial culture or "form of life" in the United Kingdom, as opposed to Japan, where it would be unthinkable for the directors of an engineering company not to have engineering experience and expertise?

How do we separate our descriptions of the levels of skill required for particular manufacturing jobs from definitions of social class in terms of employment? In taking a human- centred approach to manufacturing systems, whether computer aided or not, we are challenging the established orthodoxy. What are we putting in its place? These social questions must be considered by those who are challenging the technological orthodoxy.

How do we arrive at consistent descriptions of skills required for different jobs in different industrial sectors? Is there some universally acceptable description language, which enables us to escape from the complex cultures that have developed around craft skills? Is it coherent to look for such a universal description language, or should we rather be seeking to offer tools to workers in their cultural context? This implies developing models of users and their cultures, with the technology adapting to the user rather than requiring the user to conform to, or be programmed by, the machine.

One model is offered by the British National Council for Vocational Qualifications, who are developing a competence-based system of qualifications at different levels, based on descriptions of vocational fields drawn up by designated Industry Lead Bodies. As some of these bodies are having to be created for this purpose, we can conclude that there may have been no pre-existing common occupational culture in some industrial sectors, even within one country. What cultural assumptions will be embedded in the NVQ system, which would not necessarily survive transplantation to another country and culture?

To what extent are essential concepts of skill captured by the competence-based model? How can we assess the prior learning and achievement of a student or worker? Do we need to form a model of his knowledge, or is it enough to note that the desired behaviour has occurred?

Is technical skill only really defined when its absence is noted? In the United Kingdom we appear to have reached a general realisation of a skills crisis just when the means of responding with high quality education and training are being removed. The country may be seen to be entering a post- industrial phase, a pioneering case study from which others may learn salutary lessons.

What are the implications for working life of the use of powerful learning workstations? Is training to become embedded in the practice of work? Will the use of computer networks constructively reinforce or cut across workplace relations? Will the enhanced use of computer-based systems distort percep-tions of the nature of work and workplace relations? How much do we understand about the practical human context into which intelligent technol-ogy is to be inserted? How far will current trainees be involved in the design of the intelligent framework and workstation? Such involvement itself would have considerable implications for future work practices.

To what extent is it possible to seek to define generic training configurations, when manufacturing contexts and training needs very so greatly? Do we have a set of case studies to which we can refer?

Is our definition of training to exclude general education, when the level of general education in the work-force varies greatly across Europe? The use of intelligent tools requires a structured framework of human intelligence. Are we to assume ongoing support through means other than the intelligent training systems?

Do we see training as focused on delivery of narrowly defined competencies in the context of individual tasks, or as providing conceptual underpinning and understanding which goes beyond the particular situation? The AI perspective is more attuned to the latter, while CBT has focused on the former.

Where, as in the UK, the apprenticeship system has crumbled there is a tragic gap where skilled master workers, competent to supervise and train new entrants to the craft, should be. Such a gap can only be filled in part by technology, and only satisfactorily so if the technology is used alongside the skilled master worker, not as a replacement. The Scandinavian research evidence suggests that some three years after the departure of the human skilled worker, the absence of his human skills and judgement can become evident and irreversible. It is not sufficient to offer widespread but low-level training, and to devalue the definitions of mastery: that is to undermine the foundations of manufacturing industry. That destruction has taken place in the UK, and will not be reversed by training technologists. Training is becoming recognised as of vital importance, but responsibility tends to be devolved to others, without the power or financial resources to effect change.

At a more practical industrial level, Adam Smith noted that the ideal production line worker would have limited intelligence, so that he would not resent the restrictions his work imposed on his humanity. This assumption is not shared by advocates of Human-Centred Manufacturing Systems. What is more, it is no longer acceptable as the basis for modern manufacturing industry.

One consequence of Adam Smith's approach to production and market economics was the Taylorist pursuit of scientific management, involving the fragmentation of tasks into ever more specialised subtasks, to be performed repetitively by low grade operatives. This method reached its climax in the production lines developed by Henry Ford, delivering large quantities of a limited range of products. Manufacturing industry, particularly in high technology, is now required to be highly flexible, adjusting production methods and details to the demands of different products and markets. Work practices and training methods have not necessarily changed; indeed, old approaches to the workplace and work based learning persist despite the near-extinction of the focus of their efforts.

It appears to be the time to move beyond the division of labour to the integration of skills and specialist functions through the restoration of control to the worker. The division of labour, and the automation of fragmented sub-tasks, have been to the detriment of the dignity of skilled labour. It is only through the restoration of that dignity that the needs of modern manufacturing industry can be met. The ARTISAN project deals with KBS, where the knowledge is that of the skilled artisan. Knowledge Engineers are there as an extension of tools which he will require. After decades of de-skilling, supposedly in the name of progress, the time has come for the empowerment of the worker. Advances in AI have made us more aware of the limitations of intelligent machinery, and the unplumbed depths of human skills.

Accordingly we must provide the skilled worker with a range of new generation tools (or "extensions", to use Bernal's term), rather like the artist's palette, from which he can choose as needs arise. Similarly, in the training context, we must enable the trainee to gain confidence, experience and competence in the use of both generations of tools, drawing on the models and frameworks favoured and developed by skilled workers. This implies the need for a new integration of the work of skilled workers and those in training, mediated by knowledge engineers and represented on successive prototype systems. The skilled worker is given a new status ever close to perfection, without the possibility of arrival. Technology and the process of automation in general are relegated to their proper subordinate position, subject to the judgements and experience of the expert skilled worker.

What lessons have we learnt from the Alvey KBET (Knowledge Based Engineering Training) project at Kingston College, which brought together KBS, Interactive Video and CNC Milling tasks? We are certainly now much better able to define the parameters of what is theoretically and practically possible in this complex area, and to identify the skills required of researchers and workplace supervisors. One clear outcome is a renewed appreciation of the knowledge and the skill of the craftsman, together with the realisation that new technology components of the training system have to be authentic to the culture of the workplace. Neither the skills of the craftsman nor the culture of the workplace could ever be defined in precise terms. They are perhaps most clearly identified by their absence, in purportedly stand-alone systems for both work and training.

The less you know about education and training, the easier it seems to be to urge the application of KBS. Can such systems ever get beyond the stage of toy examples in demonstration mode? Does it really help to demonstrate the potential of a technology without addressing the human problems which have to be resolved before that potential can be realised? At what stage do the toy examples run into difficulties? Can they still perform a useful function? What might that function be? Do we need full working models of institutional structures within which to test and then demonstrate our infant and adolescent systems? This is the context for the work of the ITDU at Kingston College, and then of Advanced Training Research at Kingston Polytechnic. Both have worked closely with industry in evolving the means of working and the approaches to KBS which industry can begin to incorporate into the culture of the workplace. The Swedish Centre for Working Life in Stockholm has evolved a methodology of action research case studies [7] to address such situations.

The most ambitious users of AI technology in education and training have sought to implement Intelligent Tutoring Systems (ITS). Are these doomed to failure? Could we know what needs to be known to build effective systems that people would choose to use? Can we define what constitutes intelligent teaching and training, or do we simply recognise it when we see it? If the latter, how do we capture the successful and effective methods and strategies in program form? Where have ITS been applied with success? Can we find examples outside initial military training, where the objectives include learning to follow instructions in a mechanical manner if in doubt, rather than developing habits of questioning? Where have they failed, and what were the real reasons for the failures?

What has been the real impact of expert system shells? They have lowered the entry price to AI, offering advanced computing facilities on personal computers, but have they misleadingly raised expectations to a level which cannot be satisfied? To what extent have they tackled real questions of professional skill and expertise, as opposed to adding minor functionality to conventional systems? To what extent is it necessary to understand the limitations of your tools in order to make good use of them? How many people in industry understand the limitations of KBS? Is disillusion likely to halt the pace of commercial development? Are the limitations in explanation facilities which are inherent in small-scale rule-based systems fatally damaging to their utility in education and training?

When KBS have failed to find a commercial application, the developers then take a new interest in the education and training market. Does it make sense to view education and training in normal market terms? What alternative models can we suggest, which do not rely on the provision of substantial funds from agencies without financial resources, such as schools?

All too often the literature on KBS applied to education and training reveals a knowledge of either the technology or of the human context, but not of both. This is hardly surprising for "first generation systems" developed by people from diverse backgrounds and without a common frame of reference. There was a similar problem in first generation expert systems for industry, which is only slowly being resolved. Can we expect the benefits of greater mutual understanding in the education and training systems now being developed?

How does the situation change if one adopts a Human-Centred approach to the use of KBS technology in education and training? Can we hope to give the learner the tools to enable him to get on with the job? Should we be programming the learner or should we be enabling him to take control of his environment? Are we seeking to provide "Training Solutions", or rather "Mental Puncture Repair Outfits"? Can we identify the kinds of thinking and actions that our intended users will want to perform, and provide them with a supporting environment in which to operate? Do we then in effect design the workplace as a learning environment? Can this leave the workplace, and ultimately the company, unchanged? Depending on our answers to the above, then we may be taking an approach to knowledge bases that is driven by a meta-level approach to structure, both of knowledge and its processing. This carries considerable implications for the knowledge bases and the systems in which they are articulated. Certain standards of logical rigour in the underlying implementations are required, if there is to be flexibility for logical transformations and changes of representation. Standards will have to be addressed with regard to languages, operating systems, environments and interfaces.

We are now proposing to ask a great deal from industry. Certainly in the UK it is unusual for companies to have devoted great attention to KBS or to training, and the chances of a company having done both in a way which hands control to the employee are slight indeed. There are profound questions here regarding knowledge, power, control, trust, and decision-making within organisations. The questions themselves are far from new, but intelligent technology when applied raises them with new urgency. Directors and managers demand high levels of qualifications and training for their recruits, and are being given responsibility for Training and Enterprise Councils in their local areas, while themselves being largely untrained. How will they respond to a technology which may show up their inadequacies? Are they equipped to understand the issues we are identifying as important? Can the technology itself help? Are today's Luddites to be found in the boardrooms and City financial institutions?

Can we improve the situation by adding more layers of technology? What successful examples can we point to where expert systems have been interfaced to interactive video in a training context, beyond the pilot or demonstration stage? Is it helpful to provide the ill-informed user with powerful knowledge engineering tools whose facilities and limitations are not properly understood? Would we not be better advised to work with tried and tested tools on which we have learned not to place undue reliance? Is it at this stage of the introduction of technology that the hidden cost of educational cuts may be revealed? We can only operate with safety within the limits of our understanding.

Can we imagine a user interface, or a learner workstation, that could offer access to the full range of possible tools and facilities that might be wanted in an industrial training context? Perhaps we have to see it as a front end to the user, an extension of his senses, providing him with an interface to external facilities and activities, and supporting his decisions and reasoning. This then implies a highly developed dynamic user modelling system, and restrictions on the portions of the outside world for which interaction is fully supported.

The user is sustained within a model of the world, which may turn out to differ significantly from reality. This approach is likely to preclude direct interfaces to real time systems except under the overriding control of the user, and suggests the value of an intermediate simulation stage within which the areas of difference between the model and reality can be addressed. Brady, in a lecture to the Royal Society in London [151], described automatic sheep-shearing systems, which operate by comparing their pre-programmed model of the "ideal sheep" with the struggling animal between their sensors. If we instead have the objective of intelligent, rather than automatic, cutting, and the human operator is always in control, our human-centred model can be introduced.

British industry is interested in systems which promise a rapid return on capital, and allow them to cut costs in the short term. They want quick results followed by sustained continued improvements, and they neither want to become dependent on scarce technical skilled staff nor obliged to train their own staff in-house. To the extent that the development of KBS takes time and effort, and KBS require a sound basis of knowledge, prospects for the future are bleak in an environment where time, effort and knowledge are at a premium.

What types of KBS can then be identified as appropriate to industry? Industry wants low initial purchase and maintenance cost, availability on industry standard personal computers, early demonstrable benefits in terms of cost savings, and, ideally, compatibility with and interfaces to, current systems. User interfaces must be flexible and friendly, and system operation must be free of technical jargon. This depiction makes industry sound like children in the world of intelligent technology, impatient, uninterested in accounts of the complex problems to be resolved, and unable to defer gratification while seeking to maximise personal gain. Success will only come with industrial maturity, which entails taking a longer term view, investing in education and training of staff to take full advantage of the opportunities afforded by the technology. Industry has to escape from the tyranny of quantitative judgements driven by the demands of accountancy to the higher level of qualitative modelling and decision-making as practised by skilled engineers, including knowledge engineers. Creativity must be nurtured across the work-force, and not just among the accountants.

Chapter 5

Computer Systems

Introduction

The results of successive generations of AI research have been assimilated into software engineering practice, though the origins are not always acknowledged: examples include time-sharing, operating systems, desktop user interfaces with windows, icons, mice and pointers, natural language front ends to databases and rule based programming languages.

AI is often described as the part of computer science that does not quite work yet: it is provisional and exploratory. Software engineering, by apparent contrast, is concerned with adding structure and reliability to each stage of the software life cycle. As expert systems, based on "toy examples" in the laboratory, have proved to have commercial applicability in particular well-understood domains, their status has become ambiguous. The expert systems tools which are available on the market may have been the product of rigorously controlled software engineering, but they will be applied in the uncertain environment of the real world.

Completely reliable complex systems could never be possible in the real world. We are thus inevitably reduced to making the best of an imperfect job, improving the engineering of our software, and making use of whatever tools may be appropriate to make our systems correct, on time and to budget.

To what extent can the latest results of AI be applied to computer-aided software engineering (CASE)? Do AI and CASE offer the solution to the software crisis, or do they rather threaten a greater danger, as the scale of our uncertainty increases?

The Two Cultures of Artificial Intelligence and Software Engineering

The two fields have different backgrounds and traditions: even now they find it hard to come together in the development of, for example, third generation integrated project support environments (IPSEs). There are respectable reasons for this. Derek Partridge [152], now Professor at Exeter University, has sought to bring the fields together with a common perspective:

Software Engineering problems are a subset of AI problems: the subset of well-defined problems.

Whereas, in his view, software engineering problems are well defined, have correct solutions, quite good static approximations, quite good modular approximations, and can be accurately circumscribed, AI problems are ill-defined, with only adequate solutions, have poor static approximations, are resistant to modular approximation and poorly circumscribable.

The two traditions have evolved different methodologies, which he described as "Specify and Verify" for software engineering and "Run Understand Debug Edit" for AI.

Tom Khabaza [113] of Sussex University takes a similar view, working from more of an AI background:

The AI researcher often undertakes a programming task when the problem to be solved or the method of solution is not yet fully specified. The researcher uses the activity of programming to clarify the problem, and to explore and develop representations and algorithms for its solution.

As Khabaza suggests, this methodology is sharply in contrast with that used in conventional computer programming, where to begin coding before the problem has been properly specified and appropriate algorithms developed would be considered poor practice.

This analysis is borne out by Sheil [153], writing on programming environments in the *Encyclopaedia of Artificial Intelligence*:

Being out of control is the standard operating procedure in AI programming. Not because the programmers are bad … but because the size and difficulty of the problems that they are dealing with always threaten to overwhelm them.

Conventional programming methodologies are intended to limit exploration and enforce adherence to a known valid design. The AI tradition accepts the need to explore a problem in order to find out what works. Whereas conventional programming techniques restrain the programmer in the interests of orderly development, AI programming systems try to amplify the programmer in the interest of maximising his range. We have here a clash of cultures. As Sheil remarks:

To those accustomed to the precise, structured methods of conventional system development, AI software development techniques will seem messy, inelegant and unsatisfying. But it is a question of congruence: precision and inflexibility are just as disfunctional in novel, well-defined ones. For AI or any problem which shares its levels of uncertainty, the efficiency of the AI software development techniques has been clearly demonstrated.

Artificial Intelligence and CASE: The Analogy of Pottery

AI is an exploratory activity. Progress towards discovery is by trial and error (what Robinson [154] called "benign kludges"), yet these discoveries are justified after the event in clean theoretical terms with apparent logical structure.

Once AI works, its status changes. Those who argue "if it works, don't fix it" subsume the successful product into software engineering. The true AI researcher turns his attention to something else that doesn't work.

We have here a new instance of the classical division of labour, this time in the intellectual sphere. AI researchers are like innovative potters, working this time in knowledge rather than clay, making something solid out of what is apparently nothing, but has deep cultural roots.

AI and CASE have yet to find their Josiah Wedgwood, the man whose marketing and commercial skill was a model for the first industrial revolution. He had a number of lessons to teach us. Quality, or the image of quality, sells products. Research and development are worth pursuing, with an extensive experimental programme, and a reputation for rigid quality control. The company owner should be involved in product research, rather than just focusing on sales. Royal patronage, combined with good design and influential friends, provided a customer base, which was satisfied by maintaining a skilled work-force and well kept accounts.

We have an industrial culture clash between AI and CASE which can only be resolved through a human-centred approach, suited to post-Fordist industry. CASE is based on traditional task and problem decomposition, the division of labour and clear control structures. In contrast, AI is based on transferable thinking agents, preserving a degree of autonomy.

Wedgwood pioneered "bespoke pottery" while also exploiting the technologies of ceramic mass production. He accommodated creative artists within his operation, and sold products on the strength of their established reputations. He was prepared to set artistic trends, carefully appealing to social snobbery. He gave the impression of order and tradition, while constantly experimenting with new methods and materials.

The New Concern for Methodology

In the early cavalier days of computer science and its applications, systems were developed with little attention given to their maintenance or future adaptation.

We now face a crisis, not just in terms of the expense of software development and maintenance, which has led to an applications backlog, but in terms of the behaviour of the systems themselves. This is now being made worse by the addition of AI to what was already poorly understood. As Partridge writes [152]:

Conventional Software Engineering has led to a software crisis: computer programs can produce results that are unexpected, incorrect and inexplicable. In other words, large computer programs, which are in control of ever increasing portions of society, can be both unreliable and incomprehensible. AI software extends the domain of problems addressed into that in which there is typically no complete specification of the problem, no clear-cut correct or incorrect answers, and a necessity for self-modification.

Early work in AI, and in particular expert systems, gave little priority to methodology in the urge to advance the frontiers of knowledge through experimentation. Concern has been expressed by researchers such as Max Bramer [49] of the British Computer Society Expert Systems Group:

The need for a satisfactory methodology for all aspects of the development and maintenance of Expert Systems and the importance of placing consistency maintenance, reasoning with uncertainty etc. on a sound theoretical basis seems little appreciated by many of those developing systems in the field.

Software engineers like Alan Montgomery of SD-Scicon [155] have pointed to the problems of American-style unstructured AI programming, with poor documentation, difficulties as applications grow, a lack of structure which impedes validation and maintenance, and domination by the use of particular tools. Instead he has argued the case for a controlled teachable method for teaching and integrating KBS, including a method independent of tools, a set of computer-aided development and application generation tools, case study reports and training schemes.

Current Difficulties in Introducing New Tools and Methodologies into Industrial and Commercial Use

We can describe the problem in general terms, and even assign names to its mode of solution. A vocabulary is developing of CASE, IPSEs, ISFs (Information System Factories), CADIS (Computer Assistance for the Development of Information Systems). Pious hopes can be expressed, as by Richard Barker [156] of Oracle:

CASE is the application of computer technology to focus development effort on business needs and to automate many of the systems development tasks. Applied correctly, CASE will improve communications and understanding between users and developers, and increase development productivity and the quality of the systems built.

These hopes are predicated on some ambitious assumptions concerning the quality of methods followed by analysts and designers:

CASE is based on the premise that developers of complex, computerised business systems must be following some structured method of work to guide them through all stages of the life-cycle .... It is, of course, vital to educate your analysts and designers on the approach needed to communicate effectively amongst themselves and with their users.

David Parnas [157] of Victoria University has highlighted the severity of the personnel problem in software, which threatens the continuation of the industry and the society it serves:

Worsening the difference between software and other areas of technology is a personnel problem. Most designers in traditional engineering disciplines have been educated to understand the mathematical tools that are available to them. Most programmers cannot even begin to use the meager tools that are available to software engineers.

The evidence is overwhelming that, at least in the United Kingdom, the method and underlying educational foundations have all too often been absent. New quality standards required by the Ministry of Defence cannot be met by major software houses, who are still reluctant to use the methods developed in the past decade, and to invest in quality training. It cannot be assumed that new "intelligent" technology will make up for fundamental human failings and short-term unintelligent financial management.

Reverse Engineering, Reuse and Repository

It is attractive to think that mountains of accumulated computer code need not go to waste, but can be reverse engineered to derive a clear specification of what was intended, or reused with minor modifications. However, the success of the process depends largely on the rigour with which the system was specified and designed in the first place. Systems that have developed incrementally and without the aid of formal tools are unlikely to respond to treatment.

The true repository of knowledge in an organisation is not a part of the computer system, but is the sum total of the tacit knowledge of the work-force. Where the work-force are not broadly consulted on the installation and use of a system, full advantage cannot be taken of their repository of knowledge.

Security, Privacy, Viruses and Hacking

The weakness and vulnerability of computer systems has become increasingly apparent. We hear less confident assurances of complete reliability, more anecdotes concerning penetration of computer security, invasion of privacy through access to confidential information in databases. In general terms we now understand that no system could ever be completely secure, that within each system lie the means of its own penetration. There could be no foolproof check for viruses in a software system, merely a check against known viruses or bugs.

The problems derive from people, and cannot be solved with technology. If someone is sufficiently determined to breach security, to invade privacy, to unleash viruses or to hack into systems, they can succeed. The technology offers a means of communication between consenting adults: individuals can take unilateral decisions which damage others, and without necessarily incurring redress.

Prospects for Adding Artificial Intelligence to CASE Tools

From a software engineering perspective in the British Alvey programme, AI was to be added in third generation IPSEs. This work reached the stage of a Study Report [158] by the end of the Alvey Programme in 1988, and the recommendations have not to date been followed in the subsequent Information Engineering Directorate Programme. The Study investigated the Information Systems Factory, incorporating knowledge bases and "intelligent tools", with the definition of an ISF:

an organisation in which various information systems (tools and/or applications, hardware and/or software are integrated within a CADIS architecture to form a CADIS virtual machine, which is programmed to support activities in the organisation.

It is illuminating to see how the same level of technology is viewed from an AI perspective. Ken Kahn [159] of XEROX PARC gives more emphasis to ideas and programming methodologies:

AI is an important source of ideas and tools for building sophisticated support facilities which make possible certain programming methodologies. These advanced programming methodologies in turn can have profound effects on the methodology of AI research.

Paul Freeman [160] of Hewlett-Packard sees a synergy from a more defined technical perspective:

In technological terms, it is the synergy of logic programming and database methods which hold the greatest promise. In the short term, this synergy will manifest itself in loosely-coupled systems which will be demanding on the analytical skills of those who use them to implement systems.

Wendy Rauch-Hindin [161], introducing AI to the world of business, warns them not to expect too much:

Because AI is so labour intensive, it is not likely to be the basis of an economic revolution. For AI market success, AI technology must be used to hide the AI.

There are areas where agreement can be found. It is generally recognised

[162,163] that AI languages offer considerable advantages for prototyping, as they can be used to express executable specifications and they can support evolutionary prototyping.

Opinions are divided on the virtues of advanced hybrid tool environments. Those in favour talk from American experience of LISP workstations, and assume substantial financial and equipment resources. Kunz and his colleagues from Intellicorp [164] are explicit about what must be sacrificed in the cause of flexibility:

The premise of hybrid tool environments is that uniformity of representation and programming methodology can be sacrificed safely to improve naturalness of expression, efficiency and flexibility.

They acknowledge the difficulties in meeting the full range of user needs:

It is difficult to design a simple and efficient system that will provide almost all of the features that most users will ever need, and users are constrained both intellectually and technically when they have limited ability to explore alternative problem representations and manipulation approaches.

Robert Worden of Logica [165] combines extensive experience of both traditions, and is well placed to survey the problem from the perspective of a major systems software house. Significantly, he sees it as a matter of knowledge and uncertainty:

The main problem is one of managing uncertainty – because, at present, developing a KBS involves much more uncertainty (in project cost, and in the quality of the result) than developing a conventional information system ... this uncertainty is not merely a consequence of the immaturity of Knowledge Engineering and its tools, but follows inevitably from the nature of knowledge: it will always be there.

He has no doubt that implementation problems of integrating expert systems with information systems are soluble now, and that product solutions will emerge. He places more importance on the problems of managing the greater inherent uncertainty of expert systems development within a conventional system life cycle. Here we reach the nub of the problem, which will test management skills in the new information systems factories, how to derive maximum benefits from the strengths of the two cultures while trying to minimise their weaknesses.

The bigger and more hazardous the project, the more dangerous it is to rely on software. Herb Lin [166] of MIT, echoing David Parnas [157], Edinburgh Computing and Social Responsibility [167] and Richard Ennals [118], has expressed particular worries about the software aspects of the enormously ambitious Strategic Defense Initiative, and the limits to which technical advances could resolve fundamental problems. Lin reviews the suggestion that automatic programming could provide the answer:

Automatic programming systems are said to enable people with little or no programming expertise to program computers, and to enable professional programmers to generate code with much greater ease than if they had to do so without computer assistance.

The cases of successful use of this approach are limited and few, and rely on a clear problem description. Providing a clear description will not always be possible, as the human imagination cannot anticipate all possible circumstances a complex system might encounter. Lin also notes that expert systems hold considerable promise in domains in which extensive empirical evidence provides the basis for expertise and for tasks in which humans can intervene in the event of inappropriate system behaviour. The problem of defence against missile attack does not meet these conditions.

Issues remain over.sharing information, controlled access, managing inconsistency and contradiction, non-monotonic reasoning, security. These are issues inherent to human institutions – unless solved for humans we should not expect solutions for or by technology.

One might conclude that expert systems have current pragmatic applicability, but limited significance for the future of large-scale software engineering. A radical alternative prospectus has been offered, which we now consider.

"New Generation Software Technology" Based on Declarative Systems

The alternative to adding AI to conventional software engineering is to develop a new generation approach to computer systems in general, and then to make that available to conventional software engineers. This was the approach adopted by the Japanese in their Fifth Generation computer project. The director, Kazuhiro Fuchi [35], identified logic programming as the core technology, writing:

Logic Programming is the "bridge" connecting Knowledge Information Processing and Parallel Computer Architecture.

Using Logic Programming a whole new programming methodology was under development at ICOT in Tokyo and in collaborating laboratories around the world, in which:

a system is constructed of layers of meta programs, utilising the expressive power of meta programming, and is executed after transformation into a one layer program by partial evaluation.

This perspective had long been pursued by the logic programming community, and in particular at Imperial College, London, by the group led by Robert Kowalski. Writing with Chris Hogger [168], he has argued that logic programming offers the means of uniting the two traditions outlined above. He takes long-standing principles of computer science, but extends their practical application beyond AI into the field of software engineering:

The separation of knowledge from use, which is characteristic of rule-based languages such as PROLOG, is especially well suited for heuristic, trial and error programming. It facilitates the assimilation of additional heuristics and the correction of errors. The traditional Software Engineering methodology aims instead to eliminate errors by the sound derivation of programs from specifications.

Kowalski stakes the claim of logic programming to meet the needs of both traditions:

Logic programming is conducive to both styles of programming: indeed, because of its declarative nature based on formal logic, it has greater potential for rigorous program development than have conventional programming formalisms.

Taking a line adopted by the Japanese Fifth Generation programme and the European ESPRIT programme, he claims the central place in new software technology for logic programming:

Logic Programming attempts to unify different formalisms in different areas of computing. Logic Programming is generally regarded as a development of AI. However, it also has important links with Formal Methods of Software Engineering and with the field of Databases.

The Logic Programming Initiative

The present writer managed the national Logic Programming Initiative [119] under the Alvey Programme whose mission was to provide the foundations for this new generation software technology. This was in association both with the ESPRIT Programme and, indirectly, with the collaborative research at the European Computing Research Centre in Munich by ICL, Siemens, and Bull. Collaborative research projects addressed improved logic programming language implementation, development of advanced declarative programming environments, database systems, as well as parallel declarative systems bringing together logic programming and functional programming on the FLAGSHIP family of parallel systems. That work has already led to commercial software and hardware prototypes, and shows excellent commercial potential. At the user interface level the PROLOG Education Group [91,94] has extended our experience of a declarative approach to knowledge based systems in an educational context: the work thus far on sequential microcomputers provides useful lessons for parallel systems to come.

In light of the account of the prevailing methodology of AI research and development, it may appear paradoxical to try to mount a collaborative managed programme in logic programming, as was done as part of the British Alvey Programme, with the writer as coordinator. Certainly the attempt came as a culture shock to the academics and industry research groups concerned, who were accustomed to small scale experimental work, and had developed a degree of competitive rivalry with colleagues in other groups. The Logic Programming Initiative required individualists to learn to become team players, to accept standards set by others, and to meet externally set deadlines.

As one of the architects of the Initiative, writing some five years after its inception, I can try to set it in context. The small AI community, and in particular the devotees of logic programming, had kept to their research objectives during the thin years of the 1970s following the Lighthill Report in 1972 [169], which terminated funding for many projects. The sudden upsurge of interest internationally in the 1980s meant an explosion of research projects, but with a hazy concept of shared objectives and support infrastructures. The Alvey Report in 1982 [170] recommended a ten year programme in Intelligent Knowledge Based Systems (IKBS), but there was limited experience in industry on which to build. The first range of projects approved were diverse and lacking focus, representing a selection from proposals received, rather than reflecting a strategy. Indeed, given the emphasis on logic programming in the Japanese Fifth Generation programme, and the influence of Japan on the establishment of the Alvey committee, the absence of a nucleus of logic programming projects provoked the question in 1984, "what happened to the Fifth Generation?"

A further problem arose at national level with the establishment of four directorates for IKBS, software engineering, man–machine interface and very large scale integration. Links between the directorates were weak, except in the Demonstrator Projects, whose job it was to pull the technologies through in real world applications.

The challenge of the Logic Programming Initiative, and the associated Parallel Architectures programme, was to give coherence to innovative work across the directorates, giving a new urgency to the leading edge of the Alvey Programme. Crucially, links had to be made with the software engineering community, if there were to be real effects on the process of software development in the medium as well as long term. The new technology of logic programming was intended, in the views of Kowalski and of Fuchi, to have a major impact on software engineering methodology as well as on AI.

Among the most important aspects of the Initiative were cultural and institutional changes. The provision of workshops and collaborative projects helped foster an active research community, with increased links as a matter of routine. Industry and academic researchers developed new relationships and understanding, spawning a new set of projects. At long last, effort was put into agreeing standards for PROLOG, enabling tools and applications programmes to be used with different implementations. Young researchers were given broader horizons, rather than assuming long term continuity in the same group. As before in the history of AI we have seen technology transfer between groups through the transfer of people. The flow of expertise from Edinburgh to Imperial College and Sussex University, the Open University and Essex University, which had characterised the 1970s, now extended on into industry and smaller groups. The other lasting impact of the initiative is likely to be the integrating work in parallel architectures, declarative languages and formal methods in new programming languages and environments. The research group of which I was manager at Imperial College combined expertise in these areas, and with a set of external commercial partners provided the nucleus of a national programme.

Research management concerns both process and product. Software engineers and Treasury officials tend to focus their attention on products. The crucial element for AI researchers is the process: a structure of linked projects and workshops provided a series of by-products, as well as enriching the process.

Problems of Knowledge and Problems of People

The advances we have considered have used AI and its technological products to move from user descriptions to working systems. We must remain conscious of the difficulties of arriving at adequate descriptions, and the limitations any such descriptions have, once they are seen merely as models, rather than as reality. Jane Hesketh [171] of Edinburgh University reminds us of this fundamental restriction, which carries through to any systems we construct:

All the systems we can produce will rely on models of the world and the tasks they are to perform. Models can never wholly match reality. So we must always be aware of the limitations of our systems.

The limitations of our systems are ultimately human, rather than technical. This has begun to be realised by the Study Team for the Alvey Information Systems Factory [158], as the system which they began to specify has both human and technological components. There is little apparent expertise in what is clearly as much a matter of social engineering as it is software engineering. As long as the software engineering community remains bound by quantitative and commercial considerations the potential will not be fulfilled. Complex knowledge based systems require experience of the sharing of knowledge for collaborative problem solving. This issue has been addressed to some extent in the innovative Alvey IKBS Community Clubs, bringing together companies and technical specialists in particular commercial sectors (such as Finance, Transport, Data Processing) to jointly address problems of common interest with the aid of IKBS technology. That joint experience is now being pooled to address issues of methodology in the GEMINI Project [155].

Methodology alone will not suffice: we also require an understanding of organisations and institutions. This will not be derived from computer science, but from practical experience and social science.

Chapter 6

Social Institutions

Changing Technology and People

As the technology of computing matures, it becomes apparent that the effective management of complex systems depends on the solution of problems with people. It is an illusion to imagine that software automation enables us to somehow bypass problems with individuals and groups, whether of employees or users. Rather, if people problems are not addressed, the inappropriate use of software automation could mean corporate or social suicide. Where both people and technology can be enhanced in collaborative systems development and use, the prospects for cultural and economic growth are attractive. Good human relations are not obviated by effective software automation; they are the precondition. The model of technological change and innovation which we seek to explore is "human centred", located in the culture of the workplace.

Some issues of the introduction of new technology are not specific to information technology and computers, but raise more general questions regarding participation in decision- making and policy planning. Given that the role of technology should be to extend the effectiveness of the human worker, it might seem obvious that the worker should be involved in decisions with potentially fundamental implications for his own working future. Where technology is seen as a tool in the hands of the skilled worker, we need an appreciation of those skills and of the appropriate division of labour between man and machine.

With the advent of more intelligent computing systems it is increasingly white-collar and junior management tasks which are amenable to automation. There are signs of executive Luddism breaking out as offices are under pressure to move on from the hand-loom stage of software systems. It would be easy to cast advanced computing tools in the role of the power looms of the second industrial revolution, and to envisage an era of discontent.

Skilled people are increasingly scarce, and as the scarcity becomes generally perceived with discussion of the "skills crisis" it is realised how difficult and time-consuming it is to develop skills. Where workers are replaced or de-skilled their morale may be broken, and the chances of restoring or enhancing the skills may be lost. Skilled staff may choose to leave and offer their services to competitors if they are not appreciated and allowed to develop.

People tend to be more effective and productive when working in a team, rather than as isolated individuals. The same applies to computer systems. The challenge is to bring together people and technology into a single harmonious working system. It is unlikely that this objective can be achieved simply by implementing a top-down division of labour based on the Taylorist decomposition of tasks. Experience of computer technology suggests different appropriate models of collaborative working, and the power and flexibility offered by distributed processing on individual workstations.

Human Centred Systems

We face a conflict between the imperatives of technological advance and the needs of both the individual worker and the workforce as a group. In the United States the tendency has been to emphasise the role of advanced technology, and to minimise the requirement for advanced skills from the worker. In West Germany the skilled worker can turn his hand to a variety of tasks, where he uses the technology as a tool rather than tending it as a minder. In these two contexts the priorities for technical development and training are different. These issues have been more explored for manufacturing industry and computer integrated manufacturing, but are fundamental to the consideration of the future of computing applications.

Jon Young has addressed the question of human centred knowledge based systems design [172]. Note that most of his description applies to human centred systems in general, of which computer systems are a critical example:

A human-centred system provides an environment in which as much decision-making is given to the user as possible; in which increased performance as a function of the growth of the user's skills in manipulating the system; in which an increased level of human skills is thereby fostered; and in which personal responsibility has real and direct applicability in achieving and maintaining the productive process.

One system cannot be considered in isolation, for human centredness has implications for human skills and links between workplaces:

A human-centred system is considered to be a physical artefact whose design is influenced at fundamental levels by our considerations of human-centredness. As a system, it must preserve precision and interrelatedness of the individual workplace with others in a combined productive activity. At the same time, its human-centredness must enable and require the considerable deliberative judgement, cognitive skills, and self-pacing, self-planning of the workload which constitute the specifically human component available from every person involved in the productive process.

Commitment

The concept of commitment is given a central place in Terry Winograd's and Fernando Flores' book *Understanding Computers and Cognition* [19]. Winograd was one of the pioneers of natural language understanding research in AI [18], while Flores served as Finance Minister under Allende in Chile. They argue that technologies have to be understood in context:

All new technologies develop within the background of a tacit understanding of human nature and human work. The use of technology in turn leads to fundamental changes in what we do, and ultimately in what it is to be human. We encounter the deep questions of design when we recognise that in designing tools we are designing ways of being.

When we use tools, we do so in a social and cultural context:

Writing is an instrument – a tool we use in our interactions with other people. The computer, like any other medium, must be understood in the context of communication and the larger network of equipment and practices in which it is situated. A person who sits down at a word processor is not just creating a document, but is writing a letter or a memo or a book. There is a complex social network in which these activities make sense. It includes institutions (such as post offices and publishing companies), equipment (including word processors and computer networks, but also all of the older technologies with which they coexist), practices (such as buying books and reading the daily mail), and conventions (such as the legal status of written documents).

They argue that considerable work has to be done if we are to understand the impact of computer technology, including drawing on insights from the humanities and social sciences:

In order to become aware of the effect that computers have on society we must reveal the implicit understanding of human language, thought and work that serves as a background for developments in computer technology.

We ourselves cannot stand outside our own cultural tradition as we write or use computers:

We always exist within a pre-understanding determined by the history of our interactions with those who share the tradition.

In order to build a theoretical approach to this problem, they draw on work in speech act theory, regarding the use of language as an act of social creation. To this they add a sceptical approach towards rationalistic models of problem solving, severely limiting their expectations of intelligent systems, except as aids to intelligent human agents:

Models of rationalistic problem-solving do not reflect how actions are really determined, and ... programs based on such models are unlikely to prove successful. Nevertheless, there is a role for computer technology in support of managers and as aids in coping with the complex conversational structures generated within an organisation. Much of the work that managers do is concerned with initiating, monitoring, and above all coordinating the networks of speech acts that constitute social action.

Herb Simon has analysed how human decision-making will always fall short of the rational model, in his book *Administrative Behaviour* [173]. Rational decision-making entails listing all the alternative strategies, determining all the consequences that follow upon each of these strategies, and a comparative evaluation of the sets of consequences. He concludes:

It is impossible for the behaviour of a single, isolated individual to reach any high degree of rationality. The number of alternatives he must explore is so great, the information he would need to evaluate them so vast that even an approximation of objective reality is hard to conceive .... Actual behaviour falls short, in at least three ways, of objective rationality:

1. Rationality requires a complete knowledge and anticipation of the consequences that will follow on each choice. In fact, knowledge of consequences is always fragmentary.
2. Since these consequences lie in the future, imagination must supply the lack of experiences felt in attaching value to them. But values can be only imperfectly anticipated.
3. Rationality requires a choice among all possible alternative behaviours. In actual behaviour, only a very few of all these possible alternatives ever come to mind.

Winograd and Flores draw on the work on Speech Acts by Austin and Searle in the Wittgensteinian tradition. They quote Austin in *How to do Things with Words* [174]:

It is essential to realize that "true" and "false", like "free" and "unfree", do not stand for anything simple at all; but only for a general dimension of being a right or proper thing to say as opposed to a wrong thing, in these circumstances, to this audience, for these purposes, and with these intentions.

Searle, in his book *Speech Acts* [175] identifies five categories of illocutionary point: assertives, directives, commissives, expressives and declarations; and his work has influenced much recent work in situation semantics, such as that by Barwise and Perry [176].

Habermas takes the point further in his book *Communication and the Evolution of Society* [177], emphasising the centrality of dialogue and commitment in speech act theory:

The essential presupposition for the success of an illocutionary act consists in the speaker's entering into a specific engagement, so that the hearer can rely on him. An utterance can count as a promise, assertion, request, question or avowal, if and only if the speaker makes an offer that he is ready to make good insofar as it is accepted by the hearer.

This requirement for dialogue extends even to the process of description of objects in the real world:

I may ascribe a predicate to an object if and only if every other person who could enter into a dialogue with me would ascribe the same predicate to the same object.

In his earlier work, "Technology and Science as Ideology", in the collection *Towards a Rational Society* [178], Habermas had traced the social effects of the rationalisation which has accompanied the institutionalisation of science and technology:

To the extent that technology and science permeate social institutions and thus transform them, old legitimations are destroyed. The secularization and "disenchantment" of action-orienting worldviews, of cultural tradition as a whole, is the obverse of the growing "rationality" of social action.

Drawing on the work of Marcuse, he observes that:

Because this sort of rationality extends to the correct choice among strategies, the appropriate application of technologies, and the efficient application of systems (with presupposed aims in given situations), it removes the total social framework of interests in which strategies are chosen, technologies applied, and systems established, from the scope of reflection and rational reconstruction.

Winograd and Flores emphasise the need for a new orientation to the use of computers, and see commitment as a central issue:

There is a pervasive misunderstanding based on the failure to recognise the role of commitment in language. For example, a computer program is not an expert, though it can be a highly sophisticated medium for communication among experts, or between an expert and someone needing help in a specialised domain.

They urge:

a shift from an individually-centred conception of understanding to one that is socially based. Knowledge and understanding (in both the cognitive and linguistic senses) do not result from formal operations on mental representations of an objectively existing world. Rather, they arise from the individual's committed participation in mutually oriented patterns of behaviour that are embedded in a socially shared background of concerns, actions and beliefs.

The current misunderstanding of computers has broad implications:

An understanding of what a computer really does is an understanding of the social and political situation in which it is designed, built, purchased, installed and used.

Programmers are frequently unaware of their own limitations:

The programmer acts within a context of language, culture and previous understanding, both shared and personal. The program is forever limited to working within the world determined by the programmer's explicit articulation of possible objects, properties and relations among them. It therefore embodies the blindness that goes with this articulation.

Kathleen Christensen, in her paper "The Ethics of Information Technology" [179], makes related points:

Information Technology, like all technology, is entirely value-laden. It must be seen as a process in which values have shaped the creation, design, and application of the device, product or service .... The longer we avoid explicating the value dimensions of computer technology the greater will be our risk of serious political and moral consequences.

She notes that the emphasis on technology has implicit dangers for people and society, particularly in contexts such as social work:

> Technology is driven by efficiency, whereas social work is defined by a professional code of ethics that specifies particular relationships among the agency, the professional and the client.

Much of this code of ethics is never made explicit in the form of rules, but is embodied in the culture of the institutions concerned.

John Diebold explores these issues in his book *Making the Future Work: Unleashing our powers of innovation for the decade ahead* [180]:

> The technology is changing far more rapidly than the rules that are supposed to contain it, often leaping over national as well as regulatory boundaries. Dealing as they do with the principal determinant of human organisation – information and its communication – this technology promises to change the very fabric of society, and in the process a wide range of the most basic ethical, legal and moral questions must be faced if we are to make our future work.

These issues are not easy, as Donald Christiansen argues in his 1984 paper "The issues we avoid" [181]:

> It is much easier to design a new microprocessor, or even a fibre optic communications system than to deal with their ultimate application in a bureaucratic or international context. In practice, greater knowledge often helps freeze our inaction: the more we learn about the societal or institutional aspects of an issue, the less likely we are to know where to start in finding an answer.

Winograd and Flores argue that understanding must itself be redefined in terms of commitment:

> Understanding is not a fixed relationship between representation and the things represented, but is a commitment to carry out a dialogue within the full horizons of both speaker and hearer in a way that permits new distinctions to emerge.

Following from this they develop a theory of management and conversation:

> Every manager is primarily concerned with generating and maintaining a network of conversations for action – conversations in which requests and commitments lead to successful completion of work.

Their account of conversations represents a social version of speech act theory which offers considerable insights into organisational behaviour:

1. Organisations exist as networks of directives and commissives. Directives include orders, requests, consultations and offers; commissives include promises, acceptances and rejections.
2. Breakdowns will inevitably occur, and the organisation needs to be prepared. In coping with breakdowns, further networks of directives and commissives are generated.
3. People in an organisation issue utterances, by speaking or writing, to develop the conversations required in the organisational network. They participate in the creation and maintenance of a process of communication. At the core of this process is the performance of linguistic acts that bring forth different kinds of commitments.

Lessons learnt from this approach to computing and speech acts can be applied more widely, with implications for education and social theory:

There exists a domain for education in communicative competence: the fundamental relationship between language and successful action. People's conscious knowledge of their participation in the network of commitment can be reinforced and developed, improving their capacity to act in the domain of language.

Artificial Intelligence and Voluntary Sector Groups

Voluntary groups are having growing difficulty in recruiting volunteers to continue and expand their work in the current context of growing poverty and deprivation. Government is devolving responsibility for large areas of social policy to the voluntary sector, but without providing the necessary level of resources. Indeed, whole new concepts have been introduced, such as "Care in the Community", which greatly amplify the significance of the voluntary sector as a replacement for, as opposed to in addition to, statutory provision.

Economic difficulties make it harder for ordinary people to take on major voluntary commitments, when family budgets are hard to balance. This leaves voluntary groups increasingly in the hands of professionals and middle class volunteers, whose personal experience may be remote from that of client groups.

It is therefore necessary for voluntary groups to reassess their positions, functions and means of support. What role should be played by technology in general, and AI in particular? Is there a place for central consultancy?

Some moves to increase the level of technology used are superficially attractive, but are opposed by voluntary groups for understandable reasons. Specialist groups such as the Child Poverty Action Group (CPAG) derive much of their income from sales of their reference manuals on Welfare Rights and Housing Benefit. To replace such manuals with freely available advice systems would damage their financial base unless, that is, CPAG were to be the vendors or providers of such systems. Many voluntary organisations have developed an umbrella coordination and information dissemination function which they do not wish to relinquish, and they may be reluctant to modify their mode of operation.

The emergence of credible advice systems obliges us to reconsider the process of giving and receiving advice, and the respective roles of expert advice workers and various forms of technology. CPAG manuals are used for reference by advice workers in Citizens Advice Bureaux and Welfare Rights Centres around the country, who then face clients in person. The Lisson Grove Benefits Advice System, produced with consultancy input from CPAG staff, addresses the same audience, but may also be used to support advice interviews, including provision of printout. When compared with other systems in a review of Welfare Benefits packages [182], the Lisson Grove system was described as:

More than cheap and cheerful – it is free, flexible, wide- ranging and most effective.

Of the range of systems reviewed, Rafferty et al. comment [182]:

Using such systems is an essential part of the modern practice of personal social servicing, and one of them should be in every front line office and every educational or training unit.

Very often, as in medical general practice, the first question asked by the client does not address the underlying problem which causes him worry, and the art is to "get to the root of the problem". It is not clear that a computer system could ever really do this in the real world, beyond cases based in defined administrative or organisational areas, because the system has not lived, and cannot "understand how the client feels".

In the case of welfare rights, it is relatively straightforward to compute the entitlements of a given claimant in response to a standard set of questions. What is harder is to advise the claimant how to describe himself in order to maximise his income from the system. One poignant example is the case of teenage mothers of children who were conceived before the mother was aged 16. One mode of application, when invoking the law on under-age sex, would secure the immediate arrest and conviction of the father, even though the family were now trying to live together normally. More common is the problem of student status, and whether it is advisable for the claimant to declare himself to be a student, which may result, for example, in the loss of all entitlement to housing benefit though it could attract an 80% rebate from Poll Tax.

Such issues require a meta-level reasoning capability, allowing one to talk about arguments and cases as a whole as well as details within cases, and some capacity to reason by analogy. Sympathetic humans can often do this very well, and indeed human services professionals specialise in such work. Human expertise may be partially captured in intelligent systems which can thus add heuristics to the straightforward initial representation, but the range of possible implications of changed descriptions could not be pre- programmed within a system. Advice systems are thus revealed as illuminating dynamic models, and never a complete substitute for expert human advice and contact. Their usefulness will depend on the level of cooperation from the experts, and their capacity to reflect on and articulate their own knowledge. Some human services professionals have argued [183] that it is their obligation to take the lead in such applications of IT, in order to endow it with as much social integrity as possible.

Many voluntary groups see themselves as coordinators, as bringing together information from varied sources in order to make it available to a particular clientele. They may resent the suggestion that technological progress could render their role obsolete or unnecessary. Why not use bulletin boards or on-line databases? These could be under someone else's control, or become anarchic and unstructured due to a lack of control. Information might not be seen as reliable if its source is not always apparent.

What functions are performed beyond simple information provision in response to questions? Could or should these functions be performed by a reduced staff using new technology? Do people often visit an advice centre in order to find someone to talk to, rather than to seek particular information?

Do we perhaps miss the real value of voluntary groups by concentrating on a functional analysis of their information work? Is it perhaps in the tacit knowledge which they bring together, beyond full representation in facts and rules, that their strength lies? Voluntary sector experts know how to get things done, who to contact, what alternative routes to take through administrative complexity. In some cases, this information is deliberately not made public, or would supposedly be incomprehensible to the uninitiated.

It seems that this knowledge is not directly taught, but is acquired through experience of working in the voluntary sector. Some progress could surely be made through knowledge representation and modelling techniques, possibly incorporated as an element in social work and administration training, or in induction courses for voluntary sector knowledge workers. Bevan argues [183]:

Because human services professionals at their best are concerned with people as people not as cases, with citizens not clients, they are in a position to tackle the problem of expressing tacit knowledge in the electronic age.

Retaining a level of information gives status to the voluntary sector expert, and possibly provides an insulating buffer for the public sector officials concerned. There may be complex professional relationships at the public-voluntary interface, which have more to do with status and power, possibly as a substitute for money, than with information and knowledge. How independent can a voluntary sector worker be once co-opted onto a government-funded advisory body? To what extent is the work of voluntary agencies compromised by the receipt of financial support from particular sources?

We should perhaps consider the position of local councillors by comparison to that of voluntary agencies. Their rights of access to information concerning their authorities are laid down. Much of what they learn they do not pass on. Their silence betokens assent to what is often a change instigated by central government. Where they oppose government policy they may find their powers curtailed, meaning the downgrading of elected members in favour of unelected advisers and voluntary groups. What, then, is the position of council employees, now instructed to work in close association with the voluntary and private sectors?

Institutions and Dissent

Institutional Truth

J.K. Galbraith wrote in the *Guardian* for 28th July 1989 [184], an article entitled "In pursuit of the simple truth", reprinted from his commencement address to the students of Smith College, who traditionally move on to careers in America's leading institutions. He critically analyses the belief systems to which the aspiring career professional must subscribe, or appear to subscribe. He offers the unifying concept of institutional truth, reminiscent of our earlier account of the "Civil Servant Shell", but forming an off-the-shelf belief system suitable for those who wish to remain in favour:

Institutional truth in our time bears no necessary relation to simple truth. It is, instead, what serves the needs and purposes of the large and socially pervasive institutions that increasingly dominate modern life. Institutional truth is what serves the organisations that dominate and guide our military affairs – the military/industrial complex or, in common reference, the Pentagon, and extending out through the revolving doors to the great weapons firms and on to captive congressmen on Capitol Hill. And institutional truth is what serves our great foreign policy apparatus – the State Department, the National Security Council and the CIA. It is also what serves the current interest of the great institutions of the financial world. And it is what sells products and makes money for the great business enterprises.

Individual articles of belief will flow logically from this belief system, but will themselves at times be ludicrous or abhorrent:

You will be required to believe that in an age of massive overkill we need even more nuclear weapons; you will be expected to believe that we need modernisation – a wonderful word – of our greatly redundant missile inventory; and you will be expected to believe that we must go on to ever more esoteric, ever more destabilising weaponry, including, with the departure of Mr Reagan, the partly orphaned Strategic Defence Initiative.

A bewildering world of paradoxes is opened up, particularly in the world of defence policy:

With relaxing tensions you will believe that it is imperative that the United States not relax; on the contrary, as the Communist threat subsides, you will know that we must be more vigilant than ever. Relaxation in a time of relaxation is especially relaxing and therefore especially dangerous. That you must believe or anyhow say.

When the prevailing ideology is strong, it is safest to conform with it, even if this involves the espousal of a position of impotence when it comes to social justice:

In politics you will encounter the most esoteric of our institutional truths. Here you will encounter and perhaps vouchsafe the belief that, although we are still the world's richest country, we must tolerate in our great cities some of the world's most devastating and devastated slums ... but, you will be required to believe, we can do nothing about it.

It is somehow assumed that the social order is immutable, that the poor will not gain control of the system of government. Helping the poor through expenditure would be a mistake:

More public housing, adequate welfare payments, adequately paid teachers, sufficient recreational facilities, more community action programmes would be, our wealth notwithstanding, too expensive. Additionally such expenditure would be damaging to the morals and economic morale of those so helped. All this you will be required to believe. Not believing, you will risk being considered subversive by your fellow statespersons.

As Galbraith moves from social policy to identify the convoluted justifications of the financial community, we get close to the underlying assumptions of many of those who are seeking to profit from the technology of AI:

The institutional truth of the financial world holds that association with money implies intelligence. And it holds broadly that the greater the amount of money, the greater the intelligence. And that the pursuit of money by whatever design within the law is always benign. This is the institutional truth of Wall Street; this you will be required to believe.

We know of all too many examples, in the fields of expert systems and neural networks, of Galbraith's simple rule:

In truth, the larger the amount of money commanded, the greater very often the error, on occasions even the stupidity.

The best response to the ideologies of institutional truth is to present them with a practical working alternative. As Galbraith says:

To the adherents of the institutional truth there is nothing more inconvenient, nothing that so contributes to discomfort, than open, persistent, articulate assertion of what is real .... There is something wonderful in seeing a wrong-headed majority assailed by truth.

With some relish he suggests that the truth should be wielded as a weapon in the battle against injustice:

In all life one should comfort the afflicted, but verily also, one should afflict the comfortable, and especially when they are comfortably, contentedly, even happily wrong.

Whistle Blowing

Ralph Nader was co-editor of a collection on whistle blowing [185], and presented an anatomy of the issues in terms of the ethics of individual belief and action within organisations. He points to worrying changes:

Within the structure of the organisation there has taken place an erosion of both human values and the broader value of human beings as the possibility of dissent within the hierarchy has become so restricted that common candour requires uncommon courage. The large organisation is lord and manor, and most of its employees have been desensitised much as were medieval peasants who never knew they were serfs.

He argues the need to reconsider the roles of individuals and organisations, and the extent of obligations:

The key question is, at what point should an employee resolve that allegiance to society (e.g. the public safety) must supersede allegiance to the organisation's policies (e.g. the corporate profit), and then act on that resolve by informing outsiders or legal authorities? It is a question that involves basic issues of individual freedom, concentration of power, and information flow to the public.

Dissemination of information about an institution by one of its employees can have enormous ramifications. If we are to break out of a feudal model of obedience and conformity, so that we entertain the possibility of institutions "leaking" as a matter of routine, then there needs to be consideration of guidelines and principles. Nader argues for an ethic of whistle blowing:

There is a great need to develop an ethic of whistle blowing, which can be practically applied in many contexts, especially within corporate and governmental bureaucracies .... Whistle blowing, if carefully defined and protected by law, can become another of those adaptive, self-implementing mechanisms which mark the relative difference between a free society that relies on free institutions and a closed society that depends on authoritarian institutions.

The Artificial Intelligence for Society Club

It is easier to state what one is against than to construct a practical working alternative worthy of support. The campaign against Star Wars in 1985 and 1986 [118] raised the awareness of many in the AI community, and stimulated the foundation of British chapters of Computing and Social Responsibility (CSR), on the model of the American CPSR. Concerns were shared [167,186], but little practical changed. For many of those who joined discussions of AI and Society on the fringes of Expert Systems Conferences and international gatherings of the AI community [144] a pattern of talk without action was beginning to emerge. Some structure was provided by the *Journal of AI and Society*, now well established under the founding editor Karamjit Gill. In December 1987, at the BCS Expert Systems Conference in Brighton, it was agreed that an AI For Society Club (AIFS) should be formed (using the collaborative model of Alvey IKBS Community Clubs), and Bob Muller of Digital accepted the invitation to serve as founding chairman. In the relaxed surroundings of Digital's London offices thirty founder members, from academia, industry and community groups, met and formed four initial working groups addressing topics chosen by the meeting. These groups were to meet separately over the months, coming together roughly every six months in national club meetings.

AIFS started with no budget, and with no guarantee that members, all busy people, would offer more than moral support. AI professionals wanted to support socially useful applications of their technology, but had no real perception as to what these might be. Representatives of community groups who attended the early meetings had strong feelings regarding society's needs, but little experience of the practical utility and potential of the new AI technology. It is unsurprising that the early work of the four working groups was exploratory and undramatic.

The group considering Information Needs of the Deaf was led by Jim Kielty of TSB in association with Lady Beverley Annaly of the Anastasia Trust. They held a series of meetings at the offices of SENSE, the Deaf-Blind and Rubella Handicapped Association, where the majority of those present were pro-foundly deaf, and explored ways in which interfaces to computer systems could be improved, using demonstration systems on PC portables. Their experience was similar to that reported by Miller and Cordingley in work on developing expert systems on Non-Accidental Injuries to Children [187], where the focus was on conversations between social workers and software engineers, each developing an understanding of the work and concerns of the others.

Mark Wilcock of Digital and Karamjit Gill led the group considering health applications, in association with Gordon Beavans of Leeds University. They held discussions with hospitals and medical groups trying to identify appropriate applications on which the group could work, considering areas such as diet advice. Discussions were instructive, but a direct match of application, team and institutional setting was not achieved.

John Fox of ICRF and Janet Vaux of IBC coordinated the review of current community take-up of commercially available AI and expert systems, initiating a questionnaire to identify socially useful systems. Few commercial systems were intended for socially useful initial applications, though a number of shells and tools have been put to experimental use. The questionnaire has produced few conclusive results, and companies specialising in socially useful applications have yet to emerge.

David Hopson, of Church Action with the Unemployed (CAWTU) and UNET Electronic Publishing, and Richard Ennals of Kingston College of Further Education (KCFE) coordinated work on Welfare Rights and Community Advice, building up a network of collaborating AI professionals (including teams from Barclays, BT and the DHSS Demonstrator Project) and community workers (including CPAG and the National Council for Voluntary Organisations) with early prototype systems on family credit and equal opportunities, holding weekly working sessions and periodic group meetings at KCFE. Their numbers were added to by Polytechnic MSc students interested in socially useful projects.

Community groups have increasing access to PC level systems, but rarely to AI workstations. The microcomputer revolution has meant that informal computing skills are now widespread, and use is often highly sophisticated. Well documented tools, introduced in the context of use, should find motivated users. The Lisson Grove Benefits System is being distributed free to advice centres and community groups nationwide, with periodic free updates. The KCFE "Learning with Expert Systems" Starter Pack [121] has been distributed free to British further education colleges and many of its tools translated into Scandinavian versions. PEG-Exeter Tools (KEYNOTES, LINX and MITSI) [188], are distributed internationally for classroom use. The first AIFS products, an Information Handling Starter Pack [10] and an Intelligent Hypertext Editor, were distributed at the July meeting by David Hopson free of charge, and are available for evaluation. NCVO plan to apply the new ATR TRAINER system [189], demonstrated at an AIFS workshop, to training in Housing Benefits. The Council of Christians and Jews are using the Equal Opportunities prototype system developed with BT, now focusing on the area of meat.

Community groups, like schools, have no significant budgets available for software purchase and support. Thus, if software is to be taken up it must be available without major financial expense. Community groups cannot constitute a market in the conventional financial sense, though information exchange is their business. The interface requirements for community groups may be the same as those for customers of financial services: the combination of community knowledge and institutional finance, mediated by AI professionals, is proving productive in current AIFS prototype systems.

Applications of AI will only be regarded as interesting by community groups if they work and produce useful results. An emphasis on the technology *per se* is not welcomed, and the theoretical concerns of "strong AI" are neglected in favour of the practical outcomes of "weak AI". As the results of AI research are incorporated into computing and microcomputing, the distinctive purity of AI is lost in a more general context of the intelligent social use of computers.

Prior to the identification of a socially useful application must come the development of a collaborative relationship involving the technology specialist and the domain practitioners. This issue has been explored for the humanities by Gardin and his colleagues [13, 16]. Early prototype systems may have the function of nurturing such relationships, as happened with the two most successful AIFS working groups, and will be discarded once new problems are under discussion. A premature emphasis on product may damage this critical ongoing collaborative process. Once a product is frozen and commercialised it ceases to be negotiable.

The collaborative development of a product, such as an AI system, depends on shared perceptions of the problem to be addressed, what the product is to be, and what the intended outcomes are to be. In the military or commercial world this can be simplified by conformity to superior orders or the pursuit of financial profit, but in normal human interaction and conversation, as analysed by Winograd and Flores [19], there must be a shared commitment. We may wish to describe this in terms of belief systems or ideology. We cannot expect to develop technologically-based solutions which are free from questions of commitment. The process of collaboration can take time, as trust and common experience are built up.

Practical collaboration can lead to unexpected discoveries and problems. Some of these issues have been explored in recent work coordinated in Sweden [8, 9]. Knowledge elicitation and knowledge engineering techniques take on a different and culturally richer complexion in the context of community work. The social worker, community group activist or advice centre volunteer may see information provision as their central concern, and be unwilling to contemplate replacement by an expert system. Their view of the problem domain may be different from that of the AI specialist, who thus has to be prepared to take a subordinate role. Much of their key expertise concerns how to deal with human networks, and this cannot be made fully explicit in the form of rule- based systems. Where AI can offer useful representations of complex problems, these can often be dismissed, as in the case of work in equal opportunities, as merely reinforcing the kind of stereotypes which underlie the problems in the current social system. The critiquing approach to expert systems, where the system is used to support but not replace the human expert, is clearly preferred.

Much can be learnt from the experience of the Intermediate Technology

Development Group over the past decades. Schumacher in 1962 [190] proposed
the concept of Intermediate Technology, arguing:

A technology must be evolved which is cheap enough to be accessible to a larger sector of the
community than the very rich and can be applied on a mass scale without making altogether
excessive demands on the savings and foreign exchange resources of the country.

Dave Newman of Kingston Polytechnic, with experience in both ITDG and
AIFS, has reported on Kenyan projects for developing charcoal and wood-burn-
ing stoves, and the corrosive effect of inappropriate finance. Too much money
at the wrong time can be as serious a problem as too little money, but this is
little understood with a longstanding need.

The newly established World Press Centre, directed by Peter Thompson,
offering PC-based electronic information services on Third World development
issues to the international media, could be a crucial case study. Providing a
unique commercial service, and using personal computers as an information
medium, it also supports an Educational Clearing House.

Socially useful applications of AI should not be seen as an optional add-on to
a conventional AI course. It is not enough to choose a socially useful project
from an official list. If the project is to be useful, the students must themselves
participate in the form of life, the cultural situation, which is to be assisted, and
be alerted to some of the broader issues to be addressed. Informal analysis of
recent projects suggests that the most useful systems often emerge where the
students are building on personal experience and expertise (as in AIDS
education, First Aid Advice, Ethnic Minority Diet Advice, Third World Energy
Issues, Equal Opportunities, Welfare Rights Advice, Community Information).
One neglected point is that applications in these areas may help to redress
gender imbalances in the use of information technology. Rafferty and
Glastonbury point out [191]:

Software which directly helps clients or improves the effectiveness and productivity of service
delivery, such as welfare benefits packages ... empowers the predominantly female staff groups.

One implication may be that AI courses should be broadened, to include not
only compulsory consideration of social implications and applications, but also
to encourage "bridging work" with the students' previous academic and personal experience. This implies a need for staff development support for current
lecturers, including secondments to community groups, which could be arranged through AIFS.

Why has AIFS not Achieved More?

Many will have expected that the decision by committed AI professionals to
apply their skills to socially useful purposes would have been rapidly followed
by a set of demonstrator projects, eagerly seized by workers in the field. We can
point to some cases where this has happened, and try to analyse the ingredients
for success, and how they may have been lacking in other cases. The argument

is that the objectives of AIFS entail the breaking down of a number of cultural barriers, and the learning of new styles of work and collaboration. The lasting outcomes of AIFS may be very different from the expectations of many founding members. Professionals in the field of social action deal with knowledge as a key resource: knowledge is power. This may be compounded with the advent of information technology. This works in a number of ways. They seek and demand freedom of information in order to elicit information from government and official agencies, but then see themselves as prime sources of advice and information for their clients. They are, in short, the experts, having spent years developing networks of contacts and lines of communication with those in authority and the media. In recent years they have become accustomed to rapid changes in legislation, and the creation and abolition of numerous agencies in the areas of employment, health and social services. Great ingenuity and endurance has been required of them in order that their services may continue: if their motivations were primarily financial or short-term they would have abandoned the unequal struggle long ago.

Voluntary bodies are poorly funded, so in general have been poorly equipped with information technology facilities. British universities and polytechnics have produced few specialist computer scientists, compared with the scale of demand. IT in community groups and social action organisations has been led by enthusiastic amateurs, using personal computers. The domination of mainframes and minicomputers has been an issue for relatively few, so research activities which assume such resources have been given scanty attention.

The advent of knowledge based systems tools on personal computers raises fascinating issues. At one level we have the perfect match: advice workers whose trade is in heuristic guidance in an environment of incomplete information, meeting a technology which purports to meet those needs. However, if knowledge based systems turn out to be effective, this has disconcerting implications for the advice professional. Is the dispensing of social advice to be de-skilled? Are the services of human professionals to be dispensed with, or should we be considering a remodelling of provision in the light of the new technology?

If we take the lessons from work in human centred systems, we must not let our simple and praiseworthy concerns for the poor, sick and unemployed blind us to the central position of the caring professional. If our technology is to prove truly effective, it must be taken on by the professionals. The experience in education has been instructive. The lead in the use of PROLOG and other intelligent tools has been taken by subject teachers with a vision of what was needed and what was possible. This presupposes a period of mutual familiarisation, taking months or even years. AI professionals have often made the mistake of underestimating the knowledge based expertise of practitioners in application domains. This applies particularly with community activists using personal computers. However, such use has been according to different paradigms, and in different traditions. The results are often impressive, with necessity as the mother of invention, but the developers may fail to realise the significance of what they have done, considering it obvious and trivial.

It turns out that the prime role of AIFS has been to facilitate communication between professionals in the field who had previously not found ways of working together. AIFS has become an intellectual dating agency, with offspring following after a period of gestation. Later histories of AIFS may be like family trees, or the histories of rock groups, as was Fleck's account [50] of the early days of AI. We may wish to model the collaborative process in a PARLOG parallel simulation [192], for it has been critical to monitor parallel developments and temporal sequences. We can see processes, streams, merging, lazy and eager evaluation. Building models might be instructive.

Social Applications for Artificial Intelligence

Welfare Rights for Further Education Students: A Suitable Case for Treatment

In the present context of skills shortages and demographic change, it is important to make the best use of the nation's human resources. Individual students may choose to abandon their chosen courses of further and higher education due to their financial inability to make ends meet. They are unlikely to be aware of the full range of benefits to which they are entitled, and the appropriate procedures for application and receipt of benefits. Some form of support is clearly necessary, and informed support from parents and families cannot be assumed.

Advice and support on welfare rights could be provided from different sources: college, employer, training agent, student union, local authority, central government, voluntary agency.

While the labour of young people is in demand, it is in the short-term self-interest of employers to ensure that those in education and training complete their courses or gain the desired qualifications. Provision of education and training should include advice and information on the financial means of support available for students and trainees.

This support depends on the ready availability of the appropriate advice and information materials, tailored to this area and level of need, at the appropriate level of detail and linguistic complexity. This requires development work, piloting of materials and staff development to enable education and training institutions to perform their professional function in this area and thus meet the skilled manpower requirements of the workplace.

A proposed project involving KCFE and AIFS is intended to focus on two areas:

1.   16–17 year old vulnerable young people.
2.   Students with special needs.

Neither area is addressed adequately by current reference texts. Recent major changes have been made by government, which will now affect the situation for some years. CPAG reference texts are highly respected, but more general and bulky than is practical for use by FE lecturers and counsellors.

Neither area is supported by major campaigning and advocacy organisations, and can simply be neglected through official failure to understand difficulties of:

1. 16–17 year old students in FE not living at home.
2. FE students relying on non-existent discretionary awards.
3. Implications of the Community Charge from April 1990.
4. Varying definitions of "student" and "full-time".

Government and civil servants lack personal knowledge and experience of FE, leaving home at 16, special needs, lack of parental support, being a client of the DSS, seeking rented accommodation, seeking work, and part-time study.

The National Union of Students is led by university students, usually from a secure middle-class background, enabling them to devote time to unpaid student political activity. They lack experience of current difficulties of 16–17 year old FE students or students with special needs.

There is no natural support group for these groups of FE students, beyond the FE institution. There is no generally provided support system within FE, and practice varies greatly between colleges. As the benefits system changes, students will lose significant sums to which they are entitled through lack of information and advice. As a result, the Treasury will save money in the short-term, but both individuals and society will suffer through the damage to education and training.

The purpose of the project is to provide support, by bringing together the necessary knowledge and skills to provide information and advice using a variety of technologies, and a series of seminars and workshops. The target audience is made up of the students, their families, tutors and counsellors, and their employers where applicable.

YOSSARIAN: A System that can Make Inferences About Reactions to AIDS and Stimulate Group Discussion

The current rise in the number of AIDS related problems is seen by many health workers to be the largest medical disaster ever. In addition to the purely physical and emotional problems associated with caring for people with a terminal condition, AIDS has caused secondary problems that often outweigh the medical condition itself. The issues in AIDS often focus on areas of life that are "taboo" in normal conversation. As a consequence of this, facts tend to be blurred by misinformation, invalid assumptions and prejudices, all of which conspire to fuel long running intolerances between different cultures, races and religions.

As a consequence of this situation, training needs to cause AIDS care workers to examine issues in their lives and attitudes that are normally unspoken. Thus, much training is centred on group discussion.

This project has involved the design, implementation and testing of a profiling and scenario support system, called YOSSARIAN. The purpose of the system is to profile the attitudes of a discussion group to a series of AIDS problems based on real life scenarios. YOSSARIAN then feeds back inferences intended to stimulate further discussion. Once the interaction is over, YOSSARIAN supplies a hard copy printout, drawing conclusions from the set of responses, which may be used as the basis for planning future sessions. The system has received extensive trial use with AIDS educators, and almost invariably stimulates detailed discussion of the subject matter, supporting the facilitating role of the AIDS educator or college counsellor.

Future developments of the YOSSARIAN shell by Pete Smee at Kingston College of Further Education are exploring problems in drug abuse (with the Kaleidoscope Project in Kingston) and welfare rights (with essential rights, as outlined above). Other applications under consideration include equal opportunities (with the Further Education Unit), industrial relations issues (with the Industrial Society) and humanities teaching (with the Office for Humanities Communication). The power of PROLOG and knowledge engineering techniques is such that completed applications systems can be produced with a week of intensive work.

"Meating" the Challenge: Attitudes to Meat in a Multi-Faith Context

A specialist AIFS seminar was convened by Richard Ennals and David Hopson, and following the video "Holy Meat" discussion was led by David Hopson and Margaret Shepherd (Education Officer of the Council of Christians and Jews).

David gave the context of the work of the Community Information group of AIFS, focusing on issues of equal opportunities. The group had included Orville Hemans of British Telecom, Michelle Rigby of the London Churches Employment Unit, and Marion Schapiro of the National Council of Voluntary Organisations.

Many organisations like to declare that "everybody is welcome" without realising that many of their practices may in effect exclude particular groups of people. In building a hypertext system to model and explore such issues, the group found that the narrow issue of meat would repay deeper investigation. Seminar members were provided with extracts from theological texts and newspaper reports.

An immediate matter of concern was presented to the seminar. The British government is proposing to ban the ritual slaughter of animals, purportedly on grounds of animal welfare. This decision is vigorously opposed by Muslims and Jews, for whom the manner of food preparation is an essential part of their faith. Muslim children and students have long been ignored in the provision of institutional food, meaning that many have gone hungry rather than go against their beliefs. The debate on ritual slaughter seems to have confused scientific fact with deep-seated prejudice, and the decisions of the Farm Animal Welfare Council appear to have been taken without consulting the ethnic minority communities or their religious leaders.

Food plays a central part in human culture, and in the practices of the major world religions. Deep offence can be caused through ill-considered statements, giving rise to suspicions of racism and threats of suppression of minority cultures.

Richard Ennals led the discussion on ways of working in AIFS, bringing together the diverse cultures and constraints of education, the voluntary sector and industry. Successful projects depended on eliciting from each what they could provide, and meeting the needs of each sector (or culture). The process takes time, but can be extremely rewarding.

There is an interesting comparison with work reported by Schoech and Toole, on "An approach to cross cultural knowledge engineering in the domain of child welfare" [193]. Their objective was to develop internationally transferable software on child abuse, linking information on prediction with decision-making. Based on work in the UK and USA, they propose an eight-stage protocol for developing expert systems applicable to many cultures. Their first step was to establish knowledge which is consistent across the cultures. Our work in the field of meat as a sub-field within equal opportunities suggests that the depth of cultural issues can be such that a bedrock of culture-free knowledge may be hard to find.

Organisational Preconditions for Collaborative Artificial Intelligence Activity

After long experience we can begin to identify preconditions for constructive work. Much more is required than just a single motivated individual, bearing the intellectual world on his shoulders, if work is to continue and develop.

Access to IT and AI technology

Increasingly this can mean personal computers, but traditionally involved major expense. Hardware is not enough: there must be access to a range of software tools and to technical support.

Individuals Familiar with AI Concepts and Tools

This is not the same as IT familiarity or awareness, but involves a capacity to cope with abstraction and shifting representations. Some external training and practical experience will be desirable, as even well-written books, software and distance learning packages benefit from human mediation.

Individual Delegated Responsibility and Professional Autonomy

The one-man company or domineering managing director or principal will not be conducive to the kind of organisational culture which sustains AI. The individual professional defines his own working space, and can modify his approaches and uses of technology.

Understood Vertical Lines of Reporting and Responsibility

It must be understood who asks the questions, and what would count as answers. The professional should have liberty to make his own space within those constraints. The different levels of the organisation should be open to scrutiny, so that the professional has the option of appeal to a higher authority if necessary, for example in case of professional disagreement.

Fluid Horizontal Communication Across Sections

It must be possible for professionals to talk to colleagues of equivalent grade in other sections, exchanging ideas and information. There should not be barriers of confidentiality or secrecy.

Reflective Organisational Culture

Appraisal and evaluation, at the individual and collective levels, should be a standard feature of the organisational culture. There should be a preparedness to recognise mistakes and learn from them.

Medium- and Long-Term Planning Horizons

AI cannot be relied on to give visible benefits in the short term. Organisations taking on AI tools and approaches must take a longer view, and be prepared to see the exploratory process as one of management development.

Collective Willingness to Experiment and Explore Ideas

AI cannot be run by one person, but depends on an ongoing interchange of ideas. It must be accepted that some ideas will not work, but are worth testing.

Intellectual Entrepreneurial Culture

Ideas can be traded, exchanged and packaged, in a way similar to physical goods. The goal however is understanding, rather than pecuniary gain.

Separation of Knowledge Transfer from Financial Transfer

The free flow of ideas must not be blocked by accountancy. Knowledge should be free at the point of need, and within an organisation there should be no financial barriers.

Value Given to Knowledge

The key resource of most companies, especially in the service sector, is the knowledge of their staff, yet typically no attempt is made to put a value on it. It should be seen as an investment to support an employee on an advanced course, or to write a book or filmscript. Some model could be constructed, showing the range of others influenced by the growth of knowledge in an individual. This implies a commitment to support for dissemination of innovative ideas on return from a course or learning experience.

Non-Proprietorial Approach to Knowledge

No one person or organisation can own a piece of knowledge. It must be shared in order to have visible existence, and will then be incorporated in the ideas of others. References should be made to publications, including conversations, but as part of the archaeology of knowledge, rather than as a claim of ownership.

Working in Pre-Paradigmatic Field

This is a matter of states of mind. In the same business or research field one group can see the field as clearly established, while others discern the potential for major new advances.

Network Access to People Outside the Organisation

The organisation should not be exclusive in its claims on time and loyalty. Professionals should be enabled to maintain outside links, to ensure the continued flow of ideas.

Tradition of Education, Training, Research, Development, Investment

Traditions take time, but are crucial to the organisational culture. The lead must be taken from the top, with a visible commitment to preparing for the future.

Subordinate Role of Finance Director

The finance director should have equivalent rank to directors of technology, research and training.

Common Culture

The organisation must have an active common culture. At the level of language, a high level of communication within the organisation is presupposed. There need to be corporate modes of communication and reporting, amounting to shared representations. Institutional structures need to be recognised as existing, whether organisational, physical or social. There may be conventions and customs regarding timekeeping, meals, sports and social activities, clothing and transport. There may be tacitly accepted tastes in music, decor, reading and social concerns. Crucial to success is parity of esteem between staff of an organisation, as between, for example, teaching and non-teaching, or senior and junior staff.

New Technology and Human Institutions

If technology is regarded as the extension of man, then the use of technology must be expected to have an impact on human institutions, those manifestations of human social interaction. Indeed, technology is inseparable from the institutional form which it assumes, a layer of make-up on the face of society which may appear to be beauty in the eye of the beholder, but may take on an addictive power. How can we imagine life in California without the automobile and the television? Can we envisage factories without machines? Hardly, for the institutional structures are partly a product of the technology. Is it too late to retrieve the essence of what it is to be human, to scrub off the scales of technology, to revolutionise the form of our institutions, to begin again? Our efforts may be worthy, but can only achieve partial success, as the tools which we are using, the concepts and tools of writing, and language itself, are themselves technologies of thought.

AI is of particular interest because it assists us in subjecting the technologies of thought to critical reflection. We must arrive at representations of the knowledge which concerns us, and make these explicit, tractable to processing. Such an activity cannot be independent of human institutions, for we live as members of society. This will affect our choice of subject domains, modes of representation, descriptive language, patterns of inference, styles of interaction, and the significance we attribute to any products, conclusions or outcomes. This approach has misleadingly been described as "weak AI", casting light on concepts and problems without aspiring to create working models of the human brain. Correctly understood, it is strong, even threatening to some, and can cast powerful beams of light on murkier areas of human institutional activity. That theoretical strength, however, depends on a fundamental acceptance of the limitations of technology.

Arguments about the limitations of systems and general problem solving methods have long been stated. They achieve a new significance with the advent of AI, where a working system constitutes a working model of an ideology. Design a new creed or way of life and, rather than leaving it to humans to get it wrong, entrust its working and administration to machines, programmed by an elite. Systems, ideologies and creeds are all based on organising what is known, and assuming the completeness, sufficiency and immutability of what is known. A major change, innovation or disruption may make what was certain now obsolete. AI does not get round that with the modelling of belief systems, but increases our chances of realising the limitations of what we know and can ever know.

How can we begin to describe what we cannot know? Can we know things which we cannot begin to describe? These are age-old philosophical problems which are not solved simply by the arrival of new technology. Rather, they are raised afresh for a new generation of technologists apparently free of philosophical preconceptions, but unavoidably carrying heavy cultural baggage. (Indeed, our definition of technologist gets ever broader, now encompassing philosophers, mathematicians and linguists who are working at the coalface of knowledge.)

If we reflect on our descriptions we may come to see the limits. We can build partial models of our chosen areas of knowledge, but in the real world we could never know everything. This is not just a problem of volume, that there is too much to know, but of fundamental philosophy. We cannot know what will happen in the future, though we may be unsurprised by events as they unfold. We cannot know what other people are thinking, but we take the example of our own thoughts and actions, observe the actions of others and infer the occurrence of particular patterns of thought. Our very use of language, that tool with which we frame descriptions and communicate to others who inhabit the same linguistic culture, has flawed foundations. We agree to use common terms, and assume that each is assigning common meanings. We are obliged to describe new phenomena using old linguistic tools or paradigms: we are constantly putting new wine in old bottles, and blurring the tastes of the two.

Common sense is something we can recognise in others in a given institutional or cultural context. We can describe it in terms of observed behaviour, itself indescribable in isolation from its context. At times we feel that we "know what we are doing" or "know how to go on", but we look for confirmation of that fact from others. This is the basis of ascriptions of vocational competence: a cultural rather than an individual process.

AI has turned out to be valuable in this context also, in a way which has not been sufficiently observed. AI systems typically commence by being exploratory, *ad hoc* attempts to model or simulate behaviour or reasoning in a given domain, and then undergo a process of rational reconstruction as a stronger theoretical structure is elicited from the arbitrary scaffolding. Logicist analysis has cast new light on those areas of expert knowledge which defy description.

Representing Interpersonal Knowledge Transactions

The conventional approach to interpersonal knowledge transactions is derived from transactions with physical goods, where concepts of supply and demand, producer and consumer have been developed, and financial mechanisms have evolved to support complex transactions and institutional frameworks. The transfer of knowledge is increasingly seen in terms of the transfer of money.

I want to argue that this capitalist model of knowledge transfer is fundamentally inappropriate and destructive of the further development of knowledge, technology and human institutions. We need a richer, human centred model on which to build our future.

Why is the Capitalist Model of Knowledge Transfer Inappropriate?

A business deal tends to be visualised as a two person zero sum game, with assumptions of interpersonal competition and rationality of individual decision-making. This may work in poker or the stock market, but real life problems of knowledge tend to be less two-dimensional, linear and quantitative in nature. Conversations, arguments or debates prove to be far more complex in their logical structures, and in real life include many elements which go beyond logic.

Conversation is based on dialogue, rather than buying and selling. There is a degree of mixed initiative and feedback, rather than one producer. At the end of a good conversation both sides are richer; the overall sum total of knowledge has increased. If I teach you something I still know it.

Conversations take place within the unspoken context of a shared culture, which involves shared commitments, however limited. Once we consider linguistic utterances in terms of speech acts, we are faced with consequences, causes and effects, and shared understandings. You may assign a financial price to a particular statement or piece of knowledge, but its value is far more complex.

Book and software publishing is facing new and difficult questions. When an author writes a book, to what extent should he be entitled to copyright? What is being sold when a copy of a book changes hands? Does the author pay those from whom he has derived ideas? What is the cut-off point between copying and influence? Can an individual claim and prove copyright on an idea? How could he ever prove that he had thought of something first? We are used to ascribing value to books. How do we value the knowledge in them, which could be communicated by numerous electronic means? Is it a matter of amending the copyright law, or do we have to face up to the idea that knowledge is socially constituted and cannot thus be appropriated as the private property of an individual?

Bringing Together Industry and Society Through Education

Developing socially useful systems is a learning experience. Industry needs people with system development experience. It may be sensible, therefore, to suggest that industry should pay for developing skilled people through efforts to address society's problems in educational environments.

A critical role is played by those voluntary bodies which occupy the interstitial spaces between industry, education and society, presenting different faces to their respective partners. Their multiplicity of representations is fundamental to their role, which has long been one of institutional prototyping. Successful prototypes are then frozen into a consistent representation and subsequent institutionalisation, while experimental pioneers move on, seeking more gaps and the vision to fill them.

We begin to find common concepts emerging from this voluntary experimental sector which have increasing applications in the world of industry, and can be mediated through education. A prime example is marketing, which no longer simply means selling commodities, but enhancing one's understanding of the intended audience or community context, and modifying the representation of one's activities accordingly.

Problems of marketing are not new for the voluntary sector: indeed it exists in response to perceived need, and operates without the cushions of financial support to which the private sector has become accustomed. In recent years education at all levels has been permeated with marketing talk, and professionals have learned to continue what they know to be sound practice while periodically changing the description of what they do in order to maintain their existence.

It is industry which, paradoxically, has most to learn about marketing. When individuals are simply seen as consumers, only an impoverished perception of their needs, motivations and values can be formed. The financial market-place has little relevance for those without the resources to enter the market, or for those whose affluence obviates the necessity for conscious choice. The market metaphor distorts relationships within society, while providing few genuine lasting benefits in return.

AI may again have something to offer, in the form of a unifying concept of elicitation. The market is concerned with the elicitation of money. Knowledge based systems depend on the elicitation of knowledge, derived from research methodologies. Working systems depend on human skills and institutions, often assembled through voluntary routes, andthe available premises and support environments. The voluntary sector is a ready source of problems: at last problem solving and problem finding can come together in a context of shared commitment.

Commitment is crucial. People in dialogue or in collaboration entertain expectations for the future, and need to feel a shared commitment with their partners. Given that this could never be fully articulated in advance, such commitment is best shown through unilateral but reciprocated acts, where short-term self-interest is sacrificed in the interest of the other. We are proposing economic disarmament of the market, and starting at the level of personal interaction. We are identifying as a common strand running through our work what Bevan described [183] as:

a respect for the underdog and a vocation to empower the disempowered on terms of equal citizenship.

The means are available to hand. We now have, for the first time, a common prevailing IT environment in industry, education and the voluntary sector, with *de facto* standards of IBM–PC compatibility, MSDOS and ASCII. Present government policy simplifies matters by removing the serious prospect of government public sector funding, and indeed the view of government is that it has no role in this area, as with most others. Market forces must be left to rule. The time is ripe to unveil the alternative "green market", which operates through the elicitation and barter of knowledge, skills, problems and premises, with money only as a last resort when real contributions are unavailable.

Case Studies in AI for Problem Finding

Solving problems once they have been precisely formulated can be straightforward. Finding a genuine problem which might be amenable to solution is much more complex, and depends on elements of cultural understanding which cannot be made fully explicit. Problem recognition may be resisted within a culture, for whom apparent inconsistencies and dissonances are tacitly resolved. A proposed solution may bring disruption whose effects are considered to be more deleterious than the problem itself. AI tools and techniques allow us to consider a wide range of candidate problem domains and specifications, only moving to visible implementation when culturally appropriate. Insufficient attention has been paid to the problem interface, where institutional frameworks rub together like the San Andreas Fault. The action is at the interface, the epicentre of institutional change. Bright sparks are available.

Students completing potentially socially useful projects as part of BSc or MSc courses could be eligible for secondment to voluntary organisations for six months to implement, test and modify their systems in practical institutional use prior to entering industrial employment. In many cases the course might be a "sandwich" involving the industrial, educational and voluntary sector parties from the outset, giving financial support for the student throughout. In other cases the collaboration would arise during the intensive research project at the end of the degree course, with an increasing element of joint supervision. An additional diploma for successful institutional implementation might be awarded. A lower level secondment system should be offered to augment work experience for BTEC National Diploma and Higher National Diploma students. Coordination of such a scheme might be undertaken by AIFS, possibly in association with the Community Projects Foundation and the national working group on IT and Community Development, supported by IBM and BT. Following a pilot phase it could become a national programme, cementing links between education, industry and the voluntary sector.

Chapter 7

Human Resource Development in Information Technology

The Human Resource Development in Information Technology Survey

The Human Resource Development in Information Technology (HRDIT) Survey [194] was a joint project by Kingston College of Further Education, Pergamon Infotech and IT Training Magazine, seeking to build up a picture of current practice in private and public sector organisations. Twenty-nine thousand questionnaires were sent out in November 1989. The majority were sent to senior IT and training directors and managers in industry, using lists of named conference attendees and magazine subscribers, with a significant response from IT users in education. Questions were aimed primarily at a commercial audience.

There were 642 responses to the HRDIT questionnaire from senior management in major companies, covering 3.3 million employees, drawn from a cross-section of the UK economy and from all parts of the country, as well as a number of other European countries such as Ireland, the Netherlands, Sweden, Finland, Norway, Denmark, France, Belgium, Cyprus, Greece, Turkey, Malta and Switzerland. This suggested a high level of concern for the questions addressed. Respondents were asked to: "answer as many questions as you can based on your own impressions. Our intention is to build up a qualitative picture". All responses were entered into a database, and processed with assistance from UNET Electronic Publishing and trainees at Church Action with the Unemployed. Fuller details of the sample and findings are available in [195].

The IT Skills Crisis

Managing the Skills Gap

Whereas the CBI Study *Managing the Skills Gap* [196], published on 28th November 1989, covered 40 private sector companies employing about 265,000 people, the HRDIT Survey was more focused in the skills addressed, with its concentration on IT but more wide-ranging in opinion sampled, from both IT suppliers and users.

The CBI urged companies to alter attitudes to training to prevent output being affected. Their study suggested that skills problems were being addressed in a piecemeal fashion, with little evidence of a strategy and no mechanism for pre- empting future problems. They found:

Managers were left with a feeling of helplessness to stem the tide or do nothing other than plug the gaps. Skills problems controlled the operations of the company, not the other way round.

They reported that constant fire-fighting of skills shortages left many companies with a continuous series of problems, which adversely influenced internal perceptions of the value of training. Poaching of skilled workers from other employers put artificial pressure on internal pay structures, disrupted company planning and discouraged investment in the training of those most likely to move on.

The companies with the most successful approaches to training were found to be those in which the subject featured regularly at board-level discussions, and in which training was given a separate budget.

Changing IT Skills

In 1987 the CBI IT Skills Agency (ITSA) had established a project [197] to predict the impact of developments in IT on supply and demand for staff during the next five years and to speculate on likely changes up to the end of the century. There follow some extracts from the findings of the Study, which operated through a series of seminars and workshops, involving the present author.

In all sectors of the UK economy demand for higher levels of skill is increasing at the expense of the semi-skilled or unskilled. The rate of growth in IT professional employment is limited by the capacity of organisations to absorb new trainees. ITSA research showed that, on average, the ratio of trainees to experienced staff which companies can accommodate is approximately 1 to 10. For at least the past 10 years, demand for professional IT staff has exceeded supply. The ITSA working group expected this situation to continue. They identified a growing need over the next few years for business analysts, staff with almost equal knowledge and experience of IT and fields of application, to define requirements and prepare systems specifications that accurately meet the needs of the user.

Three main factors affect the balance between supply of, and demand for, IT professional staff: the number of new entrants choosing IT as a career; the willingness and capability of employers to take on new trainees and retrain existing staff; and the ability of education and training organisations to cope with increasing (and different) demands.

New Entrants

The number of school-leavers is projected to fall by some 25 per cent over the next six years. Although the Department of Education and Science predicts the number of graduates will increase from approximately 115,000 in 1988 to about 124,000 in 1992, the pattern of degree subjects looks set to change. The number of applicants for electronics courses in 1987 was 21 per cent lower than in 1985 and for computer science 17 per cent lower. At the same time applications for accountancy rose by 30 per cent.

The fall in applications for technology-based degree courses can be ascribed to the shortage of qualified teachers of mathematics and physics essential to inspire students' interest; to the continuing decline in employment in manufacturing industry, which presents a poor image to bright young people; and to the highly-structured study demanded for success in technological, compared to other subjects.

Recruitment and Retraining

The record of many UK companies in human resource and career development planning as well as provision of in-career education and training is poor. The average age of professional staff in IT is low and prompts the question of how organisations intend to manage the maturing population. Many of the problems associated with predicted IT skills shortages could be avoided by suitable planning and career development for IT professional staff.

Many organisations still try to satisfy demand for additional or replacement staff by recruiting from the labour market. At a time of escalating demand and limited supply, this policy serves mostly to increase staff turnover and cause a salaries spiral. Growth based solely on recruiting experienced staff, particularly if low age is specified, is a policy which will lead to poor productivity and continuing manpower problems.

Trends in the European IT Skills Scene

Latest developments were reviewed at the HRDIT Conference [198]. Software costs are now the dominating element in computer system costs. Much of the cost lies in trying to maintain and extend the existing, poorly engineered, software systems. Despite the steady spread of software engineering, and the rapid growth of Computer Aided Software Engineering (CASE) tools, productivity in software development has not kept pace with the rapid development of the hardware and the market demand. Methods of automatic production of code from the specification are increasing the efficiency of production at the coding end of the business, but there is no real sign of any major breakthrough in the specification end of the software production process. The demand for Formal Specifications for secure systems, for safety critical systems, and for simple good practice in software engineering, is actually making the specification writing stage more difficult, more manpower intensive. The demand for high quality software designers is going to grow, indeed to accelerate.

Though certain applications, for example payroll, are becoming saturated, overall growth continues. The two major growth areas in the coming decade, other than communications, will be due to the spread of knowledge based systems and better human–computer interfaces.

In the UK there are believed to be some 300,000 people in employment with IT skills. Some 100,000 are employed by computer users. The figure for the software industry was 50,000 in 1988, and is growing even faster than the industry average of 8 per cent per annum. In the IT manufacturing sector the figure is about 70,000, though it is difficult to determine due to the indeterminacy of the boundary between electronics and IT.

At the HRDIT conference Brian Oakley, former President of the British Computer Society, argued that we are clearly going to face severe shortages of IT skilled personnel, perhaps throughout Europe [198]. The countries that can best keep up the supply of skilled manpower will gain considerable economic strength. We must strive to raise our IT productivity, especially in software. We must teach many more people in tertiary education some IT skills. Virtually every market should contain a significant measure of software and systems design education, especially centred round specification writing. There is already a trend to this in British universities, with joint courses in business studies and computing, languages and computing, for example. We must make more efficient use of our available manpower, particularly women.

Moving to a High Productivity, High Skill Economy

In a speech to the Flexible Training Conference on 28th November 1989 [199] the British Secretary of State for Employment emphasised the need for Britain to become a high productivity, high skill economy leaving labour intensive unskilled work to others:

People have been saying that for years, but now it is for real. That transformation is vital, and it is very urgent.

Three clear objectives were needed to achieve a better trained work-force: every job should be linked with training; every employee should be qualified and competent; and once qualified, employees need to stay qualified.

Survey Findings

Summary

To judge by responses to the HRDIT questionnaires, we found some models of "good practice", where there was a high degree of consultation, participation and training; there were good links with outside bodies in education, training and recruitment; and recruitment policies were in place which were responsive to demographic trends.

There are other cases where HRDIT had been wholly neglected – where system managers were wholly untrained, there was no apparent process of decision-making and consultation in IT and training; it was assumed that ready trained staff can be recruited; there were no links whatsoever with outside bodies; and no attention was given to recruitment from new groups in the population, such as married women, ethnic minorities, disabled people, former psychiatric patients and the unemployed.

Collaborative Links

One outcome of the survey and conference was intended to be a new set of collaborative links, between companies, and between companies and providers of education and training.

Companies identified training needs which could readily be met by their local universities, polytechnics or colleges with whom the company had no links at present. There was little sign of companies taking an active role in the new Training and Enterprise Councils (TECs) set up with government funding to replace public sector agencies in directing training at local level. Their effectiveness is to be measured in terms of vocational qualifications awarded, though relatively few national vocational qualifications have yet been agreed, particularly at the higher levels.

There would appear to be considerable scope for improved links between education and training organisations, who are otherwise reduced to relying exclusively on their own resources, with even senior staff largely self-taught.

The Role of Directors and Managers

In general the involvement of company directors and managers in IT use was limited. Decision-making on IT and training appeared to be focused at manager level, with broad involvement the exception rather than the rule. Directors decided policy, whether or not they made personal use of the technology. Often neither IT nor training were primary responsibilities of directors. Rarely were women found as DP managers.

In many cases it would appear that secretaries were the most frequent and expert IT users, but that they were not provided with training when new systems are installed, on which they might not have been consulted. Where the managing director had a terminal, the user might well be his secretary. Supervisors make major use of IT, and are responsible for the work of skilled, semi-skilled or unskilled staff, but are rarely involved in determining policy.

There was a clear picture of top-down management approaches, with strict vertical reporting. This could be contrasted with the participatory approach popular in Scandinavia and favoured by the Industrial Society.

Educational Links

Responses to questions about links with outside bodies in education, training and recruitment suggested a general lack of knowledge and awareness. There was more interest in experience than in qualifications. This division may be partially resolved with the development of "work based learning" and "competence based assessment". The Conference considered progress in National Vocational Qualifications in IT, again industry led. Few qualifications other than degrees were mentioned, though BTEC Higher National Diplomas and Certificates, Membership of the British Computer Society and BIS Aptitude Tests were cited. Such questions were apparently not seen as a major part of company culture or management concern, despite numerous recent national initiatives for closer industry–education relations. There were notable exceptions: in particular many non-UK based firms cited close links with universities, often in their headquarters country. A number of small IT-based firms had spun off from academic research and teaching activities, and remained located geographically close to their place of origin. The absence of developed educational links suggests that many thousands of employees are denied the support for part-time study from which they and their companies could undoubtedly benefit. Responses and written comments indicated a deep-seated animosity in many companies towards educational institutions and qualifications. It would be instructive to correlate these attitudes with the educational and training backgrounds of their directors and managers. This information was not sought in the survey.

Approaches to Training

There was still a widespread tacit assumption that ready- trained staff can be recruited, though few companies admitted to regular headhunting. Respondents were asked about their use of external consultants, in-house centres, on the job training, open learning at home, individual tuition, and customised courses.

Many small companies failed to respond. "In-house" and "on the job" training was frequently reported, with the implication that working time was not lost. Complete in-house training programmes were the exception, with identified needs being reported as satisfied. There was a high level of external training used. Some companies noted that one consequence of providing quality training was that a proportion of those trained might be recruited by rivals.

It was interesting to note that after a period of years when government had been extolling the virtues of open learning, especially computer-based or computer-assisted learning, the responses showed little take-up within companies. Managers showed little enthusiasm for learning at home, but neither apparently can they be spared from the workplace. When could they ever learn? There were exceptions in the returns from particular companies, many of whose pilot projects had received government financial pump-priming support. The Open University, Open Tech, Open College, and customised packages did not seem to have made major inroads into British corporate culture.

The Survey findings were consistent with the conclusions of Wood's report on DP Department Training [200]. Wood reported an increasing awareness of the need for training in Data Processing departments, but noted that the public sector set a poor example with a significantly lower level of expenditure per employee (472 compared with 638 in 1988). 2.3 per cent of the total DP spend in the private sector went on training, compared with 1.9 per cent in the public sector. Few trainees were being taken on, totalling some 13,700, only 4.5 per cent of the total DP work-force.

Wood found that most training was concerned with operating systems and programming languages, while little DP management training is undertaken. There was a heavy reliance on external sources of training, and few companies had training departments designed for DP or technical training. Although many managers claimed to offer computer based and video training, few employees used the facilities.

New Human Resources

Responses to questions on new human resources were often of the form "We are an equal opportunities employer", or "We recruit on merit". This appeared to suggest a passive or reactive approach, rather than active recruitment. Deliberate policies of recruitment from young people, married women, disabled, ethnic minorities, former psychiatric patients and the unemployed were rarely reported, though there were some notable exceptions. As with experience in the IT industry in the USA, a policy of recruiting women to senior positions in the UK tended to be driven by female company founders or directors.

The impact of demographic change on the thinking of company managers seemed limited (as has been noted by the Department of Employment and the CBI). A number of respondents noted the absence of unemployed people in their area, but few noted the decline in numbers of young people entering the job market. As UK industry moves into recession and sheds labour, concern for new employees has ceased to be fashionable.

People and organisations often prefer not to respond to change. Charles Handy tells an apparently scientifically accurate story in his book *The Age of Unreason* [201]. According to Handy:

A frog, if put in cold water will not bestir itself if that water is heated up slowly and gradually and will let itself be boiled alive, too comfortable with continuity to realise that continuous change at some point becomes discontinuous and demands a change in behaviour.

He describes the present demographic change as the "−23 per cent: The Vanishing Generation". It will, he contends, be necessary to reconsider the way in which we live and work more fundamentally than at any other period in modern times, and which he links to the combined impact of demographic change and IT. Handy talks about the difference between "incremental change", which is what we have been used to, and "discontinuous change", which, in his view, requires "discontinuous, upside-down thinking to deal with it, even if both thinkers and thoughts appear absurd at first sight."

The Government White Paper "Employment for the 1990s" [202] states that "These demographic changes have important implications for employers, Government and individuals." The White Paper may not offer such imaginative responses to this situation as Handy does, but there is still the recognition that "we are not yet using the full potential of all of our people".

The experience of individuals, and the results of special IT training and employment projects have made plain the levels of achievement that previously marginalised groups of people can attain. Straightforward training in common commercial applications such as word-processors, spreadsheet, database and DTP software, can open up many work and employment options. More than this, learning highly-valued skills brings its own personal rewards of achievement and confidence among groups of people where frustration and resulting low morale, can be common.

This positive aspect of computer training has been of particular benefit in mental health rehabilitation [203]. Mental illness is a term loosely covering both a wide range of medical conditions and episodes of personal distress. The rehabilitation process gives support to individuals who need it, to overcome, among other problems, the personal and social isolation inevitably experienced as a consequence of mental health problems. In this context the recent introduction of computers has helped people to regain confidence in their abilities and raised self-esteem. However, few survey respondents showed any interest in employing former psychiatric patients.

Training Needs

Many companies identified unmet training needs. Computer Assisted Software Engineering (CASE) was not normally given high priority. As with expert systems, the companies which mentioned an identified need often suggested that the need had been satisfied. Recognition of the need may have itself been useful. Word processing was generally deemed to be no longer a problem. This may be because the respondents were largely managers, while word processing had been delegated to the secretaries, who were rarely consulted on IT training policy.

The difficulties appeared to be focused in between, in areas such as programming methodology, information management, databases, and desktop publishing. Where programming methodology and desktop publishing were singled out for special mention, it was where needs had been identified but not fully satisfied.

Companies that had recently moved from mainframes to a proliferation of personal computers had not necessarily addressed the problems of maintenance, technical support, and above all, training. Companies that have chosen personal computers without a prior background in mainframes have not addressed issues of IT expertise and training. Maintenance and training costs have not been given due priority in budget planning and allocation. Hardware purchases are often made at times of the year when capital is available, and are not accompanied by commitments of staff time and training.

IT Qualifications

Qualifications, expectations and requirements of trainees, programmers and analysts varied widely between companies. There did not appear to be a stable and accepted professional structure in IT, and indeed many respondents stated a preference for experience over qualifications. The practical demands of specific posts did not easily correspond to existing qualifications. This finding was consistent with the findings of the IT Industry Lead Body, seeking to establish National Vocational Qualifications in IT, and failing to identify generic competencies. Job titles and descriptions were far from uniform. Few IT staff of whatever level could claim many formal qualifications: they had learnt through experience. Some respondents challenged the language of the survey, suggesting that for them IT was a tool, and that they had little feeling of membership of the IT industry. Users of IT could be anywhere in the economy, and their activities might not be best described in terms of IT.

Such a conclusion does not make for well-formed survey results or for the ready acceptance of IT-based qualifications. It undermines the basis of "Competence in IT", and the competence approach itself, which was the starting point for current UK government training policies.

The National Council for Vocational Qualifications (NCVQ) [204] has been asked to "hallmark" qualifications awarded to individuals who successfully demonstrate standards of competence designed to meet the real needs of employers. Progress was described at the HRDIT Conference by Stewart Judd of the CBI and IT Industry Lead Body.

An important element of NVQs is the so-called "underpinning knowledge and understanding". In areas where this required knowledge and understanding cannot be satisfactorily assessed through performance alone, evidence of them has to be obtained in some other way. Training and assessment on the job cannot provide the complete answer.

NVQs are not the only qualifications of interest to employers, neither do employers recruit exclusively on the basis of qualifications. Nevertheless employers will have to improve their planning and management of selection and retention, if they are to overcome shortages of IT staff during the coming period of significant demographic change. NVQs could be an effective aid in this process.

It has to be recognised that employers do not, and will not, recruit staff on the basis of qualifications alone, although some use qualifications (or rather a lack of a qualification) as a recruiting "filter". It is also clear from previous studies that some employers express preference for graduates for jobs for which possession of a degree is entirely inappropriate. In their 1988 survey of IT skills shortages the National Computing Centre (NCC) [205] reported that while 15 per cent of employers of professional systems staff feel that a degree is necessary for trainee recruits, 65 per cent expressed preference for those educated to degree standard. Little thought seems to have been given to the reaction of highly educated individuals if they are given undemanding tasks. It remains difficult for holders of BTEC National Diplomas in Computer Science to gain proper access to the job market, despite the need for their skills. Since the NCC report was published employers have become increasingly aware of the impact of demographic changes on the future labour market, and attitudes are changing, albeit somewhat slowly. A market survey of IT training, carried out by IT Strategy Services in 1988 [206], revealed, however, a confusing mix of courses and standards in a wide variety of IT subjects. Since then there have been indications of increasing support from employers for the development of standards of performance, provided that the validity and quality of assessment are properly controlled.

Within the United Kingdom, apart from medicine, finance and the law, possession of a vocational qualification, particularly in technology, has not been a prerequisite for a job in industry or commerce. Compared to our major competitors, a high proportion of the UK work-force is poorly educated and trained. Too many employers regard the acquisition of a qualification signifying the possession of transferable skills as a threat, having no confidence in their ability to manage careers development which would retain well-trained staff. In spite of the broad consultation with, and support from, many IT employers, a major concern for the ITILB remains: "will employers endorse the new scheme, pay to monitor and maintain the new structure and pay for training in transferable skills?"

The procedures for NVQs published by NCVQ [204] state:

Performance must be demonstrated and assessed under conditions as close as possible to those under which it would normally be practised.

This has considerable implications for education and training organisations. So too has the need for underpinning knowledge and understanding. There will, therefore, be opportunities for innovative educators and trainers to contribute to this major programme to improve the relevance and flexibility of UK vocational education and training.

There are many problems yet to solve, but increasingly, aspects of IT systems performance such as security, safety and integrity, will lead to demands for IT projects to be staffed by suitably qualified individuals as a condition imposed by insurance indemnifiers.

Change

IT systems had almost universally changed in the last 2–5 years, while very often company management structures had stayed the same. Among the exceptions were research and development groups, who had made the transition to individual workstations some years ago, but were having to adjust their management structures in difficult economic circumstances.

The lack of correlation between technology change and management change might be related to the finding that few directors and senior managers themselves used IT. Some differences in responses might be correlated with the differences in hardware systems used. Long-term users of mainframe systems may prove, on closer analysis, to have different experience from more recent users of personal computers.

Richard Sharpe [207,208] noted at the HRDIT conference that, while operating behind a mask of progress, the computer world is deeply conservative in its approaches, its internal operations and its impact on the world around it. The public face of the computer world is one of change. While it seems dynamic itself, the computer world is also the driving force of change in other industries; the adoption of computer technology is seemingly revolutionising other sectors one after the other as office automation, robotics and computer-controlled networks spread out and are employed. The benefits of adopting the products of the computer world are there for all to see, such as networks, computer-assisted manufacturing, accounting and decision-making.

The strongest force in the market is the push by vendors, not the pull by users. Only the very strongest users, operating together and exerting all their force, can get what they want from the computer industry. Technical decisions will be made by vendors in the development process and in marketing which make it difficult for the user to hold on to the old equipment: maintenance charges will increase for the older equipment, spares will become scarce, skills as well as products are made obsolete as new products are launched. The real historic continuity between past, present and future in the computer world is under threat all the time as each seemingly new product is launched with all the enthusiasm that marketing staff can put behind it.

The computer world is a conservative one. On the outside the main tools of the conservative world are used to conserve power. They are employed by the largest and most powerful political and economic forces in the world to continue their exercise of power. The technology itself is bought in increasing amounts by these already powerful operations to slim down their work-force, to increase their share of markets, to get closer to customers and so shorten development times, indeed for a host of reasons that are central to the continued survival and growth of large organisations.

The largest users have their reasons for welcoming more change and less revolution. They may have their problems in getting applications up and running on time and on budget, but they have a big base of existing applications written in old technologies running on existing hardware under existing and proven systems software. This cannot all be torn up overnight. To do so would be to put the life of the corporation in jeopardy in pursuit of a technical benefit which is far from guaranteed.

The gender composition of the computer world mirrors that of the larger world. There is little difference between the computer industry and other occupations, despite the revolutionary mask the computer world likes to wear. Key jobs are done by men in metropolitan areas and the less important ones by women on the periphery: geographically, economically or racially. Low paid work is switched to the lowest paying country.

The HRDIT survey indicates that management control had clearly increased in recent years, while worker autonomy and the influence of trade unions had been reduced. Many respondents suggested that trade unions played no part in their companies, sometimes following take-overs from other companies. Some respondents indicated that questions about trade unions or equal opportunities were not relevant to their companies.

Most respondents were directors or managers, and might be expected to reflect a management view. For them IT is a management tool, and an organisational technology, though it did not appear to have assumed strategic significance in decision-making at board level.

Workplace Relations and the Role of Management

The complete survey did not give statistically reliable overall results, but was intended to provide a qualitative picture, offering insights into corporate culture. Company communications were such that one respondent could not usually speak with authority for the company as a whole, and there was rarely a general policy framework. Rarely will more than a few senior managers have been responsible for IT and IT training policy, and those policies may not be widely known or understood.

The diverse range of hardware reported by many companies suggests a lack of consistency in purchasing, reflecting an absence of a guiding strategy or policy. We hoped to detect some interesting variations between the experiences of companies with different sizes, and in different sectors of the economy. Further detailed work is required, possibly taking case studies at local level. Feasibility studies are under discussion for practical collaborative case study work, in the UK and overseas.

There appears to be significance in the perceived size of unit within which the respondent works, and his or her place in the power structure of that unit.

Some respondents felt able to respond for their company as a whole, while others made it clear that they only spoke for their small group.

Work by the Industrial Society, reported at the HRDIT Conference by their Director, Alistair Graham [209], has shown the importance of workplace relations and worker involvement. The Industrial Society finds that companies are now giving more attention to how their employees are managed and developed. They carry less spare capacity since the slimming of numbers in the early 1980s but the business environment is getting even tougher; technology is developing fast; and skill shortages are increasing.

Competitive advantage can mean getting ahead of rivals who have access to the same technology, similar cost structures and numbers of employees and who pay similar salaries. The obvious answer is to make better use of the talents of all employees and constantly update their technical skills. In any organisation training and development must be planned to support the business strategy and to take account of individual development needs. Leading companies see the quality of their staff as a strategic resource in an increasingly competitive world market-place. Given that industry in general is short of IT skills at all levels, for many employers the traditional response has been to poach from others with the bait of higher salaries. The result has been an underinvestment in training in IT skills by employers fearful of losing their newly trained staff. In many companies IT professionals earn well above their peers as measured by internal job evaluation schemes and this causes considerable resentment. This is particularly true if the employer does not offer any IT training to existing staff but insists that these people must be recruited in the market- place at high salaries.

Much of the problem lies with the lack of hands on knowledge of IT at the senior management level of many organisations. Those who see all aspects of IT as largely incomprehensible are only too ready to hire IT experts to install systems while giving little training to the vast majority of their staff who will be using them. As the problems in the City of London in the months following Big Bang have demonstrated, ignorance can prove to be enormously expensive, particularly where it involves dependence on a technology which is not understood. Managers are effectively held as hostages by their systems.

Issues of management, IT and management education are now dynamically intertwined. Organisations need to reflect on their handling of knowledge, the role of individuals, approaches to education and the strategic place of technology. Success will require additional effort and new frameworks.

The traditional problem of IT in many organisations has been with implementation of the IT strategy. Often IT specialists misunderstand and do not communicate directly with the users but resort to mandatory instructions via memos. Meanwhile the users do not understand the capabilities of the system, and IT people may need training to enable them to communicate with non-technical staff, understand people's real needs and help them to get the best out of the systems. Like specialists in other fields they may also need to acquire leadership skills to manage and lead their own team. Human resource development in IT involves the formation of new teams and the development of new approaches, but building on old principles.

The Industrial Society commissioned MORI (Market & Opinion Research International) to survey employed people to establish their perceptions and attitudes to work [210]. They were looking for evidence that employees who feel involved at work and reasonably satisfied with their jobs are also more committed to helping their company to be successful. The survey covered just over 1000 employees in the private sector. The evidence from the MORI survey is that employers who are effective at communicating with and involving their employees and providing them with satisfying jobs will be rewarded with a more highly motivated work-force, greater commitment to the company and support for its management.

Studies in the United States have shown that committed employees are more likely to remain with the organisation and have better attendance. This is of considerable importance to employers concerned about today's increasing labour and skill shortages.

The MORI survey found that job satisfaction was highly correlated with working as a member of a team, involvement in problem solving and feeling well informed. Having a job which was interesting and enjoyable was the most important factor, coming well above pay. However MORI also found that only three out of five respondents said that they were usually told the reasons for what they were asked to do. Only half of those interested got feedback about their performance. Only one third of those interested were given information on company plans for the future.

The survey confirmed that most employees prefer to get their information direct from the person they report to rather than through house newspapers, videos and other impersonal means. There are clearly times when technology can get in the way.

One third of employees believe that they could do more in their current job without too much effort – and they are less committed to their company. Only three in five feel able to express their ideas and contribute to solving workplace problems. Those involved in problem solving are twice as likely to rate their company as well managed and are more committed to helping it to be successful.

As Alistair Graham said at the HRDIT conference:

The evidence from the MORI Survey is that employers who are effective at communicating with and involving their employees and providing them with satisfying jobs will be rewarded with a more highly motivated work-force, greater commitment to the company and support for its management.

The HRDIT Survey showed some evidence of poor communication within companies. Two respondents with the same job title from the same site of the same company gave very different responses. In another case the responses from one manager were clearly changed to make them more consistent with those of his colleague from the same organisation. As with IT and information handling generally, it is a question of access to information within institutions, and thus a question of perception.

Case study work is required to test further the general conclusions reached by the Industrial Society in the specialist context of IT. Work reported from the Swedish Centre for Working Life [8,9], based on long-term case studies, suggests that the culture of the workplace is fundamental to the successful use of technology, and that broad participation is essential if risks of alienation and de-skilling are to be avoided.

Conclusions from the HRDIT Survey

The Survey results give a useful indicative qualitative picture of current practice in human resource development in IT though the mode in which the Survey was conducted, by postal questionnaire, and the somewhat arbitrary nature of the sample, suggests that detailed statistical analysis would add little to our general level of understanding reported above.

A large number of studies and consultants' reports have been conducted in this field in recent months, and the conclusions show a remarkable consistency concerning the deficiencies in the current position in the United Kingdom, and the kind of changes which would be required to make British industry competitive in its use of IT and human resources. Unanimity regarding conclusions has not led to changes in policy in either the private or public sectors.

While policy on long-term training and investment is left to market forces and the decisions of individual companies and managers, concerned with meeting short-term financial objectives, little improvement can be expected. Respondents show little sign of taking action to follow the conclusions of governments and consultants regarding demographic change, human resource development and IT.

There is an inclination among managers to seek a technological solution to a human problem. Problems of dealing with technology cannot necessarily be "fixed" through the use of a new technological device. It is necessary to reflect on the human context of technology use, and to change attitudes and workplace relations, possibly taking the theme of "Human Centred Systems" [141,142]. This requires both increased management understanding of technology, and greater involvement of the work-force in decision-making. We need more working models of successful good practice.

Chapter 8

Politics

Observing Patterns of Behaviour in Human Institutions

Computer programs are merely the latest medium in which patterns of human behaviour can be described and modelled. AI practitioners have much to learn from those other media if they are to understand the fundamentals of politics and take full advantage of their own tools for both understanding and action. Politics is a curiously dynamic environment, where a descriptive or critical remark can be construed as a political act, and there can be no such thing as a completely outside observer.

Committees

Committee procedures have been designed to give a manageable structure to the conduct of many and various organisations, enabling people to work together in a common institutional framework. Standard practices are applied across a whole culture, irrespective of the domain of concern. Agendas are drawn up, minutes taken and approved, motions moved, amendments considered, procedures invoked. Institutions acquire bureaucratic methods, and are subjected to external inspection and audit. Similar approaches can be noted in churches, political parties, academic committees, community relations councils, companies and government departments.

In addition to understanding general committee procedure, the new member needs to identify where the power lies, the informal system which underlies the surface formality. Clues will often be through language, whether verbal or body. Understanding what is going on in a meeting may require complex skills of decoding the situation semantics. It will become necessary to know where different committee members "come from", and what relationships may exist between them. The new member will say little at his first meeting, and monitor closely the responses of others to his early contributions. If obliged to speak before his chosen moment, he may be hesitant and driven by perceived feedback from individual phrases, before he settles into more relaxed communication.

A skilled experienced committee member "knows how to go on", how to effect change by means of a formalised structure. He can "make the system work for him" or "play the system". Typically, such an "operator" will have a clear picture of their goal state, and a "game plan" by which to reach it. This involves recognising the salient characteristics of the situation, and acting accordingly, as the expert chess player handles an end game.

The success of a committee system depends on the consent of the membership, and the tacit shared commitment to common objectives, which may or may not be enshrined in the constitution of the body concerned. Often the explicit objectives are less important than the latent objectives, or the process of meeting itself. Achieving a consensus, or supporting an appropriate system of delegation may be no mean feats.

Keeping the system running smoothly may require skills of social engineering. There is an art to devising amendments and ways round official obstacles. After the event it will be described in terms of rational justification, as an instance of management science.

Constitutional reform or institutional innovation is akin to software design and implementation. New structures must be built capable of coping with change over time, with organic connections with the institutional past and accessibility to individuals in the present and future.

Software engineers could usefully study the process of developing constitutions for the newly independent colonies of the British Empire and Commonwealth. The constitutional structures needed to draw on the traditional past, the experience of the colonial period, and the aspirations of the independent future. Just designing a constitution is not enough: it tends to need maintenance and updating over time.

Humorous and Satirical Writing

Stephen Potter has produced a series of books [211] outlining *Gamesmanship, Lifemanship, Supermanship* and *Oneupmanship,* all based on descriptions of stereotypical (and very British) situations in which the "Lifeman" can take advantage. Methods, gambits, tricks and devices are offered, as a form of notional training for the rigours of modern life. His art is to capture in a humorous description a situation familiar to each of his readers (the "script" is well-known).

George Mikes specialises in advising the outsider, whether as tourist or intending citizen, characterising Britain and the British from the perspective of a professional "alien" [212]. Many of his pieces of advice would translate naturally into an expert system, thus giving visible interactive form to the caricature of knowledge. We should perhaps ask how we distinguish between knowledge representation and caricature: can it be other than by intent, i.e. not in the surface form?

Mikes sums up Italian cathedrals [213] by offering a unified guide to all of them: Schank [71] would take this up as a "cathedral script" fit to rival the "restaurant script". We might consider that guide books like Berlitz and Baedecker have been offering this provision through words for over a century, offering an intermediate representation which both relates to reality and is comprehensible to readers. Cornford produced a guide for the young academic politician *Microcosmographia Academica* [214]. The humorous intent does not mask the parallels with Machiavelli's *The Prince* [215], shrewdly analytical of character traits and political methods. The academic humour makes implicit links with research methods in the humanities and social sciences.

Lewis Carroll provides a further example of humorous writing for young people as a veneer to the creative ideas of a theoretical logician. Conventional exposition of logical paradoxes does not reach a mass audience. Conjuring up magical micro-worlds for Alice enables him to give expression to ideas which defy description at the object level.

Anthony Jay and Jonathan Lynn [77,78], with their series *Yes, Minister* and *Yes, Prime Minister*, on television and in print, have provided a fictional framework within which the modern day world of Whitehall politics can be described and understood. There is an additional edge to this, as Jay also served as an adviser to Government ministers, writing speeches and advising on television technique.

Their closest predecessors were Gilbert and Sullivan, writing musical comic opera often based on the political issues and personalities of the day. Nowadays the music and stories are enjoyed, while the political context has been lost.

Shakespeare might be invoked as a further precedent, making the link to the broader classical theatrical tradition. Shakespeare's history plays gave insights into recent events for the audience of the day, and tragedies such as *Hamlet* and *Macbeth* traded on contemporary assumptions and morality.

Non-Literal Communication

Much of the strength of human institutional culture is derived from non-literal communication. The use of language is essentially enriched by the use of metaphor, allusion and reference, appealing to common experience to motivate new assertions or suggestions. Where such use of language provokes an appropriate response, the relationship is strengthened.

Thus many business and diplomatic negotiations depend on the preliminary niceties, identifying common ground (perhaps seen as common perceptions or compatible representations) within which assertions can be made, generalisations developed, qualities ascribed and quantities measured. Diplomacy and business provide institutional settings for such niceties.

Inferences, conclusions and explanations have no real-world meaning without an institutional environment. Literature may conjure this up through words. Social science makes it the object of study.

Artificial Intelligence and Politics

"Politics", wrote R. A. Butler [216], "is the art of the possible." AI provides us with tools to model and explore alternative possibilities, conducting experiments with ideas prior to practical implementation with people.

We are accustomed to discussions of political ideology, often in the form of adversarial debate which may obscure the finer points of detail. Where the ideology in question can be represented as a consistent set of beliefs, it could be run as a program and subjected to interrogation.

Two further points need to be made. Just as ideologies can be regarded as programs, so programs must be considered in the context of ideology. Automatic systems running in real time have the status of ideologies in themselves – they are presumed to contain the answers to all questions in advance of them being asked or even formulated. Computer systems to be used in a support role with the possibility of human intervention have to be seen as operating in an environment affected by the beliefs of the human agents. To consider the operation of systems in isolation from their context of use is dangerous in the extreme, though it is frequently justified in terms of standard professional or scientific practice.

"There is no Artificial Intelligence without Central Intelligence"

It is notable that a large proportion of AI research, particularly in the United States, has been funded from military sources. In the early years it appeared to the academic researchers that their work had no practical applications, so the ostensible objectives of their paymasters were not to be taken seriously. In the 1980s the balance shifted as it appeared that the Department of Defense accepted the claims for the technology made by those seeking funding, and a new implementation phase was added to the customary research and development. We need not doubt that work on speech recognition, for example, has been of use in the automation of telephone tapping, or that advances in database systems have been applied to the maintenance and updating of intelligence databases. Simulation systems have helped in planning for different eventualities in situations such as terrorist hijackings and sensitive arms control negotiations. Battle management systems and autonomous military vehicles have helped distance human agents from detailed decision making in hostile conditions. The computer hardware itself would not exist in its current form without vast investment of military funds, forcing developments at a speed which normal market forces in the civil economy could not match.

"From Big Brother to Little Sister"

The imperatives of military systems are for command and control, with orders issued from the top followed without question below. This approach to management can be carried over into civil production industry, as has been the tradition in the military industrial complexes of both West and East, where defence contracts have served to subsidise and corrupt civil work. To change to a more democratic approach with horizontal communications and initiatives from the work-force, requires a major upheaval in management structures and associated systems. AI may hasten such changes, as it can place more power in the hands of individual workers at whatever level, and subvert conventional power structures.

To what extent can we see IT companies taking advantage of the opportunities for worker autonomy? On balance the major vendors retain a centralist approach, their conservative management attitudes belying the liberated image emblazoned across their corporate advertising. The imperatives of moving to new product lines and sales campaigns require close coordination and planning with military precision. To allow excessive autonomy is to risk the secession of key groups of workers to form a rival company in the same market.

We might hope to see more enlightened approaches among user companies, but change has been slow. Management have been reluctant to weaken their power, and have remained largely ignorant of the technology with which the effectiveness of their organisations could be enhanced. Where ignorance offers the apparent promise of continued unchallenged comfort, few have opted for wisdom which might be at their own expense.

It is not surprising that similar arguments apply to governments. Change is normally demanded by oppositions, who are then reluctant to restrict their own power once in office. They have lacked prior experience of government. This excuse grows weaker as AI and simulation tools become available.

Little Sister may yet prove to be a potent force in IT and in politics. Current evidence suggests a far higher level of IT use among secretaries then among directors, yet minimal consultation of these experts on IT policy issues. Demographic change is forcing changes in the workplace: more women are likely to have the chance of taking control of key jobs, in which they may show different characteristics to their male predecessors.

A Case Study in Politics and Artificial Intelligence : Star Wars

Research Management

I came into personal contact with the issue of Star Wars in my capacity as research manager in the Department of Computing at Imperial College,

London, and coordinator of Logic Programming for the British Government Alvey Programme, and I resigned these posts in opposition to the British secret Memorandum of Understanding to participate in the American SDI programme [118].

As research manager seeking to develop the research strengths of our group, concerning logic programming and parallel computer architectures, limited alternative strategies were available. Academics like to pursue "pure" research, but government and industry are reluctant to pay. There can be "spin-off" from large mission-oriented programmes, such as administered by DARPA in the United States, or the space programme which landed men on the moon and accelerated research in a number of technologies. Alternatively, direct applications can be the focus of attention, pulling in the necessary technologies. The Alvey Programme constituted a mixture of these approaches, a national collaborative programme to develop the enabling technologies for a new generation of computer systems. It offered attractions from a research management point of view as long as the objectives of projects were attainable and consistent with ours, the necessary resources were available to support our work, the timescales envisaged were appropriate to the technical obstacles to be overcome, the complexity of the research problem was sufficiently broken down into manageable sub-problems, and the research environment permitted technology transfer between collaborators and the normal pursuit of research and teaching.

Approaches to Artificial Intelligence Research

The work of our group concerned fundamental tasks of AI, supporting systems and concepts which could be considered from many different perspectives. At its simplest AI offers the means of animating ideas, of adding a dynamic dimension to discourse. This can be located in the context of what Simon called the "Sciences of the Artificial" [63], providing a framework for the artificial constraints of economics, social and management science, and a common environment in which graduates of many disciplines may work. Alternatively AI technicians see themselves as developing the tools and techniques which can be used in diverse contexts. In the 1960s there was enthusiasm over the prospect of developing general problem solving systems [217], whereas the emphasis in expert systems is on capturing the particular aspects of individual specialist problems. Others see AI as a tool for aiding the understanding of problems, many of which cannot in fact be solved, but must be lived with. In commercial, industrial or educational applications AI can reduce the complexity of human problem solving, enabling a naive user to perform tasks which would previously have required scarce and intricate knowledge. Increasingly there is concern for issues of language and culture, and systems are designed to be addressed in natural language, and to operate in culturally appropriate ways. In general AI can be seen as extending mankind's thinking power, just as machines extend mankind's physical power. Finally and crucially, AI should be seen as a social activity, involving the free exchange of ideas and information, always provisional but increasingly practical.

Insights from Wittgenstein

Wittgenstein's ideas on philosophy are particularly germane to the problems of handling concepts given concrete realisation through AI, and informed my attempts to unravel the issues of Star Wars, trying to show a lot of confused "flies" the way out of the "fly bottle". He illustrated the idea of "seeing as ..." with his example of a duck–rabbit, which seems to be first one, then the other [66]. Different collaborators in a project will often see it as very different things: the contribution of their own past work and the preparation for future plans. Where they arrive at a clear agreed description there may be great variations in its use: a description may lead to, or imply, a prescription; it may constitute a solution of a problem or a recognition of the impossibility of a solution.

As rules and rule-based systems gain in prominence we do well to recall Wittgenstein's account of what it is to follow a rule [218, 219]. People may be described as following a rule though they are not aware of so doing: this may be a characterisation of their form of life. Rarely will it be the case that simply taking those rules to build a system will give an adequate model of the rule-following behaviour first described. Work in machine learning has confirmed Wittgenstein's insights into the limits of what can be taught and learnt. One knows how to follow a rule when one knows "how to go on", when one has acquired what appear to be appropriate judgements. The tacit knowledge involved here cannot be fully described or automated, yet it is essential. The examples of games emphasises the social nature of this knowledge and the processes by which it is transferred. I have heard accounts of Wittgenstein teaching the rules of basketball to students among the trees in Cambridge, by demonstration but without a ball. In my book *Star Wars: A Question of Initiative* [118] I have written about "Celestial Snooker" and "Celestial Poker", taking the metaphors of games to demystify complex events and concepts.

Enabling Technologies

The enabling technologies of AI can take many different forms when implemented in the context of different programmes. Unifying them all, we can depict a general elicitation symbol of a pentagon, chosen as the symbol of the British Alvey programme, unifying three government ministries, universities and industry. The programme was a means of eliciting money, people, ideas and facilities, with which diverse projects and applications could be supported.

The same symbol is associated with the American Department of Defense, and a reliance on the power of technology. "We have the technology"; "The force is with us": there is a naive view that, protected by technology, we are safe from our enemies. Less naively, but with some cynicism, there are many companies who see military projects as a source of money which can then be deployed for diverse purposes, including financing civil research programmes.

Sometimes military funding can be used to help develop successful civil products. Automobile manufacturers such as Ford and General Motors are major SDI contractors, and military contracts help bear their research and development costs. The transferability of technical advances across application domains can be critical. As research manager at Imperial College I met with representatives of United Technologies (Sikorsky) who were interested in our research in AI and expert systems for use in SDI contract. On the same visit they were seeking to purchase part of Westland Helicopters, valuing research on composite materials for building space-based mirror platforms. At Imperial College we had researchers seconded from both Westland and from British Aerospace, who were concerned to add intelligence to their satellites. Putting these technologies together we can begin to see how a component of the overall SDI scheme would draw on advanced research from disparate fields, initiated for other purposes.

Alternatively, we could focus our attention on a Strategic Health Initiative [220], seeking to ameliorate the situation of medical professionals and their patients. Finally, we can take the technology of thought and seek to enhance our work in education and training.

In each of these cases we should be aware of the complexity of the problems we are addressing. In Star Wars, for example,President Reagan asked us to believe that his automatic defence system would successfully destroy all of 10,000 or more incoming missiles, without fail, without practice, and without being able to test the system in full as we do not have a spare planet. We consider this to be a game of Celestial Snooker, and in space we have no safe pockets into which the missiles can be "potted."

In general, whatever our choice of application focus, we have a number of common requirements of new generation computers. We want parallel processing, reliability, AI, very large databases, non-monotonic reasoning, correctness, modularity, verification, speech input, real time expert systems, low cost, natural language understanding, and robustness. If control of these enabling technologies is monopolised by a single interest such as defence, and access denied to potential aggressors or their trading partners, progress in other areas may be sacrificed. Thus proposals from American SDI contractors had to be considered rather cautiously: I informed them my colleagues were busy on applications with industry, health and education.

Versions of Star Wars

Further caution is required when considering the Star Wars programme in which our involvement was solicited. There are five different versions, with different objectives and susceptible to different critical opposition.

President Reagan in 1983 announced his intention of building a "Peace Shield" to protect the civil populations of the USA and her collaborators: the

United Kingdom, Italy, West Germany, Israel and Japan. In essence a technological condom was to be placed over their territories, repelling all incoming Inter Continental Ballistic Missiles but not bombers, Cruise missiles or terrorists. Such a system is inconceivable: we cannot describe what it would be for it to work. It is an ideological construct – the owner is presumed to have all the answers before knowing the question, and the system will respond automatically.

By 1985 it was clear that this was not what the Pentagon were building. General Abrahamson, who was then in charge of the SDI Programme, talked in discussions with me on British television, of his plans to build a partially leak-proof umbrella to protect missile silos, enhancing nuclear deterrence rather than making nuclear weapons obsolete. Partially leak-proof condoms are of little value: in the Star Wars case one missile penetrating the umbrella could produce a nuclear winter as well as precipitating retaliation. In addition, the technical complexity of producing a credible system is horrendous, with many millions of lines of computer code [157,166] and numerous interconnecting pieces of hardware on earth and in space, required to perform perfectly within seconds. Established Pentagon experts on space technology rebelled against the project [221].

A third, more attainable, version of Star Wars thus appeared: the building of autonomous battlestations in space, each responsible for protecting a finite area, but in communication with other systems. Such systems could indeed be implemented and deployed crudely today, but offer no more assurances of overall protection, as well as being in breach of the 1972 Anti-Ballistic Missile (ABM) Treaty.

There has been interest expressed in the United States recently for a more limited, ground-based, system against missile attack. This could possibly be limited to one main site, consistent with the provisions of the ABM Treaty, and would maintain the momentum of realistic research.

More loosely, many European countries and defence contractors retain an interest in the enhancement of current defence technologies, though defence of Europe against attack from the East would have little to do with space-based systems other than communications satellites.

These five different versions of Star Wars also have to be seen in various contexts. Apart from considerations of defence policy, which I do not deal with here, there are issues of science and technology policy and practice, of politics, economics and philosophy. These have already given scope for diverse debates and multifarious publications.

The Politics of Star Wars

Star Wars provides us with a classic fairy tale example of "naked imperialism". The Emperor, President Reagan, had no clothes, yet his friends and allies refused to acknowledge the fact in public, and indeed accepted contracts as his tailors. No other NATO country saw SDI as consistent with NATO strategy, unless redefined as versions 4 or 5 above, yet none felt able to break ranks and criticise the President, Leader of the Western Alliance.

Room for manoeuvre has been limited by the ongoing cycle of arms reduction talks. At the time of writing Star Wars remains an obstacle. The USA will only agree to Strategic Arms Reductions if Star Wars stays. Gorbachev will only agree if it goes. This provides a rationale for the game of redefining Star Wars to save the face of all concerned. Something must continue, describable as SDI. The 1972 ABM Treaty must continue, and not be breached by SDI tests or deployment. Allies remain nervous, but solutions are readily available if the will to negotiate and coexist is there.

The silence of the Allies has cost them possibly irreparable damage to industry and education. In the UK the continued favouring of military research and development has been at the expense of civil industry. The lack of the expected Star Wars £1 billion has meant the virtual cessation of space research and support for IT as the Treasury had assumed US finance and cut British government funding. European collaboration under programmes such as ESPRIT and EUREKA was delayed and damaged. American technological imperatives have been at the expense of European co-determination.

The Economics of Star Wars

It is now generally accepted that income from the research stage of SDI for European companies has been and will be extremely limited. Contracts for major research and development are only awarded outside the USA if no American company can do the work. Implementation, if it is to happen, is a distant issue, apart from the battlestation hardware which High Frontier companies want to deploy immediately.

Unlike the Space programme concerning landing men on the moon, prospects for spin-off look poor: IBM describe it as "drip off". Companies see better routes, already in place, for exploration of their technologies, and they see grave dangers in contractual terms which give effective control of their work to the Pentagon. City financiers do not see defence electronics, or electronics in general, as a worthwhile investment.

Trade Wars

We are now accustomed to what President Eisenhower called the "Military Industrial Complex". We are aware of the dominance of military interests in NATO. Less of us are familiar with the power of COCOM, the Coordinating Committee which controls trade in strategically significant technologies between the NATO allies and Japan, and members of the Warsaw Pact, or those who might sell to them. Through COCOM the US government exercises American law extraterritorially in allied countries, controlling the movement of computers, and restricting the freedom of commercial rivals in the transfer of any technology with American components or classified status. It is Pentagon policy to maintain strict strategic trade controls, and to enforce these they produce a Militarily Critical Technologies List (MCTL), covering technologies to be controlled by the Pentagon as an extension of COCOM.

It was in order to update this MCTL with British and European research, and using the British Memorandum of Understanding as carte blanche permission to classify any British work, that a Pentagon team led by commercial consultant Clarence Robinson was sent to Britain in March 1986. They were apprehended seeking illicit access to British classified defence research, forced to leave the country, and Secretary of Defense Weinberger had to visit in person to apologise (on 17 March 1986). Industrial espionage on such security grounds is not appreciated by European governments or companies.

Science and Government

The modern British disease is secrecy. The old Official Secrets Act was all-encompassing but unenforceable – much of my book on Star Wars is trivially in breach of Section 2 of that Act, but the first edition was banned and pulped as lawyers advising the publishers feared the possibility of libel action from British Defence Secretary Michael Heseltine, Trade and Industry Secretary Leon Brittan, and Pentagon Consultant Clarence Robinson. Although it is now clear that Heseltine and Brittan had vigorously opposed British involvement in SDI, and that the Prime Minister had told them other explanations would have to be given for their resignations [222], it was not safe to say so. The Robinson incident was reported each day in Parliament by Tam Dalyell MP, but my writing was not protected by Parliamentary privilege.

The obsession with secrecy stops people talking to each other, and in consequence the complexity of policy and attempts to control it can get out of hand. Information technology policy decisions have effects right across government, yet these are not considered in narrow departmental meetings, shrouded in secrecy.

There is only a limited sense in which the UK can still be considered a democracy. Ordinary people are denied access to information, and developments in technologies to aid information provision in education and research are curtailed. There are general elections every four or five years, but few are given access to the crucial information on sensitive issues: even Cabinet Ministers were denied the opportunity to discuss the Memorandum of Understanding to participate in SDI.

Alternatives for Technology

Professor Moto-Oka, Chairman of the Japanese Fifth Generation Programme, was in Hiroshima when the atomic bomb fell, and was saved from death as he was standing in the shade of a pillar. He died of cancer some two years ago, having concentrated on benign applications of advanced technology. He spoke of a "Human Frontier Programme", to exploit Fifth Generation Computers for social good. Instead Japan signed a Memorandum of Understanding in 1986 to participate in Star Wars.

We have to go to the other extreme. Instead of seeking to build enormous perfect systems to replace human decisions we must use intelligent tools to assist human decisions. This was the argument behind the "Strategic Health Initiative" [220] which remains only a proposal. In the UK, health provision is being cut: it is not seen by government as meriting increased funding and research support.

We have made progress in education and training. At Kingston College of Further Education and in the PROLOG Education Group we have produced books [94, 108–110, 223] and low-cost software [10, 121, 188] to aid teachers and students in knowledge exploration, and to help companies address training problems.

The technology can work, and work with working people, but only if it is their choice and under their control. It can only be used with a basis of knowledge: artificial intelligence must be led by human intelligence.

Lessons from the Star Wars Experience

Rational argument plays only a small role in the determination of defence policy. Advertising and public relations techniques can have more impact on the general public, and become instruments of state policy. A further example of this phenomenon is the series of privatisations in the UK, where media images are constructed to sell the most unlikely products.

It is perfectly possible for governments and individuals to adhere to policies that are incoherent, or to sets of policies that are internally inconsistent. The political process does not expose policies to sufficient scrutiny for consistency or coherence to be required. To adhere to a policy does not necessarily imply belief in that policy, merely a pragmatic choice of labels with which to be associated.

The power of the military industrial complex continues to dominate government decision-making, and few ministers or civil servants feel able to resist. The "revolving door" system means that ministers and civil servants are assured of lucrative posts in defence companies if they develop close relations prior to leaving public office.

Politicians are happy to remain ignorant of science and technology. Scientists are merely able to influence the political system, largely from the outside. Dissident groups continue to fail to communicate effectively, meaning that governments prevail over divided opposition. Having the ear of expert advisers is not sufficient when expert advice is disregarded.

Behind the scenes, at expert level, the situation is often very different, with a good level of understanding between East and West, for example in the scientific and arms control communities. There is then a problem of educating the perceptions of the general public to accommodate policy changes and reversals.

"Star Wars" was curiously evocative of Orwell's *1984* [224], with the heavy propaganda emanating from the television screen. Military measures have to be justified in terms of perceptions of an external threat: when that threat loses credibility, as with the recent changes in Eastern Europe, military policy and technology is left exposed and vulnerable. Perhaps each generation encounters a similar conflict between fact and propaganda. Certainly the First and Second World Wars, and the Vietnam War, indicated how the truth was an early casualty. Wars fought through technology may be all the more dangerous if the technological premises are themselves based on falsehood.

It helps to model the institutional systems interacting in Star Wars. This enables one to translate or decode the utterances of individual agents, identifying both illocutionary and perlocutionary forces. This approach has been taken by diplomats and arms control negotiators for many years, and modelled with decision theory, game theory, and computer-aided simulations. I found it particularly useful to decode the attitudes of and speeches to Parliament by Ministers, and to identify the key areas of interest of finance directors of defence contractors.

The Star Wars episode offers us insights into other more general problems, such as mistaken views of the power of science and technology, the effect of individual human greed, the tyranny of ideology, difficulties in technology transfer, funding of scientific research and development, secrecy and freedom of information.

Modelling Policy and Institutions: The Case of Welfare Benefits

Increasingly civil service policy teams are making use of computer models, some incorporating AI techniques, to model the working and effects of different policy options. At the time of the Budget, Treasury models are cited, and effects of particular tax changes on families in different circumstances are quoted.

It can be interesting, and even illuminating, to run the process the other way, and consider the use of computer modelling techniques to uncover the policies. This kind of approach has become established in the logicist school of French humanities researchers, who seek to reconstruct the arguments and modes of reasoning of published scholars as revealed in their writings.

I have previously used this technique to try to uncover the policy questions behind British government complicity in the American Star Wars programme. Denied access to classified information in a policy area where little is made public, I had to form and test hypotheses, posing questions to ministers and officials. My conclusions in that case were at variance with the officially stated policy position: informed members of the British government never believed in SDI but were not allowed to say so, and felt obliged to resign when the pretended policy was in conflict with their view of British interests.

What, then, are we to make of the current position in the complex field of welfare benefits? As with Star Wars, the issue straddles several Whitehall ministries. In this case we are concerned with Health, Social Security, Education, Employment, Environment, Home Office and Treasury. Ministers come and go, and civil servants are restricted in the extent to which they can confer across departmental boundaries. The lives of millions of ordinary people of limited means are affected, and the use of billions of pounds of public money overseen by the Treasury.

Can we identify elements of consistent policy? There are some generally comprehensible principles which, taken singly, are clear enough.

1. Benefit support should be targeted on those in greatest need.
2. Public spending on welfare benefits should not be open ended.
3. Market forces should be allowed to operate wherever possible.
4. People should be encouraged to work, even at low wages.
5. Public sector institutional care should be replaced by care in the community.
6. People should be encouraged to invest in their own futures.

Taken together these policy principles provide guidelines for dismantling the traditional welfare state, analysing current structures and suggesting changed directions. They derive from considerations of cost and accountancy. Within a given department, and in closely circumscribed administrative domains, they may be judged cost-effective and efficient. It is when the policy area is more complex and diverse, spilling over into the areas covered by different ministries, that problems are more likely to arise. We can describe anomalous situations which result from the application of the six principles above, but which are not explicitly intended outcomes of stated policy.

"Student" is defined differently in different pieces of legislation, leaving the situation of, for example part-time students in further education or full-time students dependent on non-existent discretionary grants, unclear. Can "students" still be at school or Sixth Form College, or in Tertiary College?

With the abolition of rates, and the change to community charge to be paid by individual adults, we might expect a fall in rents where these have included an element for rates. This is unlikely.

The freezing of student grants, the introduction of student loans and the suggestion of charging full tuition fees for higher education is likely to make it impossible for many students to follow the courses they had intended before the changes. However, government says that student numbers in higher education should double without an increase in government funding. The proposed loans system would involve considerable increased short-term government expenditure without corresponding benefits or increases in student numbers.

The government has accepted the recommendations of the Griffiths Report that Care in the Community should be coordinated by local authorities. Their changes in the social security system make care in the community extremely difficult financially, and no new funds have been announced for local authorities to ease the situation.

Young people are not eligible for most benefits, and are encouraged to take places on Youth Training if they do not stay at school, go to FE College or enter employment. If they leave home, work often requires accommodation, accommodation requires an income in order for payment to be made, and any benefits to support accommodation costs are limited and retrospective. There is a new vicious circle of deprivation, but it is alien to the experience of those who make the rules.

Many of these problems are compounded by the Community Charge or Poll Tax, which seeks to force responsibility for payment onto many who lack the necessary resources.

If we are to avoid imputing villainy to government policymakers, we have to try to explain this anomalous situation by considering the representations used for modelling society for policy making. The representation, the language and associated metaphors, will greatly influence practical outcomes. Our understanding of the thinking of politicians may help us to persuade or remove them.

Markets (redescriptions of problem domains in financial terms) themselves must be carefully defined to suit the purposes of the ideology, omitting embarrassing or complicating elements. Where a new market is described, it is with financial objectives in mind.

We are about to see the management of unemployment benefit and job centres handed over to market forces, in a return to eighteenth century methods of tax farming. Similarly, community care is to be given over to the private and voluntary sectors while financed and coordinated by local authorities. The clear financial assumption is a reduction in government expenditure in this area, to be justified in terms of increased efficiency and a diminution of the problem as defined.

Policies predicated on a view of society in terms of the working of market forces will inevitably focus on quantitative issues of payment and ownership, cost-benefit analysis and unit cost. If we describe people more qualitatively, and in terms of their relationships with each other within society, we reach different conclusions.

We must also note a separation between the governors and the governed. Increasingly they inhabit different worlds, of private affluence and public squalor. Without deliberate malice, administrators can be led to oppressive acts. Pursuit of the market model is made easier if one does not have to meet the people concerned, but can safely regard them as numbers, as members of a different life form, part of a problem for administrative solution.

It would seem that our policy modelling must include the subject area, the modes of representation, the administrators and their political masters together with their belief systems, and the prevailing circumstances in which they work. This is complex: simple certainties would be easier. Accountancy provides a ready modern substitute, but with an accuracy which is entirely spurious, based on the selection of those aspects of reality which can be quantified in financial terms.

Life was easier in the days of empire, when administrators could run the colonies while leading their own lives with their own families safely at home, or in hermetically sealed expatriate compounds. We now face the problem that our own inner cities and suburbs are the modern colonies. One day their people may seek their independence.

It may be instructive to reflect on the analysis by the anthropologist Malinowski on modes of direct and indirect rule when practised by the British in Colonial Africa [225]. External rule could be imposed:

A scientific study of facts in this matter would reveal clearly that "direct rule" means in the last issue forced labour, ruthless taxation, a fixed routine in political matters, the application of a code of laws to an entirely incompatible background. And again as regards education, the formation of African baboos and in general the making of the African into a caricature of the European.

Indirect rule was introduced by Lord Lugard, and bears an uncomfortable resemblance to present policies applied by central government to local authorities in the United Kingdom:

The political indirect rule which was the guiding principle of Lord Lugard's political and financial policy in Africa should be extended to all aspects of culture. Indirect cultural control is the only way of developing economic life, the administration of justice by Natives to Natives, the raising of morals and education on indigenous lines, and the development of truly African art, culture and religion.

Malinowksi emphasises the importance of detailed cultural knowledge by the administrator. This is hard to maintain if the administrator is from a race, or a class, apart:

But whether we adapt in our practical policy the principle of direct or indirect control, it is clear that a full knowledge of indigenous culture in the special subjects indicated is indispensable. Under indirect or dependent control the white man leaves most of the work to be done by the natives themselves but still has to supervise it, and if he does not want to be a mere figurehead, or blunderingly to interfere in something which he does not understand, he must know the organisation, the ideas and the customs of those under his control. The statesman, on the other hand, who believes in indirect control and who wants rapidly to transform a congeries of tribes into a province of his own country, to supersede native customs and law by his civil and criminal codes, needs obviously also to know the material on which he works as well as the mould into which he is trying to press it.

The methods of the anthropologist in abstracting from the workings of political institutions, would be usefully acquired by AI researchers.

Artificial Intelligence and Coping with Change

As individuals we are used to formulating plans of action, assuming a stable framework of events and institutional structures. Classical logics encourage this approach, as they can deal with known and unchanging sets of axioms, but run into problems when non-monotonic reasoning is involved [226,227]. Even temporal logics may assume an artificially regular pattern of change over time. Change is disruptive, so we often pretend it does not occur.

Financial markets have run into problems with "programmed trading" and with rule-based expert systems driven by chartist analysis of past market performance. Events not considered by chartist analysis, such as changes in world oil prices or a break in East–West tensions, come as wholly unexpected, and can trigger market collapses if responsibility for reactions is devolved to machines. Automatic defence systems operating in real time are predicated on assumptions of an enduring real world stability, including physical constants and standard chemical reactions. Policy models assume enduring base assumptions, focusing on defined areas in which to postulate "what if?". Medical diagnostics assumes consistent correlations of signs and symptoms, causes and effects, and shared assumptions by varied users.

In the real world of political and institutional change, all other factors do not remain constant. Indeed, the extent of change may be such that fundamental reassessments of individual belief systems may be required. Old assumptions may be undermined, old animosities removed. Colby and Abelson [75,76] achieved just renown with their characterisation of the "Cold War Warrior" with his "Ideology Machine". Given the classic master script which sees the world in terms of good guys, bad guys, and those who could be influenced by either, the Ideology Machine could provide a passable rendition of the responses of a State Department spokesman as a press conference. Even that system assumed certain immutable certainties. How can the Cold War Warrior cope with the changes in Eastern Europe including the breaching of the Berlin Wall? Given that their system was based on the speeches of Ronald Reagan in support of the presidential candidature of Barry Goldwater, what light does it cast on the eight years of Reagan's presidency? Could we use their system to model the policy of those years?

There are numerous other examples: indeed, this problem is the very stuff of politics. How do lifetime Conservative or Labour supporters cope with the ebb and flow of third parties in British politics? How do lifelong Anglicans take a position on the ordination of women, or unity with the Roman Catholic Church? How do strict moralists respond to the spreading of AIDS through normal heterosexual activity? How do advocates of nuclear power react to the withdrawal of nuclear power stations from privatisation? How do advocates of the free market economy react to the failure of private sector funding of the Channel Tunnel and rail link? How do critics of industrial training by companies justify giving control over training to those companies? How do those who oppose increased salaries for teachers respond to growing teacher shortages?

Such reassessments depend on the capacity of key individuals to accomplish a paradigm switch, to adjust their mode of representing the world and thus their set of actions in response. This requires sophisticated operations at the level of meta-knowledge, themselves presupposing a capacity to represent alternative worlds, and to consciously operate within them, as a form of participant–observer. It also presupposes some layered structure of beliefs about the world, within which some are easily modified in the light of experience, while others are set firm, and may have the status of ideology. Some of these issues were explored by Kowalski in Chapter 13 of his *Logic for Problem Solving* [34].

The capacity to cope with change may be developed through a breadth of experiences of different roles in different "forms of life", where a speedy "change of hats" is required. A rich and varied career is insufficient: the individual is required to reflect, and to play several roles simultaneously or in sequence and at will. Normal life offers relevant opportunities, as summed up in Shakespeare's "Seven Ages of Man", or as developed by social theorists [228,229].

To deal with change, or even to help drive change, requires more. The individual must be prepared to take the initiative. How can this be done?

The use of language can be critical: natural language can frequently sustain multiple interpretations, and an agent can move from a position of uncertainty in a given situation by monitoring the responses to his own considered utterances. Meeting someone at a party, the face seems familiar but one cannot put a name to it. The first greetings are neutral and probing, building up a model of the other until "the penny drops", the connection is established, the two are on the same wavelength, share a common context or form of life. Such a use of language involves taking risks, it is intellectually and emotionally entrepreneurial. The ice may break with a common recollection, a common acquaintance or common amusement at a joke. Stand-up comedians have this problem with a new audience, feeling their way with their opening gags, monitoring the faces of the front row before launching into their major routines.

We need to consider this exploratory phase further. It corresponds to the sensitive stages of international diplomacy, when two or more sides are trying to gauge responses to changing events, and to move towards shared perceptions. On such diplomacy may hang the future of nations. A similar analysis could be given of industrial relations.

Rather than the traditional two-person zero-sum model derived from game and decision theory, we are looking for a model of interaction that enables all participants to emerge without losing face, and with the capacity to continue. This objective could be regarded as falling under an ideological heading, for it conflicts with normal competitive individualistic practice, and implies some fundamental concept of community or common good, if only as a context within which to come to understand individual and group differences.

Within a given problem domain or world, successful accommodation to change depends on the capacity to deal with different representations of that world. New information is then assimilated to different models in parallel, and the different models may be seen as more or less appropriate depending on the circumstances. One may achieve dominance but the others persist.

The Virtues of Virtual Systems

Institutions faced with the prevalent rate of change of the late twentieth century may benefit from realising that their apparent structural weaknesses may constitute a strength.

Britain does not have a written constitution, yet there are courses and examinations on "British Constitution". Whereas the United States has a Supreme Court which can rule, at the meta-level, whether legislation is, or is not, constitutional, in Britain such a system is lacking. All legislation is at the same level, and a majority vote in Parliament may introduce into law a new provision which contradicts, or is inconsistent with, what has gone before. The resolution of such issues is then left to the courts, whose deliberations may give rise to later legislative changes.

There are curious analogies with the contrasting methodologies of software engineering and AI. The American Constitution conforms with the rigorous systems model of software engineering, which requires full and clear specification followed by verification, the whole process being constrained by the guiding framework of the constitution and amendments. The British constitution conforms more with the "Run, Understand, Debug, Edit" model of AI as analysed by Partridge [152] and others. It is convenient to refer to it as a system, but those who work inside it know it to be anything but rational and systematic.

The official picture of a system of government makes it easier to give official explanations of events. Whereas the individual actions of people exercising free will within an institutional structure are hard to predict, events when they occur are all too easy to explain in terms of structures, rules, probabilities and risks.

The above arguments have not included the question of whether surface level institutions and activities may have different underlying purposes and meanings, possibly construed in terms of individual intentions. At the individual level we could then draw on work on illocutionary and perlocutionary forces of speech acts, and at the social level on manifest and latent functions of institutions. This can also open up the general field of conspiracy theories, as well as the rival "cock up" theories, which note that most systems do not, in fact, work.

Intelligence

We may have to focus on a different interpretation of the phrase "Artificial Intelligence". Developed in wartime, the technology of cryptography was used to break enemy codes, to understand, model and predict enemy behaviour, to provide an artificial form of military intelligence to supplement the reports from agents in the field. Intelligence here is information about others, a means of preparation for future challenges or adversity. It also had an active component: the seeding of rumours, sometimes false, to monitor their spread and consequences, and on occasions direct interventions in events.

The "Intelligence Community" may have become set in their ways, so accustomed to the standard enemy that they have failed to monitor the details of change, the cracks in the dam, and are bemused by the flood when the dam breaks. The standard enemy has been taken for granted, wheeled out in order to secure enhanced domestic funding, and almost become indispensable.

New approaches are needed, and needed at speed. We cannot repeat the experience of the 1940s, where the defeat of Hitler meant the immediate resumption of the Cold War, even to the extent of recruiting German, Italian and Japanese war criminals to serve in the new war against Communism. George Orwell described this in his novel *1984* [224], and we are still surrounded by "Newspeak", and "economy with the truth".

More flexible thinking is needed, though this of course carries with it considerable risks. The people of East Germany have effected rapid change: can the people of the United Kingdom continue to assume that "There Is No Alternative" to Thatcherism, and that they must wait until 1991 or 1992 to express an opinion in a General Election? How is the future development of the European Community affected by changes in Eastern Europe? How will the United States respond, and how will this affect the "special relationship" with the United Kingdom?

The AI community has a role to play here, assisting in the exploration of alternative realities, enabling the citizen "to boldly go where no man has gone before", i.e. into the future. How can this be done? First and foremost by AI scientists playing their full role as citizens in the political life of their countries, putting their skills and tools at the service of the policy makers and local groups, exposing the fallacies in government and opposition statements and proposing alternatives for consideration. Secondly a process of technology transfer is required, whereby the dispossessed in the education and social systems are empowered, given the means to express their ideas and participate in shaping the future. The time for standing on the sidelines as detached observers has long gone. If problem solvers do not participate in the real and changing world they become part of the problem.

The above relates to what Searle [22] has called "weak AI", but illustrates the misleading nature of the label. It is, I submit, weak and socially impotent to adhere to a mythical but instructive objective of modelling and replicating the human brain ("strong AI"), while refusing to consider the social use of the practical tools which have resulted.

The AI scientist has a responsibility as a citizen from which he is not absolved as a professional. This is sometimes obscured by the macho language of the "hard" as opposed to "soft" sciences, and the respect paid to objectivity, distancing from human emotion and consideration. Such cold "rationality" might be acceptable in an unchanging and ordered universe, but not in our world of change and human suffering. In the real world, human problems never find neat technological solutions; life goes on, and the times are changing.

Policy Perspectives

Summary

A unified policy approach is required for IT and its applications, transcending conventional departmental and subject barriers. Government must have an IT policy, even if only minimally as a major employer and purchaser. IT is of itself neutral, but can be used to support different approaches to the economy and society. It can, for example, strengthen the position of the state or of the individual.

In recent years the introduction of IT has tended to support accountants and financial control, using technology as a means of reducing both the work-force and the level of expenditure on research, development and training.

A new Government's central concern should be for people, not finance, as the driving force for technology. Attention to human resource development and collaborative working will facilitate productive economic activity, and would be supported by a coordinated IT policy.

While previous governments have focused the majority of research and development on military projects, with limited civil spin-off and damaging diversion of resources from productive use, a new government should focus on people. Major IT programmes in the fields of health, education and training will combine the enhancement of the quality of life for the people with commercially valid industrial products meeting an international market.

Towards an Alternative IT Policy

Previous IT policy has been based on supporting UK IT manufacturers. Labour governments have provided public sector backing for leading companies such as ICL and INMOS. The first Thatcher Conservative government gave preference to UK companies through national IT programmes, subsequently withdrawn as the ideological case for privatisation has been accepted.

Now UK IT manufacturers have almost disappeared and current policy is to leave matters to market forces. This naively assumes free market conditions in IT, despite the numerous trade controls imposed, in particular, by the USA. IT manufacturers have not been helped by the short-termism and technological ignorance of City financial institutions, who have at the same time recruited many of the nation's graduate engineers as financial accountants.

The UK IT industry has been dominated by defence contracts, constituting a major distortion of the market. The products and methodology of the defence industries are not easily converted to meet the needs of the civil market, and there has been a lack of government policy support.

The policy focus now needs to be support for UK IT users, noting the move from mainframes to micros, and the proliferation of IT use in society. This was recommended by the 1986 Bide Report commissioned by the DTI, but rejected by Lord Young and Nicholas Ridley.

There could be a case for major state investment in new generation technology infrastructures, such as the installation of UK-made broad band networks in schools and colleges. However, the success and rationale of the investment would depend on the appropriateness of the human dimension, as opposed to the technology. Education and training aspects would need to be given a central place, rather than being bolted on *post hoc* as with the DES Microelectronics Education Programme following the DTI Micros in Schools Scheme. Indeed, considerable management training using currently available technologies would need to precede the introduction of a technology of the future unless we are to repeat the failures of the past.

The critical component of the modern advanced system is the intelligent human user. IT policy cannot be divorced from education and training policy. The American approach to IT (and technology in general) has been to seek worker replacement, and de-skilling of production roles. The European approach (seen in West Germany, for example) has been to seek worker enhancement, seeing the skill of the work-force as the critical resource in a post-Fordist economy.

The UK is part of Europe, a multilingual community. Natural language processing is big business internationally, but is held back in the UK through timidity and linguistic incompetence. IT provides the communication medium between individuals and communities, and needs to be combined with natural language skills.

The class nature of British industry must be addressed: conventional approaches to the division of labour are in question as technology offers executive power to secretaries and shopfloor workers, and enables managers to type their own letters. Directors are seeking to avoid consideration of IT issues, which they delegate to others. Few directors or managers themselves have training, in IT or in anything else.

Union involvement in the work-force and in training should be enhanced. Worker participation should be compulsory in processes of deciding technological change in the workplace. Not only is this the view of the European Social Charter, but research confirms the economic and technological benefits of worker participation.

State-of-the-art training courses should be available in further education, using equipment provided by industry.Leaving such matters in the hands of the newly created Training and Enterprise Councils is not adequate, as they are controlled by the very companies who have failed to provide training for their own employees.

A start can be made by building on current good practice.The Shadow Labour government should identify and assess particular case studies, considering in particular the repeatability and generalisability of the structures and approaches observed, and the management training required.

Research and Development

UK research and development has had an outstanding reputation in the past, led by university-based academic research. That position has now been severely damaged by withdrawal of public funding from universities and from collaborative research and development. Long-term research cannot be sustained through a series of erratic short-term programmes, necessitating considerable wasting of research time on securing funding.

The Alvey Programme worked in natural harmony with the European Community ESPRIT programme, as part of the European Framework Programme. The failure to follow up the Alvey Programme and the attempts to delay and restrict ESPRIT-2 and Framework have damaged UK industry and the UK position in Europe. Both Alvey and ESPRIT have a major training role, as they form a critical part of the technical development of research staff. This has been of particular importance in the UK where companies do not have an established culture of research and development.

The majority of UK research and development is currently devoted to defence, with few commercial spin-off products. Furthermore, UK IT companies have developed a dependency on defence funding and modes of financial management that ill prepares them for competing in the civil market. A major programme of conversion projects and management training, designed to shift the culture from military to civil ways of thinking, is now required, and even sought by the more perceptive companies as they note the proposed cuts in US defence spending.

City financial institutions place little value on research and development, and have little understanding of technical issues. Under present accounting practice, the simplest way to improve company balance sheets is to cut research and development expenditure. Another method is to sell off advanced technology and buy into low-risk entertainment or service industries. This suggests a need for changes in company law to require publication of expenditure on research, development and training, and changes in tax laws to give incentives for good practice and to penalise shorttermism.

Few senior civil servants or politicians have a background in science and technology, and lack natural sympathy with research and development. Broader policy implications of research and development decisions are poorly understood, if at all.

Concentration on short-term profit and the demands of the market are to the detriment of long-term development and stability. UK industry has a poor tradition of investment in research, development and capital equipment. The period of collaborative working under Alvey may even have induced a dependency on a lead from government which leads to a vacuum when the government withdraws.

In the IT industry, as elsewhere, there are natural alliances in Europe. For example, ICL has a good relationship with Bull and Siemens, developing new generation computer systems and combining research at the European Computing Research Centre in Munich.

UK academics are courted by the Japanese, but UK companies have not been seen as offering great research benefits for Japan, though Japan has established alliances to secure a place in Europe before 1992 and Fujitsu purchased ICL.

Entanglements with the USA and the US military–industrial complex have been very damaging to UK interests. This view was shared by Heseltine, Brittan, Tebbit, Pattie and Lawson, and underlies their resignations.

Government backing is required for major new research institutes, building on the academic excellence of centres such as Imperial College, Edinburgh University and Manchester University, and underpinning the transition to development and commercial take-up. Cohesive management will be required if the UK is to regain a leading role in new generation technology.

Technology Transfer

The key to industrial and commercial success is the transfer of technology from research and development to product refinement and exploitation in the market-place. This requires a framework of supporting policy. The present government has withdrawn from most stages of the process, meaning that powerful ideas reach commercial fruition overseas, often in teams led by expatriate UK scientists.

Technology transfer is a delicate process, akin to planting out seedlings from a garden centre. Care and nurture are needed for a critical transition period before unrestricted market forces are left to prevail.

Experience under the Alvey Programme has given rise to a number of tried and tested mechanisms:

Demonstrator projects
Collaborative projects
Club projects
Secondment schemes

Defence presents a particular problem. Whereas in the US civil projects and products follow defence research, and may be the underlying rationale for project funding being sought, the same has not applied in the UK. Many defence projects have been technical failures, and few have led to products with a broad appeal in the civil market-place.

Technology is best transferred through people. This links research, development, technology transfer, training and education. Issues to be addressed include intellectual property rights, patents and copyright, royalties, confidentiality, disclosure, and funding of the technology transfer mechanisms. More profound is the need to rekindle an environment of intellectual enterprise, untarnished by short-termism and narrow commercialism. Government must recognise that the key resource of a country is its people, and emphasise human resource development. IT is not exceptional in this, but the all-pervasive presence of IT makes it a natural focus for initiatives with impact across the economy and society.

Meeting National IT Training Needs

Numerous reports have described the current growing skills gap. The present UK work-force is not equipped to take advantage of new technology through a lack of training.Current policy has been to leave IT Training to market forces. This fails as:

1. Companies fear the poaching of trained staff.
2. Training, research and development costs are set against current year profits, as are the bonus elements of managers' salaries.
3. There has been a move to the lowest common denominator of learning packages and narrow vocational training.
4. Small companies are reluctant to spare key staff for training.
5. Companies lack a "training culture" from the top.
6. It may seem cheaper to buy in consultancy.
7. No market value is set on work-force skills, which are only valued in their absence.

IT was oversold in the early 1980s. "Solutions" are now sold without problems being identified and understood. Salesmen seek to maximise profits rather than to solve real problems.

Training Needs Analysis (TNA) was oversold in the mid 1980s. Trainee profiles are compared with job profiles to identify the gaps to be filled. This approach coincided with radical demographic change during which human needs analysis has gained in importance. Given the people available, what jobs can be done? The TNA approach assumes fixed job descriptions, often based on the previous post-holder, and workers who can be made to change.

The Manpower Services Commission (then the Training Commission, now the Training Agency) has been emasculated in recent years. The tripartite basis was destroyed with the removal of trades union representatives, and schemes like YTS and ET were used to impose a choice of low-wage employment or withdrawal of benefits on the unemployed and schoolleavers.

Training and Enterprise Councils, which come into operation from April 1990, are likely to cause further damage, as they place public funds for training under the control of employers who have themselves given the matter little attention or financial support. Furthermore, the Training and Enterprise brief enables TECs to consider training as only one of a range of solutions to workplace problems. The learning process is to be relegated to a subordinate role compared with work based outcomes and objectives.

As IT has developed and spread it has permeated most areas of employment and training. Issues of IT training blend with issues of training in general. IT is encountered in the context of the domain of application and use, and may not be best approached through an emphasis on the technology as the focus of interest.

There are generic issues of knowledge and information handling which can be addressed using a variety of tools. Often IT has been used almost as a substitute for addressing problems of knowledge: for years we have emphasised IT awareness and computer literacy, but without clarifying the context and motivation.

The conventional entrepreneurial approach is to see information as a product to be sold for profit, and information technology as the means of production and distribution. This preserves an emphasis on the individual user.

Given the social basis of knowledge and information, we may prefer instead to see information technology as the means of distribution and exchange. Production and ownership of knowledge are complex cultural issues. Who can truly claim copyright on an idea? The idea takes product form only when used in a social context.

On this account the development and use of IT skills cannot properly be considered in isolation from the social and institutional context. This suggests a need to move away from the present product-oriented short-term skills training in the use of particular packages. A broader culture of continuing education and training is needed, in which IT plays a consistent part.

IT, and AI in particular, should be used to support a more human-centred approach to systems and the workplace, taking account of individual needs and differences. Models of good practice are available on which new policy initiatives could be built, using new technology to help build a new social order.

There is scope for an increased role for trades unions in securing improved working conditions, noting the example of Scandinavia where trades unions are in the forefront of research in this field [7–9]. This also implies increased trade union involvement in new technology training and development.

Better use can be made of voluntary sector groups and strategies. For voluntary groups, information is the lifeblood and human networks are the means of distribution. The information technology used is now the same as in the commercial and education sectors, but without the profit motive and with an emphasis on communication. We can find innovation in the field of welfare rights and citizens advice, using methods which could usefully be transplanted to education, training and industry.

The role of government here is to identify the common needs which can be met through collaborative activity by individuals and agencies. Individual commercial needs can only be met as part of a broader enhancement of the environment.

Issues of finance properly arise subsequent to the above considerations. Money is only exchanged to remedy inequities between parties to a contract or joint activity. The most successful collaborations may involve no transfer of money between the partners. Alternatively, the general tax and policy environment may be so arranged as to give maximum support to training and collaboration for the benefit of the community. Thus we could consider training taxes or levies, or transfer fees attached to key staff.

The key to the revival of IT training, and thus training and industry generally, is likely to be the Further Education system (FE), itself under severe attack from the current government. IT training covers a multitude of sins, almost all of which can be committed in FE, an environment which brings together the worlds of work and education, and which can offer more than mere vocational training packages. Programming is for machines, training is for dogs and soldiers, education is for people.

IT Tools for Institutional Change

Institutions, particularly in the UK, rarely wish to change, though circumstances now dictate that people and structures cannot stand still. Even robust buildings can be damaged by earthquakes.

Institutions may choose to coat themselves in IT to protect themselves from change. Administrative procedures may be given a new lease of life through the advent of automation. Hidden reinforcements may be added through, for example, the linking of databases. Query procedures may be modelled on current practice rather than on a fresh analysis of the problems and communication requirements. Management information systems may be built to keep information inside rather than as an aid to its dissemination.

The costs of IT tend to be disregarded in the general context of institutional change. Government declares that the costs of management information systems in education must be met from the savings produced by their use in the first few years. Pilot studies are often omitted, or their level of financial support glossed over. Support may be given to establish projects, but no allowance is made for ongoing maintenance and updating.

We have much to learn from the lifecycle model. Lehman has written of the software lifecycle, covering the different stages through which a computer software system passes, each with particular problems, needs and costs. Similar accounts have been given of social institutions. Concepts of software engineering have much in common with those of social engineering, though for cultural reasons this is rarely noted. The myth of scientific objective validity has corrupted the workings of both software and institutional systems. In both cases it is people who form the critical weak link.

IT offers people an opportunity to reflect on their institutional position. Institutions provide a human microworld in which some model or set of rules can be explored in order to gain enhanced understanding of complexity. This furthers freedom of information, but may fall foul of institutional habits of secrecy and restrictive practices. It may be an uncomfortable process for many, and thus has to be part of a longer term development process.

At this stage in the development of the technology we would perhaps not wish to separate IT from IT use. We might favour a consultancy model for a government agency: this role could have been played by the National Computing Centre had they kept in the forefront of technology developments and maintained the level of support and presence required to take a credible role.

A useful model would be the Swedish Centre for Working Life in Stockholm, with a strong IT interest in the workplace, and joint support by government and trades unions. Their chosen methodology of action research case studies is highly effective, though time-consuming as work situations are observed over a number of years of technological change.

Similar arguments can be stated in the case of humanities research, with the French group led by Jean-Claude Gardin taking the lead, reflecting on and modelling the reasoning of scholars in disciplines such as archaeology. This draws attention to the theoretical issues at the heart of the disciplines.

IT and Social Justice

The time and technology are right for IT to be used as a major instrument in the enhancement of social justice. The same computer technology is used in industry and in voluntary community groups (i.e. IBM-PC-compatible micro-computers). It is also the standard used by the Labour Party Computing Advisory Group, now Computing For Labour. Just as Labour Party election and membership software can be used in constituencies across the country, the same applies for welfare rights and medical advice systems.

One mistaken conclusion from this would be that universal systems should now be put in place, providing uniform solutions across the country. Such a centralised approach might have fitted the technology in the days of computer centres housing mainframes. It has less relevance when individuals and groups have powerful processing power on their own desks, and are keen to respond to local circumstances.

Controversy has raged over the role of electronic networks. At present, although the costs of modems for microcomputers are low and falling, the costs of telephone lines are high, rendering community use economically unviable. This could change with a return of telecommunications to public ownership or control, and with preferential rates for community use. In the current circumstances electronic networks and electronic mail are best seen as mechanisms of communication, not of remote processing. Control remains local, but using common languages and packages which conform to certain standards in order to be readily disseminated and understood.

Private enterprise, following the initial injection of military research and development funds, may have served us well in bringing down the cost of personal computer hardware to within the reach of middle income families and low income community groups. It is not clear that the same applies with software for microcomputers. Already the cost of software greatly exceeds that of hardware for typical systems, and license charges include costs for ongoing maintenance which are beyond the pockets of microcomputer users. In consequence, illegal copies and substandard "look-alikes" abound, to the detriment of sensible use. Public domain software carries invisible health warnings, as it comes undocumented, may have undiagnosed bugs, and may serve as a means of transmitting damaging viruses. "Shareware" can only be a partial solution, with the voluntary payment of license fees on receipt of a copy. The free provision of top quality professional software would antagonise the software houses which charge large fees for customised systems for clients or for competing packages. To charge the full commercial rate places powerful tools beyond the financial reach of those who need them most. Market forces cannot be left to rule when those in need cannot enter the market-place.

There is a growing collection of top quality software for IBM-PC-compatible systems, addressing issues of social justice and brought together through the Artificial Intelligence For Society Club. Systems which can be distributed free, and have been described in this book, include:

1. Lisson Grove Benefits System.
2. YOSSARIAN AIDS Education System.
3. UNET Information Studio.
4. Hyperdoc Intelligent Hypertext Editor.
5. Learning with Expert Systems Starter Pack.

Public service information and leaflets could be made available on PC disks, or as PC-based advice systems. The model of the World Press Centre and Third World Educational Clearing House could be followed in the provision of social services and welfare rights information for community groups, using regular daily updates of information from a range of sources and software to support off-line processing of queries from community users. The necessary technology is available.

IT and Education

The UK education system has been sorely abused in the name of technical progress, with obsolete micros in every school. Support for UK IT companies was the prime motivation, with the educational work of the Microelectronics Education Programme (MEP) coming almost as an afterthought. Equipment installed in the early 1980s has not been replaced, and spending cuts leave teachers and students stranded in the past, using non-standard equipment which is used neither in industry nor in overseas schools and colleges.

After an early obsession with computing, seen as programming in BASIC, government has moved from computer studies to IT awareness to IT in the curriculum. Policy has been based on ill-informed exhortation, and has depended on the voluntary collaboration and unpaid efforts of underpaid teachers. The outcome has been mediocrity and disillusion, broken by flashes of classroom creativity.

National pump-priming programmes have been followed by apathy and collapse as local authorities have lacked the means to take over regionally based national initiatives. This has been destructive of organisation and professional competence. MEP was followed by MESU, and now by NCET: a national council directed by a former civil servant as a substitute for a policy and a budget.

Alternative pilot projects have been pursued by groups such as the PROLOG Education Group (PEG) since 1980, developing educational materials in the UK and around the world with a base at Exeter University School of Education, available for the full range of educational computers. Maintaining links with advanced research, supported by a diverse range of funding agencies, and in close association with industry, PEG has kept up with the state of the art in both education and computing, and has always been conscious of the financial and technical limitations faced by classroom users.

National programmes have frequently been proposed, and favoured by the specialist national agencies, such as a programme of Knowledge-Based Systems for Schools with the Council for Educational Technology, only to meet with Treasury refusal to approve funding. The necessary experts keep in close contact. A new government will need to rekindle enthusiasm in the education community, and to provide the necessary resources to provide sound foundations in education for the future use and development of IT.

In conclusion, intellectual regeneration requires a questioning, open approach to knowledge, and not merely the injection of technology and finance: we need an intellectual enterprise culture. We can gain strength from the appropriate use of "Weak AI."

Conclusion

This book is written in turbulent times for technology, politics, and society. It has sought to show that an over- dependence on systems, whether technological, political or social, constitutes submission to ideology. A human centred approach, based on progress towards qualitative social goals, may well include the use of socially appropriate technologies. Artificial intelligence can provide the glue which links the parts of fallible models of human institutions.

Once developed, any technology achieves the value which is socially ascribed to it, and may be assigned some price to facilitate or control its onward transmission. Where systems or institutions which can advance human happiness are kept as the preserve of the few, or as a means of controlling the many, this should be understood in its economic and political context. In this way, our consideration of artificial intelligence and human institutions is inherently political. Carrying the argument further, we should expect to see future party political manifestos available in program form.

One virtue of artificial intelligence as a focus of concern is that it enables the details of technologies to drop out of consideration. Considered in the context of human institutions it can heighten our capacity to reflect on alternative ways of living and working. The very demonstration of the existence of alternatives breaks the hold of total institutions, at national, local or individual level, providing liberation of the human spirit.

More work is needed on institutional case studies with artificial intelligence. We need to improve our understanding of the means of enhancing interpersonal communication, the importance of tacit knowledge and the strengths and weaknesses of shared commitments. Technology can be transferred, and the sum of knowledge increased.

This approach does not countenance the abdication of qualitative considerations in favour of simple responsiveness to the workings of the "free market". The market can deal only in prices and say nothing of value. We now have access to richer models, involving applying artificial intelligence to the consideration and development of human institutions.

References

1. Colmerauer A (1973) Un systeme de communication homme–machine en Français. Artificial Intelligence Group, University of Aix-Marseille
2. Colmerauer A (1978) Metamorphosis grammars. In: Bolc L (ed) Natural language communication with computers. Springer, Berlin
3. Levi-Strauss C (1969) The elementary structures of kinship. Eyre and Spottiswoode, London
4. Piaget J (1971) Structuralism. Routledge and Kegan Paul, London
5. Papert S (1980) Mindstorms. Basic Books, New York
6. Hilton J (1988) Skill, education and social value: some thoughts on the metonymy of skill and skill transfer. In: Goranzon B, Josefson I (eds) Knowledge, skill and artificial intelligence. Springer, London
7. Goranzon B (1990) The practical intellect. UNESCO and Springer, London (in press)
8. Goranzon B, Josefson I (eds) (1988) Knowledge, skill and artificial intelligence. Springer, London
9. Goranzon B, Florin M (eds) (1990) Artificial intelligence, culture and language: on education and work. Springer, London
10. Hopson D (1989) Information studio. UNET, London
11. Kuhn T (1972) The structure of scientific revolutions. Routledge and Kegan Paul, London
12. Hacking I (ed) (1981) Scientific revolutions. Oxford University Press, Oxford
13. Gardin J-C et al. (1988) Artificial intelligence and expert systems: case studies in the knowledge domain of archaeology. Ellis Horwood, Chichester (translated by Ennals JR)
14. Schurer K (1990) AI and the historian: prospects and possibilities. In: Ennals JR, Gardin J-C (eds) Interpretation in the humanities: perspectives from artificial intelligence. British Library, London
15. Collingwood R (1946) The idea of history. Oxford University Press, Oxford
16. Ennals JR, Gardin J-C (eds) (1990) Interpretation in the humanities: perspectives from artificial intelligence. British Library, London
17. Godel K (1931, translated 1962) On formerly undecidable propositions of Principia Mathematica and related systems
18. Winograd T (1972) Understanding natural language. Edinburgh University Press, Edinburgh
19. Winograd, Flores F (1986) Understanding computers and cognition. Addison-Wesley, New York
20. Toulmin S (1988) The dream of an exact language. Presented at: Culture, language and artificial intelligence, Stockholm, May 1988
21. Goranzon B (1987) The practice of the use of computers. AI & Society 1(1)
22. Searle J (1984) Minds, brains and science. BBC Books, London
23. Benson I (ed) (1986) Intelligent machinery: theory and practice. Cambridge University Press, Cambridge
24. Haugeland J (1988) Artificial intelligence: the very idea. MIT Press, Cambridge, Mass

25. Graubard S (ed) (1988) The artificial intelligence debate. MIT Press, Cambridge, Mass
26. Minsky M, Papert S (1969) Perceptrons. MIT Press, Cambridge, Mass
27. Frege G (1960) Begriffschrift. In: Geach P, Black M (eds) Translations from the philosophical writings of Gottlob Frege. Blackwell, Oxford
28. Robinson JA (1965) A machine-oriented logic based on the resolution principle. J ACM 12(1)
29. Colmerauer A, Kanoui H, Von Caneghem M (1979) Etude et realisation d'un systeme PROLOG. Artificial Intelligence Group, University of Aix-Marseille
30. Anderson B, Hayes P (1971) An arraignment of theorem-proving or the logician's folly. Memo 54, Department of Computational Logic, University of Edinburgh
31. Kowalski R (1974) Predicate logic as a programming language. In: Proceedings IFIP 1974. North-Holland, Amsterdam
32. Hayes P (1977) In defence of logic. In: Proceedings IJCAI 5. MIT Press, Cambridge, Mass
33. Polya G (1945) How to solve it. Princeton University Press, New Jersey
34. Kowalski R (1979) Logic for problem solving. North-Holland, New York
35. Fuchi K, Furukawa K (1986) The role of logic programming in the Fifth Generation Computer Project. In: Shapiro E (ed) Proceedings of third international conference on logic programming. Springer, Berlin
36. Clark K, McCabe FG (1984) Micro-PROLOG: programming in logic. Prentice-Hall, London
37. Cercone N, McCalla G (eds) (1987) The knowledge frontier. Springer, London
38. Bench-Capon TJM (1987) Knowledge representation. In: Ennals JR (ed) Artificial intelligence state of the art report. Pergamon Infotech, Oxford
39. Kowalski R, Sergot M (1985) Computer representation of the law. In: Proceedings BCS Expert Systems seminar on social implications of AI and expert systems. Abingdon, 1985
40. Sergot M (1982) Prospects for representing the law as logic programs. In: Clark KL, Tarnlund S-A (eds) Logic programming. Academic Press, London
41. Sergot M (1980) Programming law: LEGOL as a logic programming language. In: Niblett B (ed) Computer science and law. Cambridge University Press, Cambridge
42. Sergot M, Sadri F, Kowalski R, Kriwaczek F, Hammond P, Cory T (1986) The British Nationality Act as a logic program. Comm ACM 29:370
43. Leith P (1986) Fundamental errors in legal logic programming. Computer Journal 29(6)
44. Susskind R (1987) Expert systems in law. Oxford University Press, Oxford
45. Susskind R (1989) Pragmatism and purism in AI and legal reasoning. AI & Society 3(1)
46. Sergot M (1983) A query-the-user facility for logic programming. In: Degano P, Sandewall E (eds) Integrated interactive computing systems. North-Holland, Amsterdam
47. Hammond P (1982) APES: a PROLOG expert system shell. Department of Computing, Imperial College, London
48. Bundy A (1987) AI bridges and dreams. AI & Society 1(1)
49. Bramer M (ed) (1987) Research and development in expert systems III. Cambridge University Press, Cambridge
50. Fleck J (1982) Development and establishment in artificial intelligence. In: Elias N et al. (eds) Scientific establishments and hierarchies. Reidel, New York (Sociology of the sciences, vol 1)
51. Gardin J-C (1974) Les analyses de discours. Delachaux & Niestle, Neuchatel
52. Gardin J-C (1980) Archaeological constructs. Cambridge University Press, Cambridge
53. Gardin J-C et al. (1987) La logique du plausible. Editions de la Maison des Sciences de l'Homme, Paris
54. Gardin J-C (1990) Interpretation in the humanities: some thoughts on the third way. In: Ennals JR and Gardin J-C (eds) Interpretation in the humanities: perspectives from artificial intelligence. British Library, London
55. Carr EH (1972) What is history? Penguin, Harmondsworth
56. Laslett P (1977) Family life and illicit love in earlier generations. Cambridge University Press, Cambridge
57. Laslett P (1965) The world we have lost. Methuen, London
58. Macfarlane A (1977) Reconstructing historical communities. Cambridge University Press, Cambridge
59. Macfarlane A (1978) The origins of English individualism. Basil Blackwell, Oxford
60. Macfarlane A (1976) Resources and population: a study of the Gurungs of central Nepal. Cambridge University Press, Cambridge
61. Collingwood R (1939) Autobiography. Oxford University Press, Oxford
62. Ziman J (1982) Basic principles. In: Rotblat J (ed) Scientists, the arms race and disarmament. Taylor and Francis, London
63. Snow CP (1969) The two cultures: a second look. Cambridge University Press, Cambridge

64. Simon H (1969) The sciences of the artificial. MIT Press, Cambridge, Mass
65. Boden M (987) Artificial intelligence and natural man, 2nd edn. MIT Press, London
66. Wittgenstein L (1953) Philosophical investigations. Basil Blackwell, Oxford
67. Stutt A (1989) Argument in the humanities: a knowledge-based approach. PhD thesis, Open University
68. Kowalski R (1978) Logic for data description. In: Gallaire H, Minker J (eds) Logic and databases. Plenum, New York
69. Feigenbaum EA (1979) Themes and case studies of knowledge engineering. In: Michie D (ed) Expert systems in the microelectronic age. Edinburgh University Press, Edinburgh
70. Minsky M (1975) A framework for representing knowledge. In: Winston P (ed) The psychology of computer vision. McGraw-Hill, New York
71. Schank RC, Abelson RP (1977) Scripts, plans, goals and understanding. Lawrence Erlbaum, New Jersey
72. Fahlman S (1979) NETL – a system for representing and using real-world knowledge. MIT Press, Cambridge, Mass
73. Doran JE (1989) Distributed artificial intelligence and the modelling of sociocultural systems. In: Murray LA, Richardson JTE (eds) Intelligent systems in a human context. Oxford University Press, Oxford
74. Doran JE (1990) A distributed artificial intelligence reading of Todorov's The Conquest of America. In: Ennals JR, Gardin J-C (eds) Interpretation in the humanities: perspectives from artificial intelligence. British Library, London
75. Colby KM (1973) Simulations of belief systems. In: Schank RC, Colby KM (eds) Computer models of thought and action. Freeman, New York
76. Abelson RP (1973) The structure of belief systems. In: Schank RC, Colby KM (eds) Computer models of thought and action. Freeman, New York
77. Lynn J, Jay A (1984) The complete yes, minister. BBC, London
78. Lynn J, Jay A (1986) Yes, prime minister. BBC, London
79. Skinner BF (1953) Science and human behaviour. Free Press, New York
80. Kemmis S (1977) How children learn. University of East Anglia, Norwich
81. Fothergill R (1987) The director's view of MEP. British Journal of Educational Technology 18(3)
82. Ennals JR (1979) Historical simulation and involving the student. In: Sledge D (ed) Microcomputers in education. CET, London
83. Self J (1986) Educational computing software. Harvester, Brighton
84. Howe JAM, du Boulay B (1979) Microprocessor assisted learning: turning the clock back? Department of Artificial Intelligence research paper no. 119, University of Edinburgh
85. Howe JAM (1978) AI and CAL ten years on. PLET 15(2)
86. Sleeman D, Brown JS (eds) Intelligent tutoring systems. Academic Press, New York
87. Self JA (1974) Student models in computer-aided instruction. International Journal of Man–Machine Studies 6: 261–276
88. Sleeman D (1982) Inferring (Mal) rules from pupils' protocols. Proceedings of European conference on AI, Orsay
89. Clancey WJ (1987) The knowledge engineer as student – metacognitive bases for asking good questions. Report no. KSL-87-12, Stanford University
90. Goldberg A (1979) Educational uses of a Dynabook. Computers and Education 3(4)
91. Ennals JR (1983) Beginning Micro-PROLOG. Ellis Horwood, Chichester
92. Ennals JR (1985) Artificial intelligence: applications to logical reasoning and historical research. Ellis Horwood, Chichester
93. Nichol J, Dean J, Briggs J (1984) Pupils, computers and history teaching. In: Yazdani M (ed) New horizons in educational computing. Ellis Horwood, Chichester
94. Nichol J, Briggs J, Dean J (eds) PROLOG, children and students. Kogan Page, London
95. Rasmussen J (1988) Using PROLOG in the teaching of ecology. In: Nichol J, Briggs J, Dean J (eds) PROLOG, children and students. Kogan Page, London
96. Sissa G (1988) Using PROLOG in the teaching of electronics. In: Nichol J, Briggs J, Dean J (eds) PROLOG, children and students. Kogan Page, London
97. Bateman D (1988) An IKBS as an aid to chemical problem-solving. In: Nichol J, Briggs J, Dean J (eds) PROLOG, children and students. Kogan Page, London
98. Goble T (1988) Using PROLOG in the teaching of geography. In: Nichol J, Briggs J, Dean J (eds) PROLOG, children and students. Kogan Page, London
99. Wittgenstein L (1922) Tractatus logico-philosophicus. Routledge and Kegan Paul, London
100. Wittgenstein L (1966) Lectures and conversations. Basil Blackwell, Oxford
101. Wittgenstein L (1969) On certainty. Basil Blackwell, Oxford

102. Wittgenstein L (1974) Philosophical grammar. Basil Blackwell, Oxford
103. Foucault M (1967) Madness and civilisation. Tavistock, London
104. Foucault M (1971) L'ordre du discours. Gallimard, Paris
105. Foucault M (1972) The archaeology of knowledge. Tavistock, London
106. Kanoui H (1982) PROLOG-II manuel d'exemples. Artificial Intelligence Group, University of Aix-Marseille
107. Ennals JR (1984) The French connection. In: Ramsden E (ed) Microcomputers in education 2. Ellis Horwood, Chichester
108. Ennals JR, Cotterell A (1985) Fifth Generation computers: their implications for further education. Further Education Unit, London
109. Cotterell A (ed) (1988) Advanced information technology in the new industrial society. Oxford University Press, Oxford
110. Cotterell A, Ennals JR, Briggs J (1988) Advanced information technology in education and training. Arnold, London
111. Yazdani M (ed) (1984) New horizons in educational computing. Ellis Horwood, Chichester
112. Yazdani M (ed) (1988) Expert systems in education: special issue. Expert Systems 5(4)
113. Khabaza T (1987) Towards an intelligent help finder. In: Hawley R (ed) Artificial intelligence programming environments. Ellis Horwood, Chichester
114. Wolstenholme D (1987) GLIMPSE. Department of Computing, Imperial College, London
115. Bundy A (1984) Intelligent front ends. In: Fox J (ed) Expert systems state of the art report. Pergamon Infotech, Oxford
116. O'Shea T (1981) A self-improving quadratic tutor. In: Sleeman D, Brown JS (eds) Intelligent tutoring systems. Academic Press, New York
117. Tompsett C (1988) Education, training and knowledge base design. Expert Systems 5(4)
118. Ennals JR (1986) Star Wars: a question of initiative. John Wiley, Chichester
119. Ennals JR (ed) Artificial intelligence state of the art report. Pergamon Infotech, Oxford
120. Clancey WJ (1984) Use of MYCIN rules for tutoring. In: Buchanan B, Shortliffe E (eds) Rule-based expert systems. Addison-Wesley, New York
121. Briggs J (1988) Learning with expert systems. Further Education Unit, London
122. French P (1988) Intelligent training. ATR, Kingston Polytechnic
123. Rahtz S (ed) Information technology and the humanities. Ellis Horwood, Chichester
124. Bentley T (1986) Embedded computer-based training: the Stewart Wrightson Open Tech project. CNJ, Harrogate
125. O'Malley C (1988) Extended computer assisted learning. In: Proceedings ISCIIS III, Izmir, Turkey
126. Howe JAM, O'Shea T, Plane F (1979) Teaching mathematics through LOGO programming: an evaluation study. Department of Artificial Intelligence research paper no. 115, University of Edinburgh
127. Wertz H (1982) Evaluation of LOGO. IREM, Clermont-Ferrand
128. Parlett M, Hamilton D (1972) Evaluation as illumination. Centre for Research in Educational Sciences occasional paper no. 9, University of Edinburgh
129. Vogel C (1983) Language and creativity. University of La Reunion
130. Solomonides A, Levidow L (eds) Compulsive technology: computers as culture. Free Association Books, London
131. Ennals JR (1988) Pedagogical aspects of multicultural information technology. Proceedings of 3rd PEG Conference, Copenhagen, July 1988
132. Gullers P, Goranzon B, Vicklund B (1988) New methods and new technology. Swedish Joint Industrial Safety Council, Stockholm
133. Mansell J (1989) Expert systems and the assessment of prior learning and achievement. Further Education Unit, London
134. Bide A (chairman). Report of the IT86 committee. Department of Trade and Industry, London
135. Mikes G (1972) The prophet motive: Israel today and tomorrow. Penguin, London
136. Schumacher EF (1973) Small is beautiful: a study of economics as if people mattered. Blond and Briggs, London
137. Dreyfus H (1990) Is Socrates to blame for cognitivism? In: Goranzon B, Florin M (eds) Artificial intelligence, culture and language: on education and work. Springer, London
138. Janik A (1988) Tacit knowledge, working life and scientific method. In: Goranzon B, Josefson I (eds) Knowledge, skill and artificial intelligence. Springer, London
139. Berry D (1988) The problem of implicit knowledge. In: Goranzon B (ed) Preparatory papers for culture, language and artificial intelligence. Swedish Centre for Working Life, Stockholm
140. Hertzberg L (1988) A perspective on culture, language and AI. In: Goranzon B (ed) Preparatory

papers for culture, language and artificial intelligence. Swedish Centre for Working Life, Stockholm

141. Cooley M (1990) The new technology and the new training: reflections on the past and prospects for the future. In: Goranzon B, Florin M (eds) Artificial intelligence, culture and language: on education and work. Swedish Centre for Working Life, Stockholm
142. Cooley M (1988) Creativity, skill and human-centred systems. In: Goranzon B, Josefson I (eds) Knowledge, skill and artificial intelligence. Springer, London
143. Jordan W (1988) Social effects of IT – past and future. In: Cotterell A (ed) Advanced information technology in the new industrial society. Oxford University Press, Oxford
144. Gill K (ed) Artificial intelligence for society. John Wiley, Chichester
145. Cross M (1988) The changing nature of the engineering craft apprenticeship system in the United Kingdom. In: Goranzon B, Josefson I (eds) Knowledge, skill and artificial intelligence. Springer, London
146. Ennals JR (1988) Can skills be transferable? In: Goranzon B, Josefson I (eds) Knowledge, skill and artificial intelligence. Springer, London
147. Bliss J, Ogborn J (1987) Knowledge elicitation. In: Ennals JR (ed) Artificial intelligence state of the art report. Pergamon Infotech, Oxford
148. Cameron B (1983) Computer based educational consultancy. Department of Computing, Imperial College, London
149. Ostberg G (1990) How to make materials data systems useful for designers. In: Goranzon B, Florin M (eds) Artificial intelligence, culture and language: on education and work. Springer, London
150. Hall G (1989) Product design: why materials matter. TV Choice, London
151. Brady M (1986) Robotics. Lecture to Royal Society, London
152. Partridge D (1986) Artificial intelligence: applications in the future of software engineering. Ellis Horwood, Chichester
153. Sheil B (1987) Programming environments. In: Shapiro S (ed) Encyclopaedia of artificial intelligence. John Wiley, Chichester
154. Robinson JA (1983) Logic programming: past, present and future. ICOT TR-015, Tokyo
155. Montgomery A (1989) GEMINI – Government Expert Systems Methodology Initiative. In: Kelly B, Rector A (eds) Research and development in expert systems V. Cambridge University Press, Cambridge
156. Barker R (1988) Computer aided systems engineering and RDMS. In: Managing change. Pergamon Infotech State of the Art Review, Oxford
157. Parnas D (1985) Software aspects of strategic defence systems. Papers for SDIO, US Department of Defense
158. Oddy G, Tully C. Information systems factory study: final report. Department of Trade and Industry, London
159. Kahn K (1987) Partial evaluation as an example of the relationships between programming methodology and artificial intelligence. In: Hawley R (ed) Artificial intelligence programming environments. Ellis Horwood, Chichester
160. Freeman P (1987) Knowledge based management systems. In: Ennals JR (ed) Artificial intelligence state of the art report. Pergamon Infotech, Oxford
161. Rauch-Hindin W (1986) Artificial intelligence in business, science and industry. Prentice-Hall, New Jersey
162. Melliar-Smith M (1986) Software technology and the new techniques. In: Benson I (ed) Intelligent machinery: theory and practice. Cambridge University Press, Cambridge
163. Ince D (1989) Software prototyping and artificial intelligence based software tools. In: Kelly B, Rector A (eds) Research and development in expert systems V. Cambridge University Press, Cambridge
164. Kunz J, Kehler T, Williams M (1987) Applications development using a hybrid AI development system. In: Hawley R (ed) Artificial intelligence programming environments. Ellis Horwood, Chichester
165. Worden R (1988) Integrating KBS into information systems – the challenge ahead. In: Duffin P (ed) Knowledge based systems: applications in administrative government. Ellis Horwood, Chichester
166. Lin H (1987) Software and systems issues in strategic defence. In: Din A (ed) Arms and artificial intelligence. SIPRI/Oxford University Press, Oxford
167. Edinburgh Computing and Social Responsibility (1986) Computational Aspects of SDI. University of Edinburgh

168. Kowalski R, Hogger C (1987) Logic programming. In: Shapiro S (ed) Encyclopaedia of artificial intelligence. John Wiley, Chichester
169. Lighthill J (1972) Artificial intelligence. Science Research Council, London
170. Alvey J (1982) A programme for advanced information technology. Department of Trade and Industry, London
171. Hesketh J (1986) Formulation of an adequate specification. In: Computational Aspects of SDI. Edinburgh Computing and Social Responsibility, University of Edinburgh
172. Young J (1989) Human-centred knowledge based systems design. AI & Society 3(2)
173. Simon H (1976) Administrative behaviour. Free Press, New York
174. Austin J (1962) How to do things with words. Oxford University Press, Oxford
175. Searle J (1969) Speech acts. Cambridge University Press, Cambridge
176. Barwise J, Perry J (1983) Situations and attitudes. MIT Press, Cambridge, Mass
177. Habermas J (1979) Communication and the evolution of society. Beacon Press, Boston
178. Habermas J (1968) Toward a rational society. Heinemann, London
179. Christensen KE (1986) Ethics of information technology. In: Geiss GR, Viswanathan N (eds) The human edge. Haworth Press, New York
180. Diebold J (1984) Making the future work. Simon and Schuster, New York
181. Christiansen D (1984) The issues we avoid. IEEE Spectrum 21(6):25
182. Rafferty J, Smith E, Glastonbury B (1989–1990) Welfare benefits packages. New Technology in the Human Services 4(4) Winter
183. Bevan E (1988) The task for a new professionalism. In: Glastonbury B, La Mendola W, Toole S (eds) Information technology and the human services. John Wiley, Chichester
184. Galbraith JK (1989) In pursuit of the simple truth. Guardian, London, 28 July 1989
185. Nader R, Petkas P, Blackwell K (eds) Whistle Blowing. Bantam, New York
186. Ennals JR (1987) Socially useful artificial intelligence. AI & Society 1(1)
187. Miller C, Cordingley E (1988) An expert system on non-accidental injury. In: Glastonbury B, La Mendola W, Toole S (eds) Information technology and the human services. John Wiley, Chichester
188. Nichol J, Briggs J, Watson L, Brough D (1988) Keynotes; LINX. PEG School of Education, Exeter University
189. French P (1989) ATR-TRAINER. ATR, Kingston Polytechnic
190. Schumacher EF (1962) Reflections on the problem of bringing industry to rural areas. Planning Commission, New Delhi
191. Rafferty J, Glastonbury B (1989–1990) IT, moral values and equal opportunities. New Technology in the Human Services 4(4) Winter
192. Conlon T (1988) PARLOG Programming. Addison-Wesley, London
193. Schoech D, Toole S (1988) An approach to cross-cultural knowledge engineering in the domain of child welfare. In: Glastonbury B, La Mendola W, Toole S (eds) Information technology and the human services. John Wiley, Chichester
194. Ennals JR (1990) HRDIT survey report. Pergamon Infotech, London
195. Ennals JR (ed) (1990) Human resource development in information technology. Proceedings of Conference. London, 19–21 February 1990. Pergamon Infotech
196. CBI (1989) Managing the skills gap. Confederation of British Industry, London
197. CBI IT Skills Agency (1988) Changing IT skills: the impact of technology. Confederation of British Industry, London
198. Oakley B (1990) Trends in the European IT skills scene. In: Ennals JR (ed) Human resource development in information technology. Proceedings of Conference. London, 19–21 February 1990. Pergamon Infotech
199. Fowler N (1989) Speech to flexible training conference. London, 28 November 1989
200. Wood A (1989) DP department training: the marketplace – trends and attitudes. Corporate Edge Publications, London
201. Handy C (1989) The age of unreason. Business Books, London
202. Department of Employment (1989) Employment for the 1990s. HMSO, London
203. Evans G (1990) Computers and mental health. Westminster Association for Mental Health, London
204. NCVQ (1989) National vocational qualifications: criteria and procedures. National Council for Vocational Qualifications, London
205. Buckroyd B, Cornford D (1988) The IT skills crisis: the way ahead. NCC, Manchester
206. Judd SV, Virgo P (1988) The state of the UK IT skills and training market. IT Strategy Services, London
207. Sharpe R (1989) The computer world. TV Choice/KCFE, London

208. Sharpe R (1990) The computer world. In: Ennals JR (ed) Human resource development in information technology. Proceedings of Conference. London, 19–21 February 1990. Pergamon Infotech
209. Graham A (1990) IT and workplace relations. In: Ennals JR (ed) Human resource development in information technology. Proceedings of Conference. London, 19–21 February 1990. Pergamon Infotech
210. Industrial Society (1989) Blueprint for success: a report on involving employees in Britain. Industrial Society, London
211. Potter S (1962) Gamesmanship; Lifemanship; Supermanship; Oneupmanship. Penguin, Harmondsworth
212. Mikes G (1959) How to be an alien. Penguin, Harmondsworth
213. Mikes G (1968) A guide to Italy. Penguin, Harmondsworth
214. Cornford J (1908) Microcosmographia academica. Bowes and Bowes, Cambridge
215. Machiavelli N (1961) The Prince. Penguin, Harmondsworth
216. Butler RA (1971) The art of the possible. Hamish Hamilton, London
217. Newell A, Simon H (1963) GPS: a program that simulates human thought. In: Feigenbaum EA, Feldman J (eds) Computers and thought. MacGraw-Hill, New York
218. Johanneson KS (1990) Rule-following and intransitive understanding. In: Goranzon B, Florin M (eds) Artificial intelligence, culture and language: on education and work. Springer, London
219. Janik A (1990) Tacit knowledge, rule-following and learning. In: Goranzon B, Florin M (eds) Artificial intelligence, culture and language: on education and work. Springer, London
220. Ennals JR (1986) A strategic health initiative. In: Gill K (ed) Artificial intelligence for society. John Wiley, Chichester
221. Bowman R (1985) Star Wars: defense or death star? Institute for Space and Security Studies, Chesapeake
222. Dalyell T (1987) Misrule. Cecil Woolf, London
223. Ennals JR, Gwyn R, Zdravchev L (eds) (1986) Information technology and education: the changing school. Ellis Horwood, Chichester
224. Orwell G (1947) 1984. Penguin, Harmondsworth
225. Malinowski B (1929) Practical anthropology, vol 2, Africa, p 24
226. Elcock EW (1983) The pragmatics of PROLOG. In: Pereira L (ed) Proceedings of Logic Programming Workshop. Lisbon, 1983
227. McDermott D (1981) A temporal logic for reasoning about processes and plans. Department of Computer Science research report no. 196, Yale University
228. Merton R (1957) Social theory and social structure. Glencoe, Illinois
229. Goffman E (1968) Asylums. Penguin, Harmondsworth

Subject Index

Name Index